AF545192

Thalen & Thalen

silver

Texts by:
George A. Larson
Jean-Claude Marcourt
Jeroen Martens
Rob & Jaap Thalen

Design & lay-out:
Rob Thalen

Translations:
Taal-ad-Visie, Brugge

Photography:
Thalen studios
Arnaud Nilwik

Printed by:
PurePrint, Oostkamp

Published by:
Stichting Kunstboek bvba
info@stichtingkunstboek.com
www.stichtingkunstboek.com

ISBN: 978-90-5856-482-5
D/2013/6407/48
NUR: 656

All rights reserved. No part of this book may be reproduced, stored in a database or retrieval system, or transmitted, in any form, or by any means, electronically, mechanically, by print, microfilm or otherwise without prior permission in writing of the Publisher.

© Stichting Kunstboek bvba, 2013
© Thalen & Thalen sprl, 2013

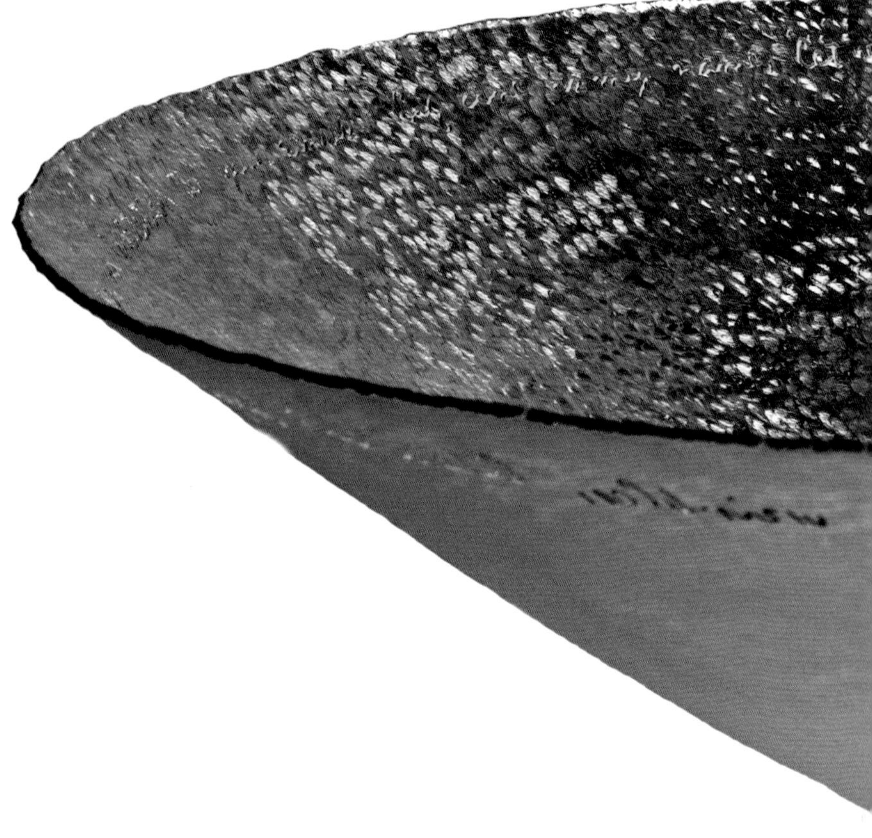

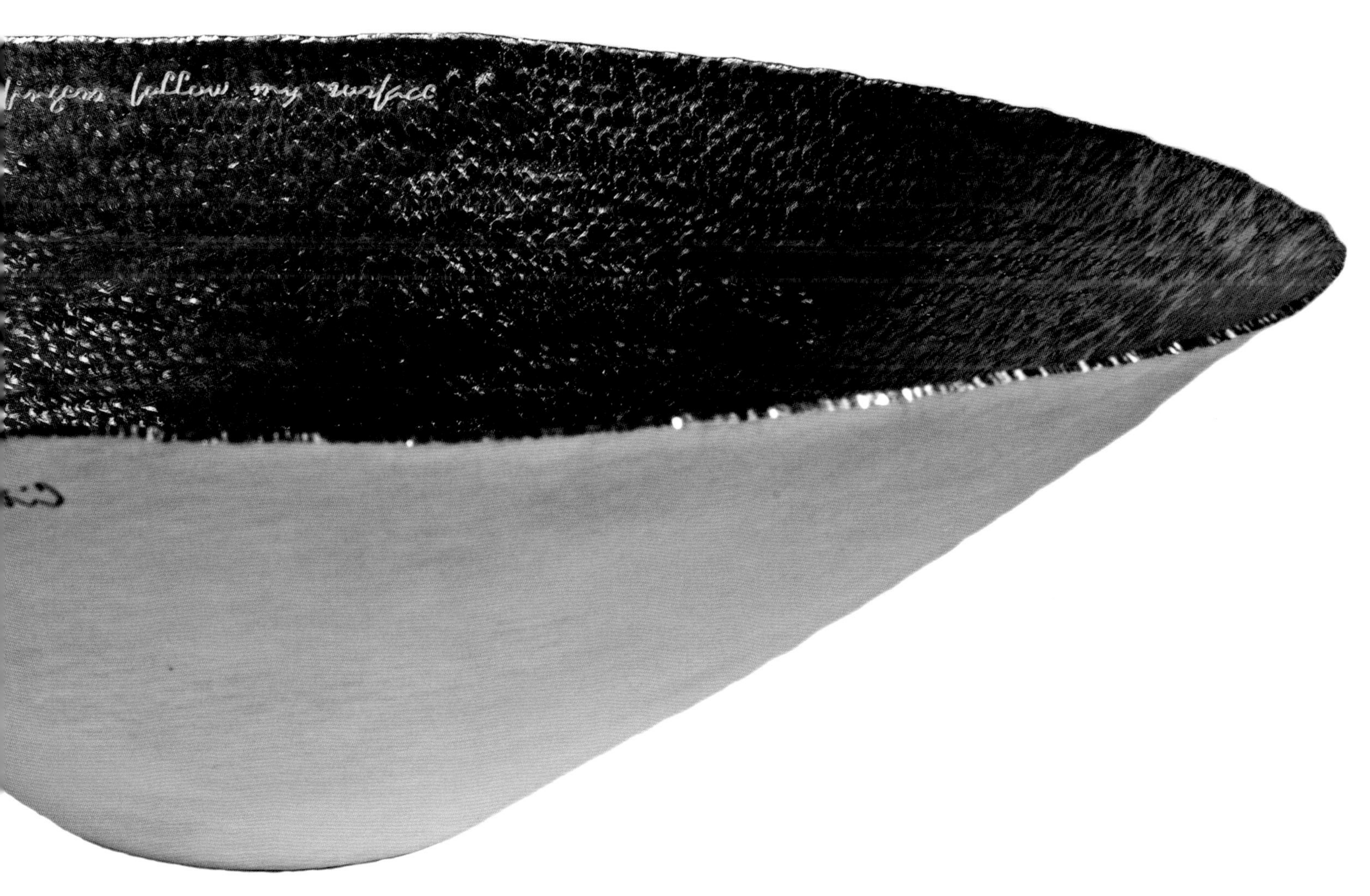
fingers follow my surface

05

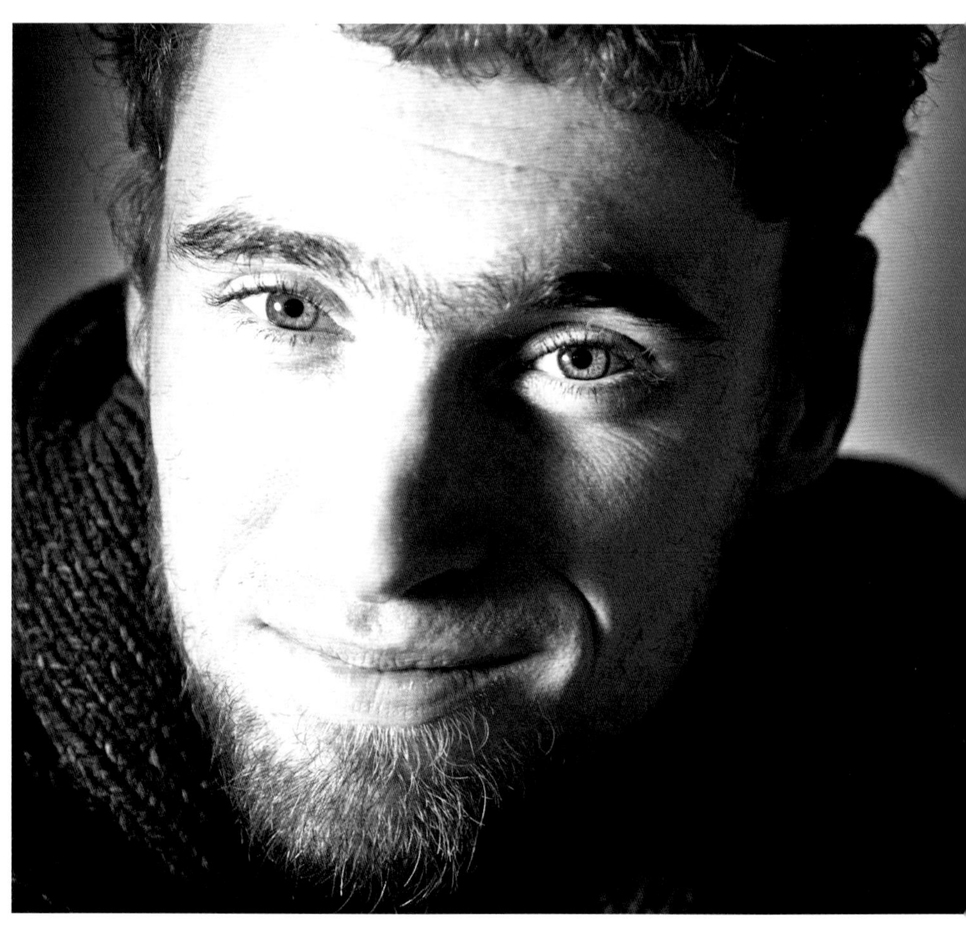

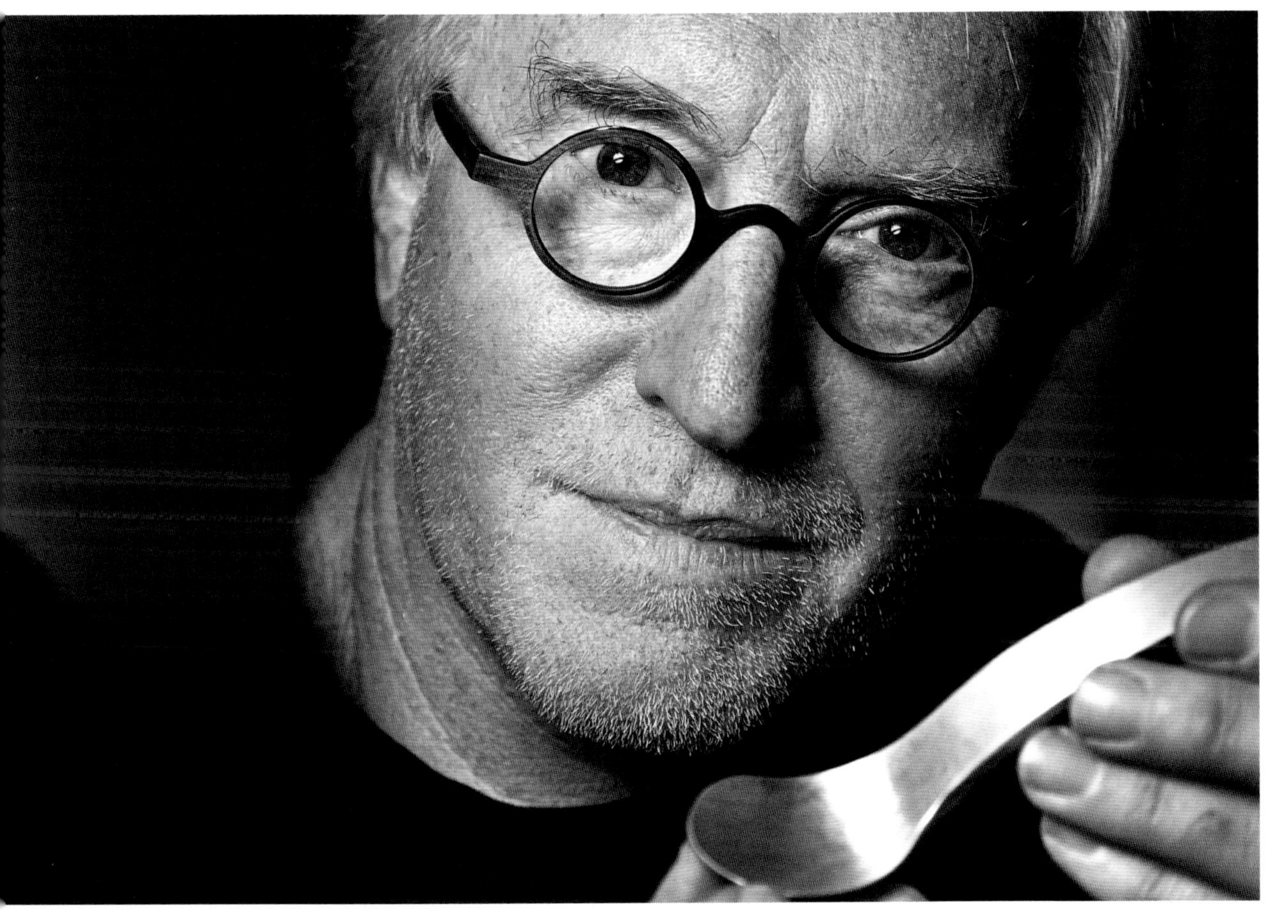

Voorwoord

Dit jaar wordt de Sterckshofopdracht voor de eerste keer uitgereikt aan een kunstenaarsduo, vader en zoon Thalen.
Deze unieke samenwerking doet denken aan de oude traditie waarin vaders hun vakkennis doorgeven aan hun zonen. Het is opvallend hoe vader en zoon Thalen uitblinken in kennis van historische en hedendaagse technieken van het zilversmidambacht. De puurheid en schijnbare eenvoud van hun ontwerpen doen hun werk moeiteloos lijken. Het is een bewijs van hun uitstekende vakmanschap. De bron van hun werk is hun passie en liefde voor zilver. Hun talent voor design en hun inzicht in de mogelijkheden van het fijnzilver maken het werk van Thalen & Thalen zo speciaal.
De Sterckshofopdracht is voor het Zilvermuseum Sterckshof een unieke gelegenheid om hedendaagse zilversmeden te steunen en de collectie hedendaags zilver gericht aan te vullen.
Jaarlijks wordt een zilversmid uitverkoren om in onze opdracht een object te vervaardigen dat opgenomen wordt in de collectie van het museum.
De allereerste Sterckshofopdracht werd in 1996 toegewezen aan de jonge David Huycke, 18 edities later kiezen we dus voor een kunstenaarsduo dat de grenzen van fijnzilver aftast en experimenteert met de vormentaal en de wijze waarop het oppervlak van het zilver bewerkt kan worden.

Wat me persoonlijk het meeste trof bij een bezoek aan hun atelier in Francorchamps was de alledaagse aanwezigheid van zilver in hun leefomgeving. Hun meest recente werk is tegelijkertijd bruikbaar en in zijn puurheid schitterend uitgewerkt.
Hun ontwerpen brengen zilver terug in het dagelijkse leven. Ze maken niet enkel onbereikbare kunstobjecten, maar ook heel toegankelijke wijn- en champagnebekers, bestek, suikerpotjes...
Het maakt me heel nieuwsgierig naar hun toekomstig werk.
Wij zijn heel blij met het resultaat van de opdracht. De vraag die het duo zich stelde bij het aanvaarden van de opdracht was hoe ver ze konden gaan met bijna 2 kilo fijnzilver. Hoe precies zij met hun hamers het zilver konden laten leiden tot een vorm die zijn eigen gewicht nog net kan dragen. Het resultaat is een staaltje vakmanschap, te bewonderen in ons museum in Antwerpen.
Het object is een typisch Thalen & Thalen object, maar tegelijkertijd toch uniek in zijn uitwerking. Een zeer mooie aanwinst voor onze collectie hedendaags zilverdesign.

Jeroen Martens
Directeur Zilvermuseum Sterckshof

Préambule

Cette année, la Commande du Musée de l'orfèvrerie Sterckshof se voit pour la première fois confiée à un duo d'artistes, le père et le fils Thalen. Cette collaboration unique nous évoque d'emblée cette vieille tradition de la transmission du savoir de père en fils. Cette façon dont le père et le fils Thalen excellent dans la connaissance des techniques historiques et contemporaines de l'orfèvrerie a de quoi impressionner. La pureté et l'apparente simplicité de leurs objets donnent à leur travail une impression de facilité. Il s'agit pourtant au contraire de la preuve de leur immense savoir-faire. La source de leur travail réside dans leur passion et dans leur amour pour l'argent. Leur talent pour la conception et leur vaste connaissance des possibilités de l'argent fin rendent leur travail si spécial, unique.
Pour le Musée de l'orfèvrerie Sterckshof, les Commandes Sterckshof constituent une occasion unique de soutenir l'orfèvrerie contemporaine et d'enrichir sa collection d'argenterie contemporaine. Chaque année, un orfèvre est ainsi élu pour confectionner un objet qui sera repris dans la collection du musée. La toute première Commande Sterckshof a été confiée en 1996 au jeune David Huycke. Dix-huit ans plus tard, nous choisissons donc un duo d'artistes, dont le travail confine aux frontières de l'argenterie, qui pousse la langue des formes et la surface de l'argent dans leurs derniers retranchements.

Ce qui m'a personnellement le plus touché lors de ma visite dans leur atelier de Francorchamps a été la présence permanente de l'argent dans leur environnement de vie. Leur travail le plus récent se veut à la fois pratique et magnifique de pureté. Par leurs projets, le quotidien se réapproprie l'argent. Ils ne réalisent pas seulement des objets d'art inaccessibles, mais aussi des gobelets à vin et à champagne, des couverts, des pots à sucre et d'autres objets qui nous semblent finalement presque familiers. Je suis très curieux de découvrir leurs prochaines créations.
Nous sommes par ailleurs extrêmement satisfaits du résultat de la Commande. La question que ce duo s'est posée en acceptant notre Commande a été de savoir jusqu'où ils pourraient aller avec deux kilogrammes d'argent fin. Avec quel degré de précision pouvaient-ils utiliser leur marteau pour façonner l'argent et lui donner une forme capable de supporter son propre poids ?
Le résultat est un petit trésor d'artisanat, que vous pouvez admirer dans notre musée d'Anvers. Si la pièce est un objet Thalen & Thalen caractéristique, elle est en même temps unique en son genre de par son élaboration. Une acquisition superbe et très précieuse pour notre collection d'argenterie contemporaine.

Jeroen Martens
Directeur du Musée de l'orfèvrerie Sterckshof

Vorwort

In diesem Jahr wird der Sterckshofauftrag zum ersten Mal an ein Künstlerduo (Vater und Sohn Thalen) vergeben. Diese einzigartige Zusammenarbeit erinnert an die alte Tradition, in der Väter ihre Fachkenntnisse an ihre Söhne weitergeben. Auffallend ist, dass sich Vater und Sohn Thalen sowohl durch Kenntnisse in den historischen als auch zeitgenössischen Techniken des Silberschmiedehandwerks auszeichnen. Die Reinheit und scheinbare Einfachheit ihrer Entwürfe lassen ihre Arbeit mühelos erscheinen. Dies ist ein Beweis für ihre hervorragende Handwerkskunst. Die Quelle ihrer Arbeit ist ihre Leidenschaft und Liebe für Silber. Ihr Talent für das Design und ihr Verständnis für die Möglichkeiten des Feinsilbers sorgen dafür, dass das Werk von Thalen & Thalen so außergewöhnlich ist.

Der Sterckshofauftrag ist für das Silbermuseum Sterckshof eine einzigartige Möglichkeit, die zeitgenössische Silberschmiede zu fördern und die Sammlung zeitgenössischen Silbers gezielt zu ergänzen. Jährlich wird ein Silberschmied auserkoren, um in unserem Auftrag ein Objekt anzufertigen, das in die Sammlung des Museums aufgenommen wird.

Der allererste Sterckshofauftrag wurde im Jahr 1996 an den jungen David Huycke vergeben. 18 Ausgaben später entscheiden wir uns somit für ein Künstlerduo, das die Grenzen von Feinsilber

auslotet und mit der Formensprache und der Art und Weise experimentiert, in der die Oberfläche von Silber bearbeitet werden kann.
Was mich persönlich bei einem Besuch in ihrem Atelier in Francorchamps am meisten beeindruckt hat, war die alltägliche Präsenz von Silber in ihrem Lebensumfeld. Ihr jüngstes Werk ist sowohl gebrauchsfähig als auch in seiner Reinheit wunderschön verarbeitet. Ihre Entwürfe bringen Silber zurück in den Alltag. Sie fertigen nicht nur unnahbare Kunstobjekte an, sondern auch sehr zugängliche Wein- und Champagnerschalen, Besteck, Zuckerdosen... Das macht mich ganz neugierig auf ihr zukünftiges Werk.
Wir sind sehr zufrieden mit dem Ergebnis des Auftrags. Bei der Annahme des Auftrags hat sich das Duo die Frage gestellt hat, wie weit sie mit 2 kg Feinsilber gehen können. Wie genau sie das Silber mit ihren Hämmern zu einer Form führen lassen könnten, die ihr eigenes Gewicht gerade noch tragen kann. Das Ergebnis ist eine Probe der Handwerkskunst, die in unserem Museum in Antwerpen zu bewundern ist. Das Objekt ist ein typisches Objekt von Thalen & Thalen, das gleichzeitig aber einzigartig in seiner Ausarbeitung ist. Eine sehr schöne Ergänzung für unsere Sammlung zeitgenössischen Silberdesigns.

Jeroen Martens
Leiter des Silbermuseums Sterckshof

Foreword

This year, the Sterckshof commission has, for the first time, been awarded to two artists, father and son Thalen, whose unique collaboration is reminiscent of the old tradition in which expertise was handed down from generation to generation. It is striking how father and son Thalen excel in knowledge of both traditional and contemporary techniques of the silversmith craft.
The purity and apparent simplicity of their designs give their work the semblance of effortlessness. It is a testament to their excellent craftsmanship. What drives them in their work is their passion, and love, for silver. But it is their talent for design and their understanding of the possibilities of fine silver that make the work of Thalen & Thalen so special.
The Sterckshof commission is for the Sterckshof Silver Museum a unique opportunity to support contemporary silversmiths and to extend the collection of contemporary silver in a very specific way. Every year, a silversmith is chosen to create an object that is included in the museum collection.
The very first Sterckshof commission was assigned to the young David Huycke in 1996; 18 editions later, we choose an artist duo to explore the boundaries of fine silver and experiment with the language of shapes and the way in which the surface of silver can be altered.

What personally struck me most when visiting their workshop in Francorchamps was the everyday presence of silver in their living environment. Their most recent work is both practical and beautifully crafted in terms of purity. Their designs bring silver back into everyday life. Their work includes both unattainable art objects, as well as very accessible wine and champagne cups, cutlery, sugar bowls, ... I can't wait to see more of their work in the future.

We are very pleased with their creation. The question which the pair asked themselves when they accepted the commission was how far they could take 2kg of fine silver. How precisely the hammers could lead the silver to a shape that was just capable of carrying its own weight. The result is an exquisite sample of craftsmanship, on display in our museum in Antwerp. The object is typical of the Thalen & Thalen work, but at the same time unique in its finish. All in all, a very attractive addition to our collection of contemporary silver design.

Jeroen Martens
Director Sterckshof Silver Museum

Wallonië, een kleine Europese regio die menigeen steeds weer versteld doet staan. Een regio die bruist van nieuwe activiteiten. Het is blijkbaar geen gebied voor grote industrieën, maar juist voor kleine bedrijven van hoogstaande kwaliteit.

Bij de ontwikkeling van Wallonië zien we steeds meer activiteiten die een duurzaam karakter hebben en die passen bij de vraag van vandaag naar specialisme en kwaliteit.

De nichemarkt waarin Thalen & Thalen opereren, is een van die specialismen die je net hier vindt.

Wie denkt dat objecten in zilver niet meer van deze tijd zijn, zou eens het atelier van Thalen & Thalen moeten bezoeken. Zij creëren voorwerpen uit het fijnste, meest pure zilver dat er bestaat. Hun creaties worden geïnspireerd door de prachtige omgeving van de Ardennen en de soms woeste weersomstandigheden.

Zoals zij het zelf zo graag omschrijven zijn de zeer tactiele oppervlakken van hun creaties een uitdrukking van krachtige landschappen, wilde bergbeekjes en zelfs opengebarsten klei in een droge rivierbedding...
Natuurelementen vertaald in zilveren objecten.

Zij brengen hun creaties, maar ook onze streek naar gebieden ver buiten onze landsgrenzen. Zij stellen regelmatig tentoon in München, London, New York, Miami, Chicago en talloze andere plaatsen.

Bij de presentatie van dit boek zijn Rob en Jaap net terug van een spraakmakend evenement in Miami en staat het Zilvermuseum in Antwerpen klaar om hen te ontvangen.

Het zijn dit soort (kleine) bedrijven als Thalen & Thalen die onze regio op de kaart zetten en meehelpen aan een duurzame ontwikkeling van Wallonië.

Jean-Claude Marcourt,
Vice-President van de Waalse Regering, Minister van Economische Zaken, KMO's, Buitenlandse Handel, Nieuwe Technologieën en Hoger Onderwijs

La Wallonie, une petite région d'Europe qui n'en finit pas d'étonner. Une région qui regorge d'activités nouvelles et d'entreprises d'excellente valeur.
Le développement de la Wallonie voit apparaître de plus en plus d'activités durables qui correspondent exactement à la demande d'aujourd'hui: spécialisation et qualité.

Le créneau de Thalen & Thalen est justement une de ces spécialités que recèle la Wallonie.

Si vous pensez que les objets en argent ne sont plus de notre temps, allez faire un tour dans les ateliers de Thalen & Thalen.
Ils y créent des objets dans un argent des plus fins et des plus purs qui soit. Leurs créations sont inspirées par les beaux paysages des Ardennes et le climat parfois rude qui est le leur.

Comme ils le décrivent si bien, les surfaces très tactiles de leurs créations sont l'expression des paysages poignants, des ruisseaux sauvages et parfois même des pierres d'argile abandonnées par un lit de rivière asséchée. Autant d'éléments puisés dans la nature et traduits en objets d'art en argent.

Ils exportent leurs créations mais aussi notre région dans des contrées lointaines. Ils exposent régulièrement à Munich, Londres, New York, Miami, Chicago et dans beaucoup d'autres villes.

Au moment de la présentation de ce livre, ils reviennent tout droit d'un événement important à Miami et le Zilvermuseum à Anvers est prêt à les accueillir.

Ce sont ces (petites) entreprises comme Thalen & Thalen qui mettent notre région en évidence et qui contribuent à un développement durable.

Jean-Claude Marcourt,
Vice-Président du Gouvernement Wallon, Ministre de l'Economie, des PME, du Commerce extérieur, des Technologies nouvelles et de l'Enseignement supérieur

Die Wallonie ist eine kleine Region in Europa, die einem immer wieder in Staunen versetzt. Eine Region voll neuer Aktivitäten und exzellenter Unternehmen.
Die Entwicklung der Wallonie geht mehr und mehr mit nachhaltigen Tätigkeiten einher, die dem heutigen Zeitgeist nach Spezialisierung und Qualität voll und ganz entsprechen.

Die Nischenprodukte von Thalen & Thalen gehören genau zu diesen Spezialitäten, die die Wallonie hervorbringt.

Wenn Sie glauben, dass Gegenstände aus Silber nicht mehr in unsere Zeit passen, dann machen Sie einen Rundgang durch die Ateliers von Thalen & Thalen.
Dort werden Objekte aus feinstem und reinstem Silber hergestellt. Die Kreationen spiegeln die schönen Ardennen-Landschaften und das dort vorherrschende, manchmal raue Klima wider.

Es wird gut beschrieben, wie die sehr taktilen Oberflächen der Kreationen bestechende Landschaften, wilde Flüsse und manchmal sogar Tonsteine aus einem ausgetrockneten Flussbett widergeben. Alles Motive aus der Natur, umgesetzt in Kunstobjekte aus Silber.

Diese Kreationen, aber auch unsere Region werden in ferne Gefilde exportiert. Ausstellungen finden regelmäßig in München, London, New York, Miami, Chicago und in vielen anderen Städten statt.

Während dieses Buch vorgestellt wird, kommen die Künstler direkt von einer wichtigen Veranstaltung in Miami zurück, und im Silbermuseum in Antwerpen werden sie bereits erwartet.

Es sind diese (kleinen) Unternehmen wie Thalen & Thalen, die unsere Region ins Rampenlicht rücken, und die zu einer nachhaltigen Entwicklung beitragen.

Jean-Claude Marcourt,
Vizepräsident der Wallonischen Regierung, Minister für Wirtschaft, KMUs, Außenhandel, neue Technologien und Hochschulwesen

Wallonia, a small region of Europe that never ceases to amaze. A region brimming with new activities and top quality enterprises. The development of Wallonia is leading to the creation of more and more sustainable activities which are a perfect match to today's needs: specialisation and quality.

The niche of Thalen & Thalen is precisely one of those specialties so typical of Wallonia.

If you think that silver objects are outdated, have a look at the studios of Thalen & Thalen. There, they create objects in one of the finest and purest silver available. Their creations are inspired by the beautiful landscapes of the Ardennes and the sometimes harsh climate that fashions them.

As they describe it so well, the very tactile surfaces of their creations are reminiscent of the harrowing landscapes, the wild brooks and sometimes even of ruptured clay left behind in a dry river bed. All these elements are inspired by nature and translated into art objects made of silver.

In addition to their creations, they also export our region to faraway lands. They hold regular exhibitions in Munich, London, New York, Miami, Chicago and many other cities.

As this book is about to be published, they are just back from a major event in Miami and Antwerp's Silver Museum is ready to exhibit their work.

(Small) businesses, such as Thalen & Thalen, are the ones putting our region on the map and contributing to sustainable development.

Jean-Claude Marcourt,
Vice-President of the Walloon Government, Minister of Economy, SMEs, Foreign Trade, New Technologies and Higher Education

Thalen & Thalen, zilver...

Zilver is voor ons niet meer dan een middel om onze vormentaal tot uitdrukking te brengen.
Zilver is voor ons het ultieme middel om onze vormen te realiseren.
In een wereld waar short lifecycles en recycling voorop staan, creaties neerzetten die blijven.
Zilver beleven.
Waarom je ultieme espresso uit een kartonnen bekertje drinken als het uit fijnzilver kan?
Tweehonderdduizend redenen om te kiezen voor zilver, begin maar met het aan te raken.
Creaties zo tactiel dat je ze wilt omhelzen...

Deze en andere oneliners ontstaan bijna elke dag wanneer we met onze klanten en vrienden communiceren over onze creaties. Tijdens een kunstbeurs enkele maanden geleden, kwam er iemand naar ons toe en zei dat hij ons werk zou willen omschrijven als 'contemporary zen'.

Onze zoektocht is begonnen vanuit het gevoel dat wij ons willen omgeven met objecten die ons als het ware begeleiden in ons leven, het aangenaam maken.
Voor sommigen zal dit in een tijd van crisis raar klinken, maar uiteindelijk zullen we ons leven beoordelen op zaken die het de moeite waard maken. Mensen en dingen die bij je horen.

En wij, wij zijn die createurs, die onze liefde voor zilver en meer nog voor fijnzilver omzetten in creaties die onze passie en persoonlijkheid dragen en die uitnodigen om mee te reizen op het levenspad.

Puur is een van de termen die ons leiden. Puur in het materiaal en de uitdrukkingsvorm. We zoeken niet naar de perfecte spiegeling die ons slechts de omgeving van het object laat zien, we zoeken naar vormen die uitnodigen om aan te raken. Simpele vormen in de juiste verhoudingen. De beoordeling daarvan is vaak een heel persoonlijke zaak. Welke vorm past? Vormen die zowel heel klein als ook heel groot mogen worden. Vormen die verwonderen...

Vanuit technisch oogpunt zoeken we steeds naar mogelijkheden om onze creaties uit één stuk zilverplaat te laten ontstaan.
Geen montage als dat niet werkelijk onvermijdelijk is.
Misschien lijkt het dat deze benadering ons zou kunnen beperken in de vrijheid van het vormgeven, maar in werkelijkheid is het juist een uitdaging om met het materiaal een communicatie aan te gaan, waarbij de grenzen van het mogelijke opgezocht worden.
En als we die grenzen bereiken laten we dat zien, uit respect voor dat materiaal.

rob & jaap thalen

Thalen & Thalen, l’argent...

L’argent n’est pour nous qu’un moyen d’exprimer notre langage des formes.
L’argent est pour nous le moyen ultime de matérialiser nos formes.
Dans un monde prônant les cycles de vie courts et le recyclage, nous concevons des créations qui durent.
Vivre l’argent, le ressentir.
Pourquoi boire votre espresso dans un gobelet en carton si vous pouvez ce faire dans un récipient en argent fin ?
Il existe une infinité de raisons de choisir l’argent. Commencez par le toucher.
Des créations si tactiles que vous vient l’envie de les étreindre…

Ces quelques slogans naissent pratiquement chaque jour lors de nos discussions avec nos clients et nos amis. Lors d’un salon d’art il y a quelques mois, quelqu’un est venu nous dire qu’il décrirait notre travail comme du “zen contemporain”.

Notre recherche est partie du sentiment que nous souhaitons nous entourer d’objets qui nous accompagnent à travers la vie, qui la rendent plus agréable.
Pour certains, cela peut sembler bien étrange en ces temps de crise, mais en définitive, nous voulons évaluer notre vie à l’aune de ce qui vaut la peine d’être vécu. Les personnes et les choses qui font partie de vous.
Nous, nous sommes ces créateurs, qui convertissons notre amour pour

l'argent et surtout pour l'argent fin en des créations qui portent en elles notre passion et notre personnalité, et qui invitent leur détenteur à nous accompagner sur le chemin de la vie.

La pureté est l'un des termes qui nous guident. La pureté du matériau, la pureté de la forme d'expression. Nous ne recherchons pas le reflet parfait, qui se contenterait de nous montrer l'environnement de l'objet. Nous recherchons des formes qui invitent au toucher. Des formes simples, dans de bonnes proportions. L'appréciation qui en découle est vague et très personnelle. Quelle forme convient le mieux? Des formes qui peuvent être très petites, ou très grandes. Des formes qui suscitent l'admiration.

Sur le plan technique, nous recherchons toujours les possibilités permettant de réaliser la création à partir d'une seule plaque d'argent. Aucun montage n'est opéré, sauf lorsqu'il s'avère absolument inévitable. Il se pourrait que cette approche nous limite dans notre liberté d'expression, mais en réalité, il s'agit précisément du défi d'entrer en communication avec le matériau, une communication au cours de laquelle nous confinons aux limites du possible. Et lorsque nous atteignons ces limites, nous le montrons, par respect pour le matériau.

rob & jaap thalen

Thalen & Thalen, Silber...

Silber ist für uns nichts Weiteres als ein Mittel, unsere Formensprache zum Ausdruck zu bringen.
Silber ist für uns das ultimative Mittel, unsere Formen zu verwirklichen.
In einer Welt, in der kurze Lebenszyklen und Recycling im Vordergrund stehen, Kreationen hervorbringen, die dauerhaft sind.
Silber zum Leben erwecken.
Warum Ihren ultimativen Espresso aus einem Pappbecher trinken, obwohl er auch aus Feinsilber sein könnte?
Zweihunderttausend Gründe, um sich für Feinsilber zu entscheiden, beginnen Sie doch mit dem Berühren.
Kreationen, die so taktil sind, dass Sie sie umarmen wollen...

Diese und andere Einzeiler entstehen fast jeden Tag, wenn wir mit unseren Kunden und Freunden über unsere Kreationen reden. Vor einigen Monaten kam auf einer Kunstmesse eine Person zu uns, die sagte, dass sie unsere Arbeit als "zeitgenössisches Zen" umschreiben würde.

Unsere Suche begann ausgehend vom Gefühl, dass wir uns mit Objekten umgeben wollen, die uns sozusagen in unserem Leben begleiten und es angenehm machen.
Für Einige mag dies in einer Zeit der Krise seltsam klingen, aber letztendlich bewerten wir unser Leben über Dinge, für die sich die Mühe lohnt. Menschen und Dinge, die ihnen gehören.
Und wir, die Gestalter, die unsere Liebe für Silber und stärker noch

für Feinsilber in Kreationen umsetzten, die von unserer Leidenschaft und Persönlichkeit geprägt sind und dazu einladen, auf dem Weg des Lebens mitzureisen.

Rein ist einer der Begriffe, die uns lenken. Rein in Bezug auf das Material und die Ausdrucksform. Wir streben nicht die perfekte Spiegelung an, die uns nur die Umgebung des Objektes sehen lässt, sondern suchen nach Formen, die zur Berührung auffordern. Einfache Formen in den richtigen Proportionen. Die Beurteilung dessen ist oft eine sehr persönliche Sache. Welche Form ist die richtige? Formen, die sowohl sehr klein als auch sehr groß werden können. Formen die erstaunen.

Aus technischer Sicht sind wir immer auf der Suche nach Möglichkeiten, unsere Kreationen aus einem Stück Silberplatte entstehen zu lassen. Keine Montage, wenn sie nicht wirklich unvermeidlich ist.
Möglicherweise scheint es, dass uns dieser Ansatz in der Gestaltungsfreiheit einschränken könnte, aber in Wirklichkeit handelt es sich nur um eine Herausforderung, mit dem Material in Kommunikation zu treten und dabei nach den Grenzen des Möglichen zu suchen.
Und wenn wir auf diese Grenzen stoßen, lassen wir dies aus Respekt für dieses Material erkennen.

rob & jaap thalen

Thalen & Thalen, silver...

To us, silver is nothing more than a means of creating shapes.
To us, silver is the ultimate way of creating shapes.
In a world dominated by short lifecycles and recycling, we deliver creations that last.
Experiencing silver.
Why should you drink your delectable espresso from a paper cup if you could drink it from a fine silver cup?
There are thousands of reasons why you should choose silver, starting with the tactile aspect.
Creations that are so tactile you want to hug them...

These, and other, one-liners are almost a daily occurrence when we communicate with our clients and friends about our creations. At an art fair a few months back, someone came up to our stand and said that our work is like contemporary Zen to him.

Our quest started from a feeling that we wanted to be surrounded by objects that guide us and inject enjoyment into our lives.
To some, this may sound odd in times of crisis, but in the end, the way we evaluate our life will be counted by the things that make it worthwhile. People and things that have a place in our heart.

And we happen to be those artists who translate our love for silver, and particularly fine silver, into creations that reflect our passion and personality and that invite to follow you on the path of life.

Pure is one of the words we are guided by. Purity in material and our way of expression. We do not look for the perfect mirror that only shows us the area around the object. We are looking for shapes that invite to be touched. Simple basic shapes in the correct proportions. The assessment of this is often a very personal matter. What shape feels right? Shapes that are both very small or indeed, very large. Shapes that are awe-inspiring.

From a technical point of view, we always look for ways of creating our works from one single sheet of silver. We avoid joints unless absolutely necessary.
It may seem that this approach could limit the freedom of creating shapes, but in reality, it is a challenge to enter into communication with the material and explore the boundaries of what is possible. And when we reach those limits, we show them, out of respect for that material.

rob & jaap thalen

31

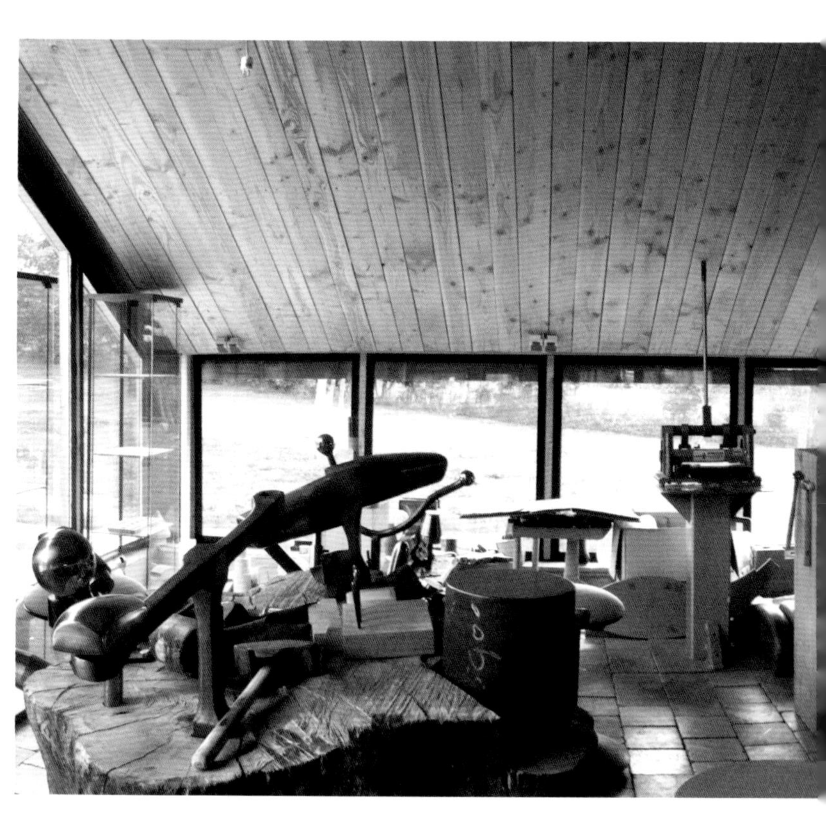

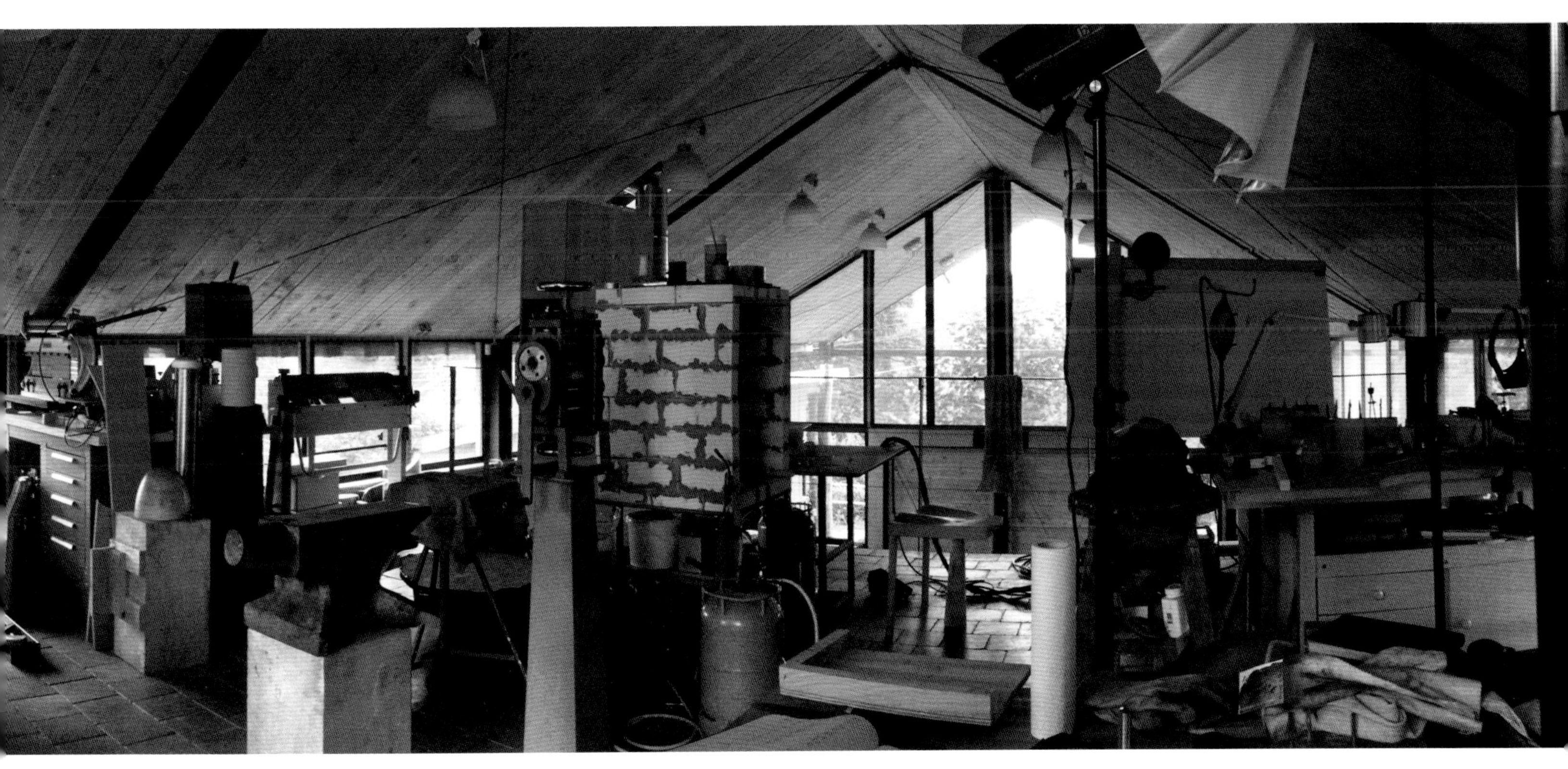

33

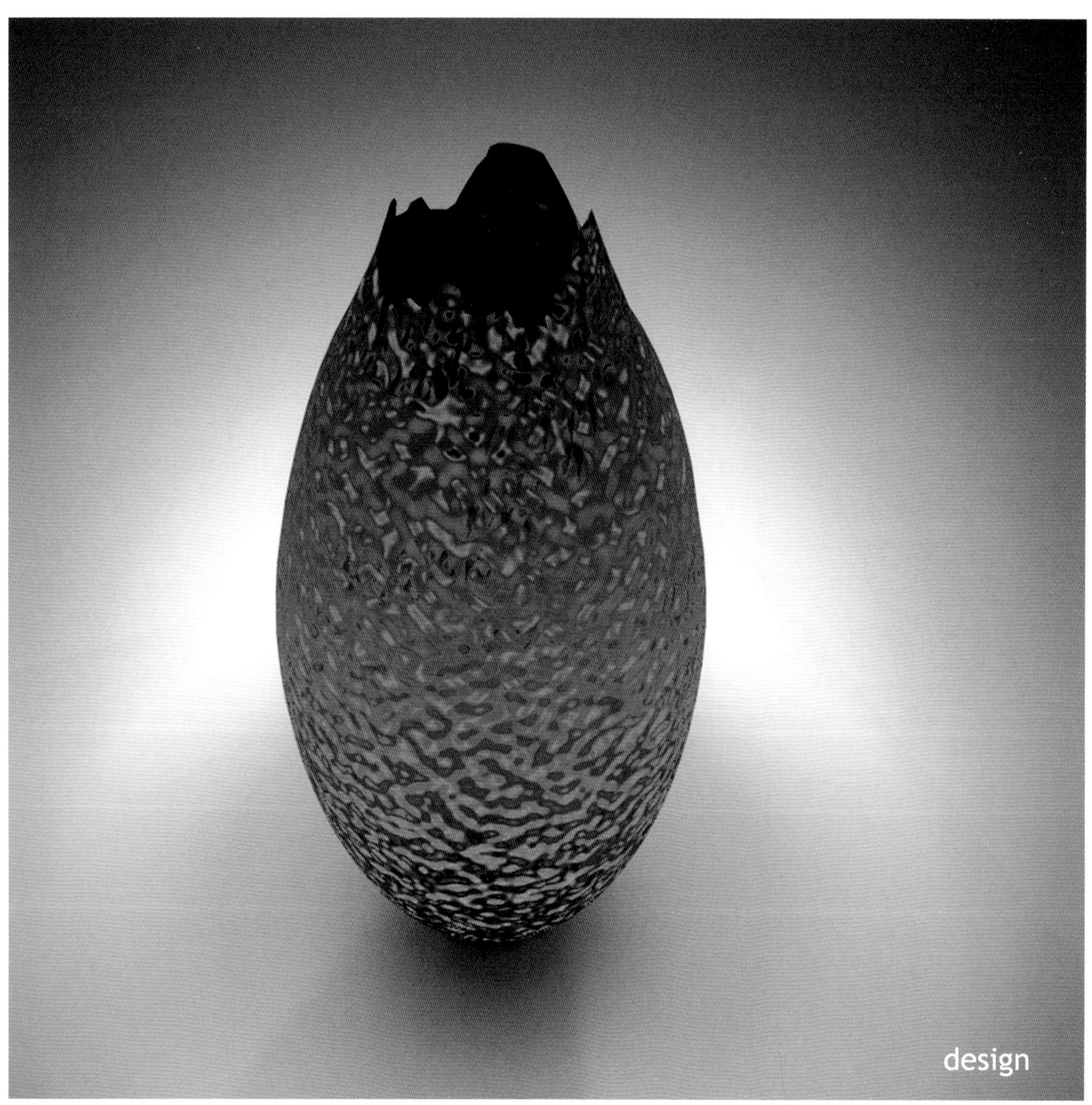

Gedachten bij de opdracht van Zilvermuseum Sterckshof

Voor de museumopdracht gingen wij de uitdaging aan om te zien hoe ver we kunnen gaan met bijvoorbeeld 2 kilogram fijnzilver, een rondel gegoten in een diameter van 11 centimeter en met een dikte van ongeveer 2 centimeter.
Hoe precies kunnen wij onze hamers het zilver laten leiden tot een vorm die zijn eigen gewicht nog net kan dragen? We hebben daarbij gekozen voor een hoge, een beetje spitse ovale vorm, waarbij de bovenrand tot bijna nul uitloopt en als het ware verdwijnt in de lucht. Dit met een oppervlak dat lijkt op gedroogde klei in een rivierbedding.

Laat de queeste beginnen!

rob & jaap thalen

Idée imaginée dans le cadre des Commandes du Musée de l'orfèvrerie Sterckshof

Pour la Commande qui nous a été adressée par le Musée de l'orfèvrerie, nous avons relevé le défi de voir jusqu'où nous pouvions aller avec deux kilogrammes d'argent fin se présentant sous la forme d'une rondelle d'un diamètre de 11 cm et d'une épaisseur d'environ 2 cm.
Avec quel degré de précision pouvions-nous utiliser notre marteau pour façonner l'argent et lui donner une forme capable de supporter son propre poids ? Nous avons jeté notre dévolu sur une forme en pointe plutôt haute à la base ovoïde, dont le bord supérieur est pratiquement inexistant et se dissipe d'une certaine façon dans l'air. La surface de cet objet ressemble à la terre glaise desséchée du lit d'une rivière.

Que la quête commence !

rob & jaap thalen

Gedanken zum Auftrag des Silbermuseums Sterckshof

Für den Auftrag des Museums haben wir uns der Herausforderung gestellt zu prüfen, wie weit wir mit 2 kg Feinsilber gehen könnten; eine mit einem Durchmesser von 11 cm und einer Dicke von etwa 2 cm gegossene Rondelle.
Wie genau können wir unsere Hämmer das Silber zu einer Form bringen lassen, die ihr eigenes Gewicht gerade noch tragen kann? Wir haben uns dabei für eine hohe, etwas spitz zulaufende ovale Form entschieden, deren oberer Rand fast zu Null wird und sozusagen in der Luft verschwindet. Dies mit einer Oberfläche, die Ton in einem getrockneten Flussbett gleicht.

Beginnen wir mit dem unausführbaren Auftrag!

rob & jaap thalen

Thoughts on the commission for the Sterckshof Silver Museum

For the museum commission, we set ourselves the challenge to see how far we could take approximately 2 kg of fine silver. A cast disc with a diameter of 11 cm and a thickness of approximately 2cm. How precisely can our hammers guide the silver to a shape that is just capable of carrying its own weight? We opted for a tall, slightly pointed oval shape, where the top edge peters out and disappears into thin air, as it were. A shape with a surface that has the texture of dried clay in a river bed.

Let the quest begin!

rob & jaap thalen

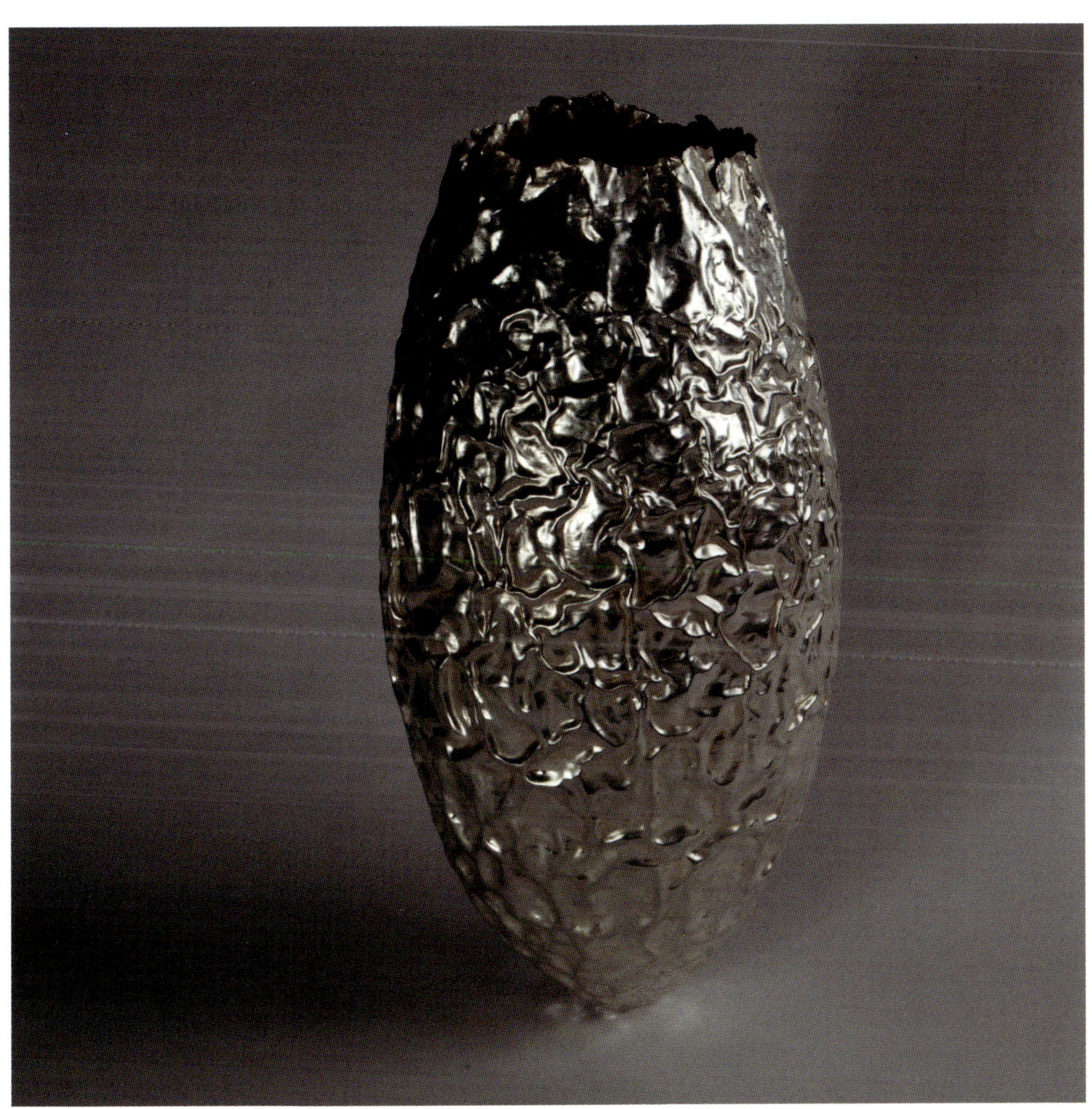

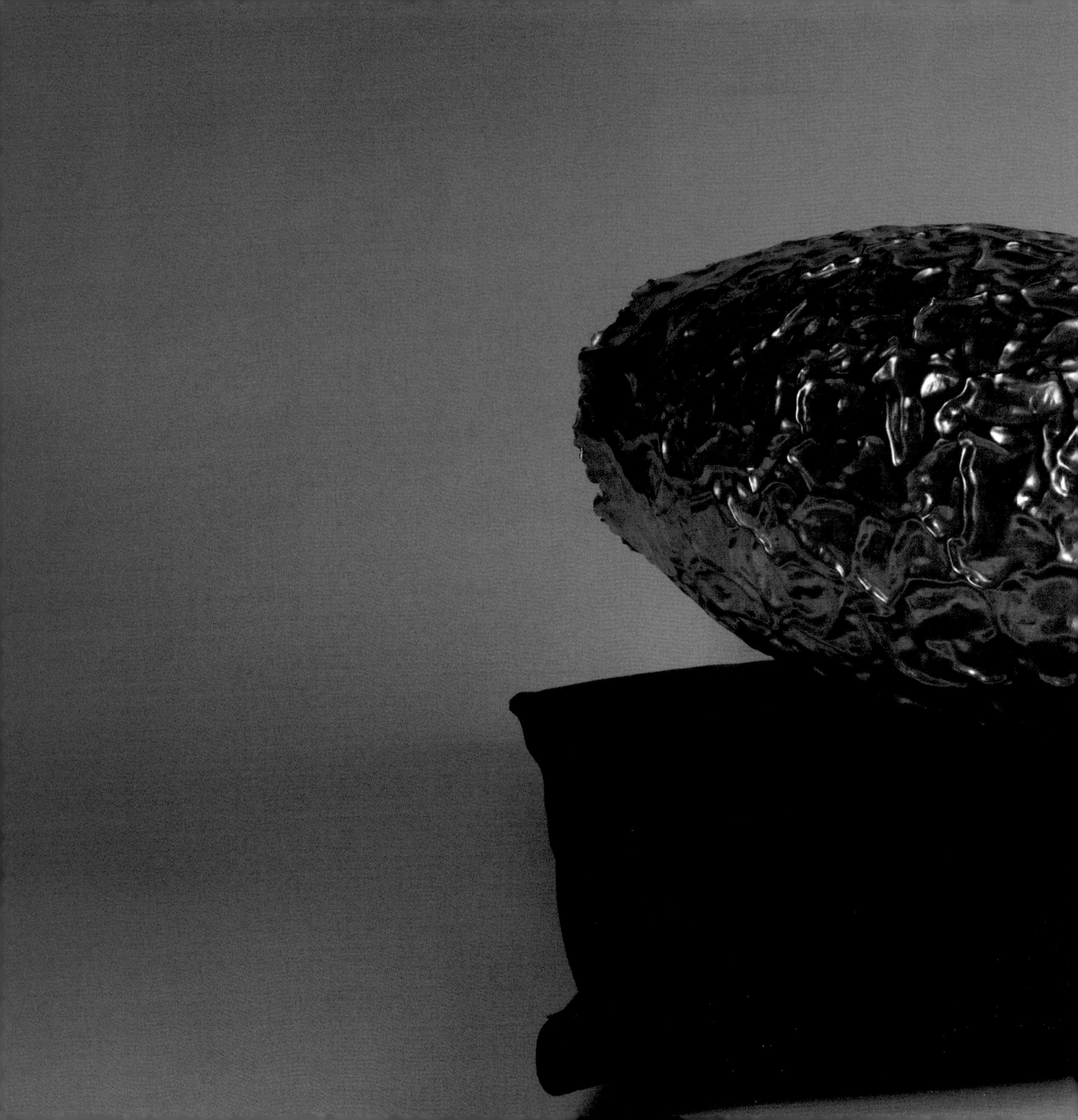

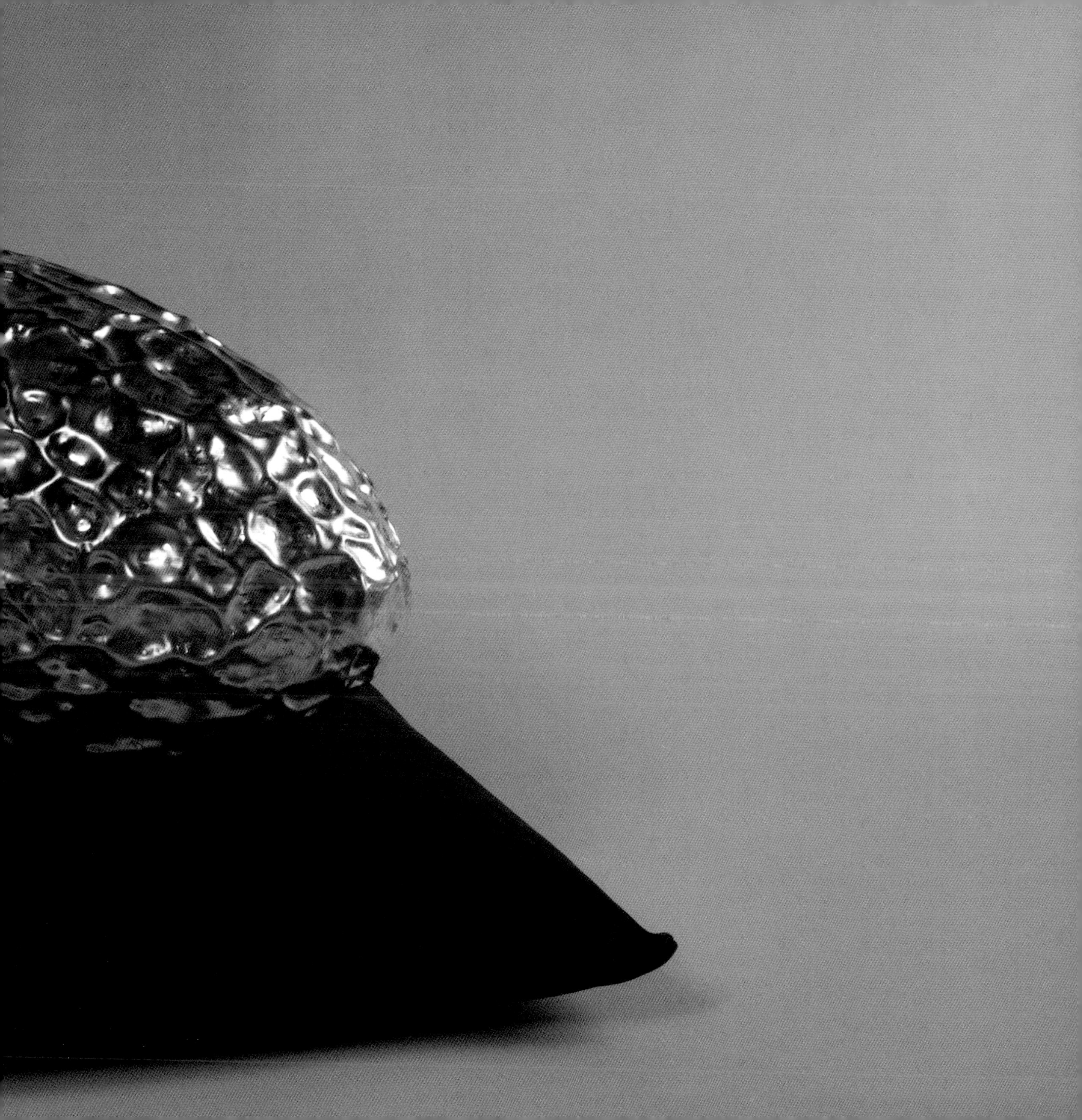

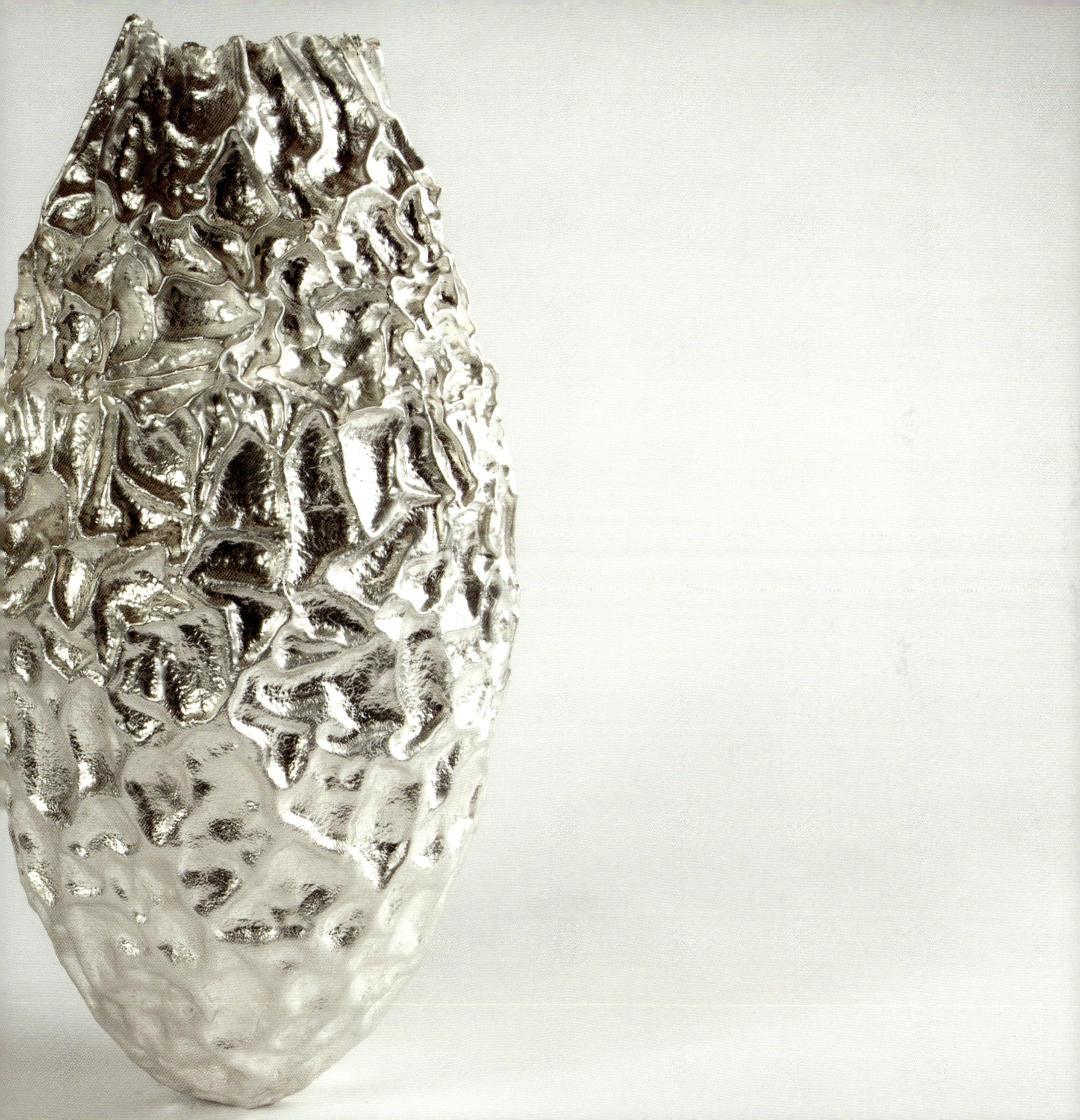

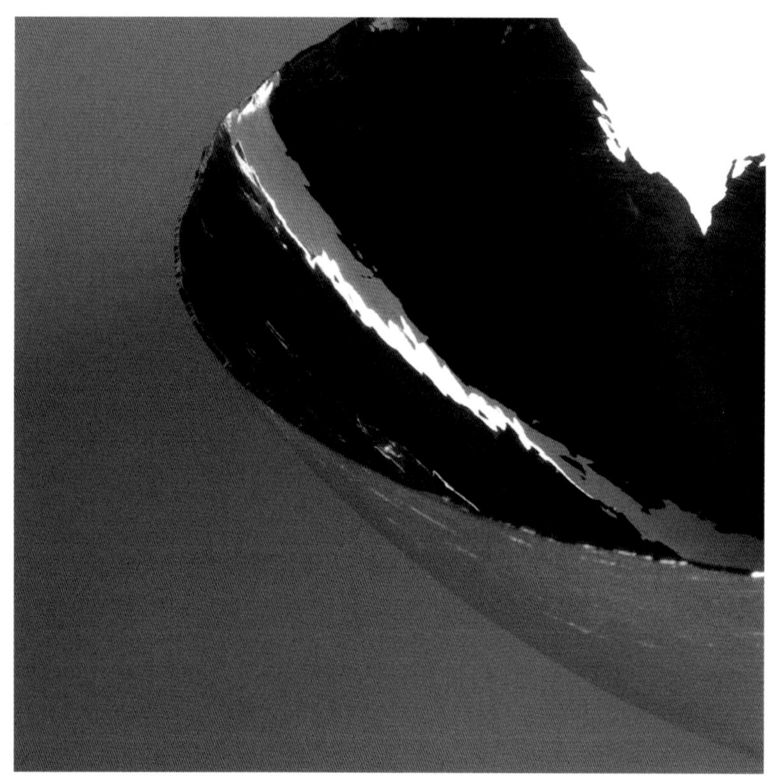

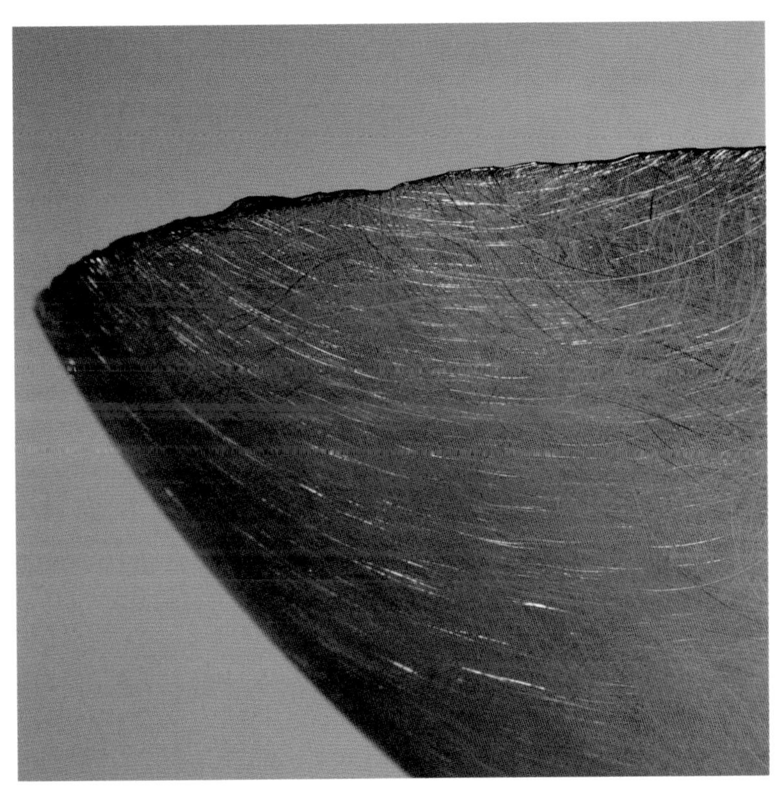

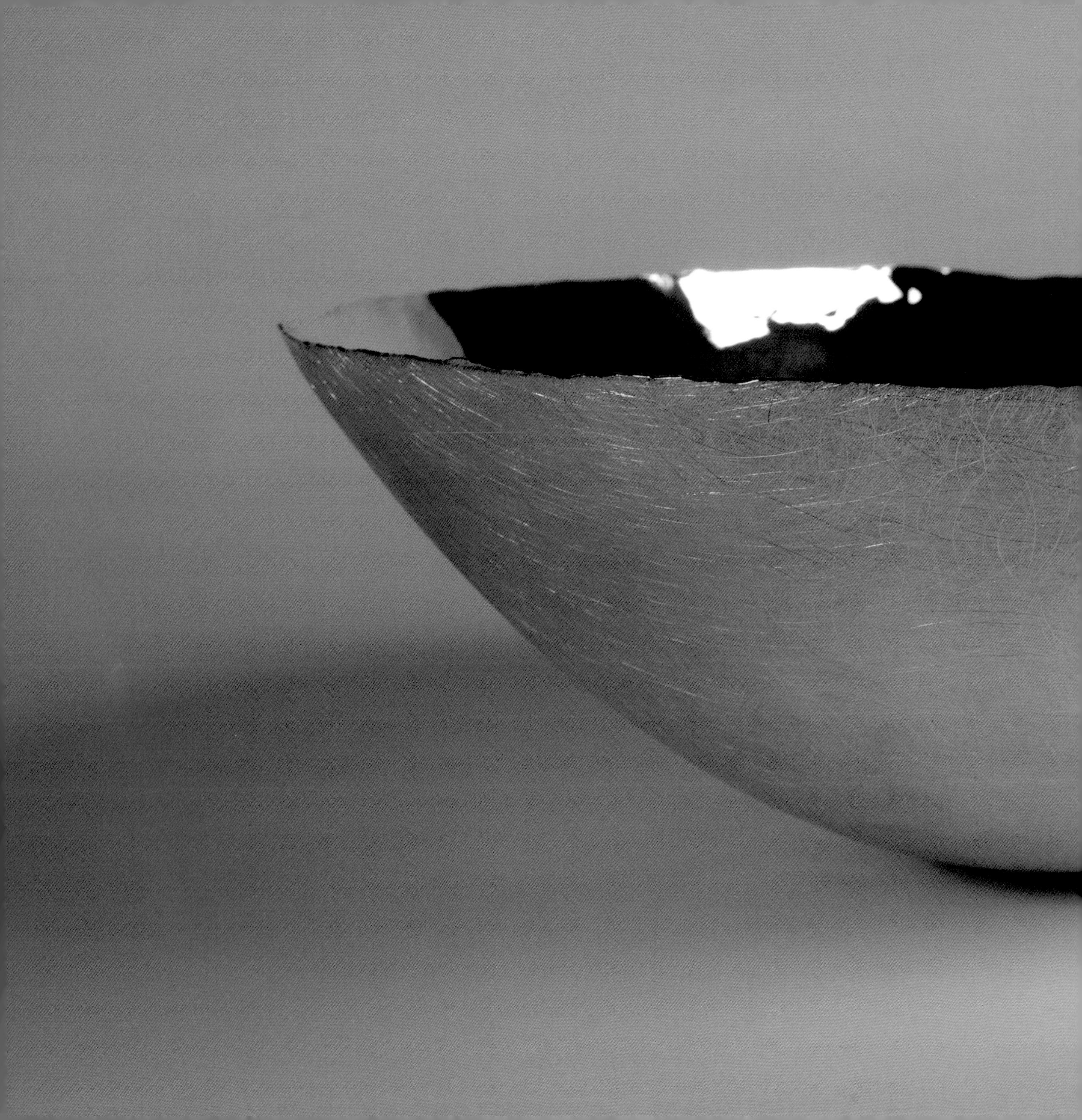

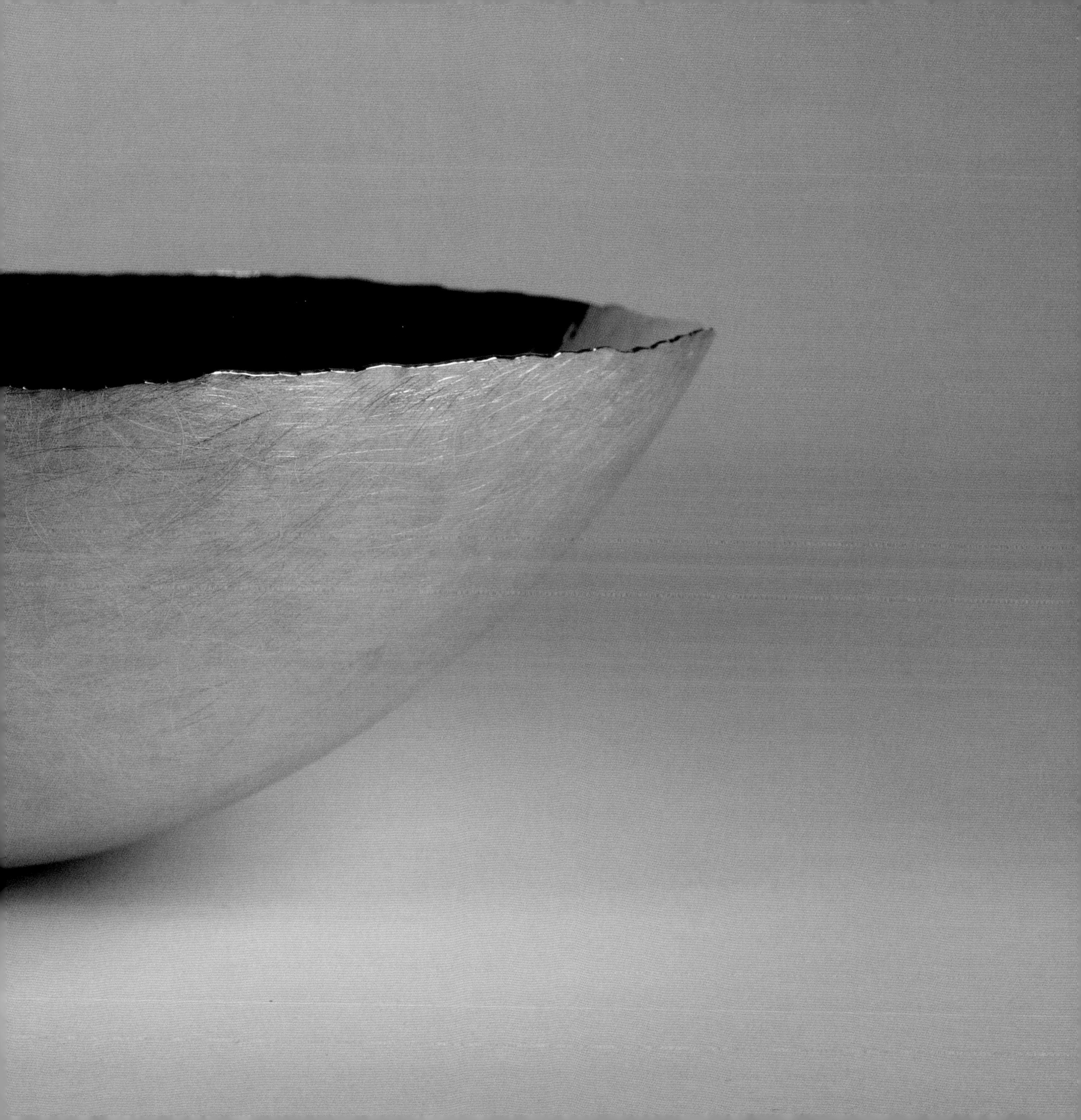

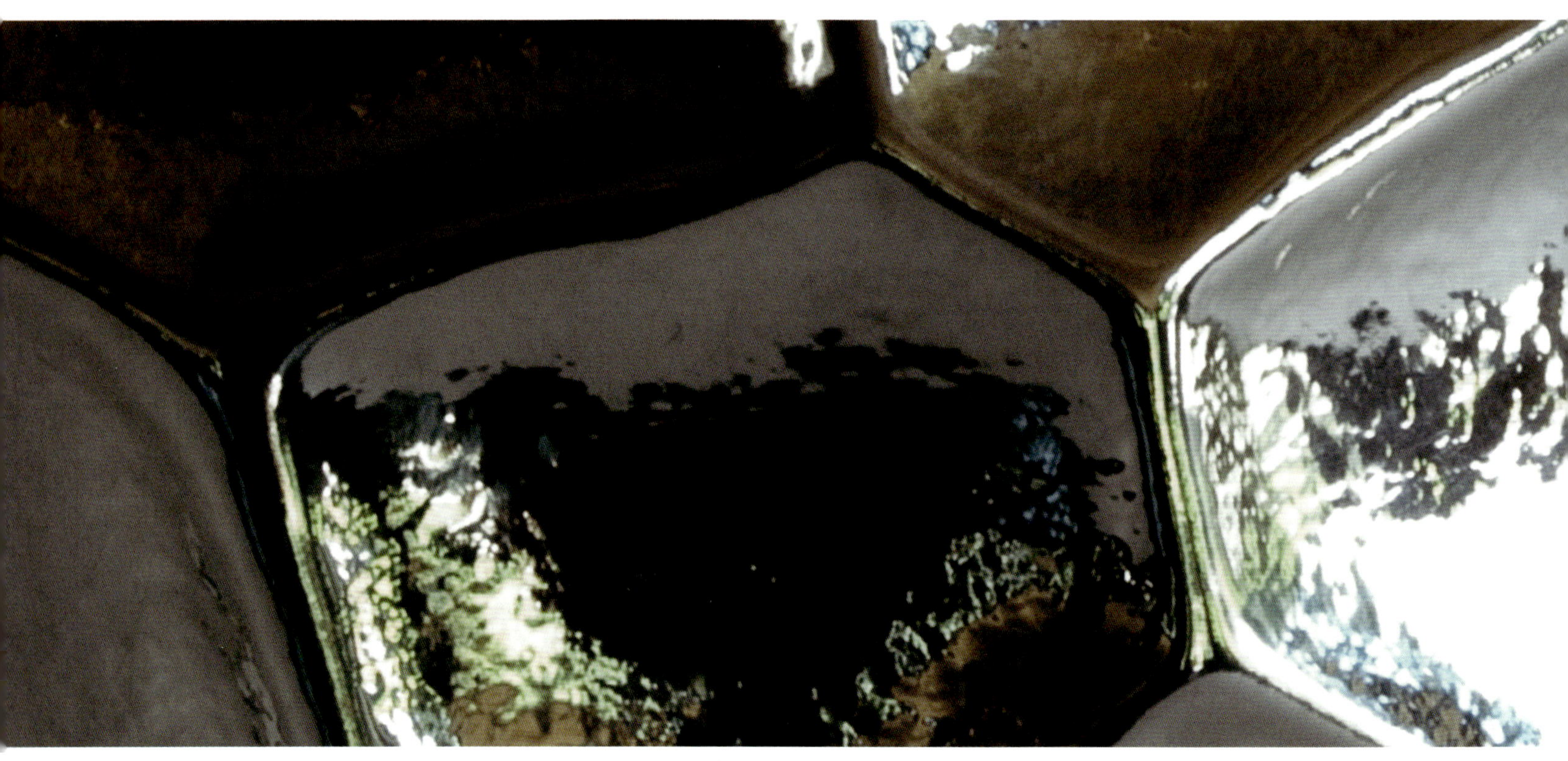

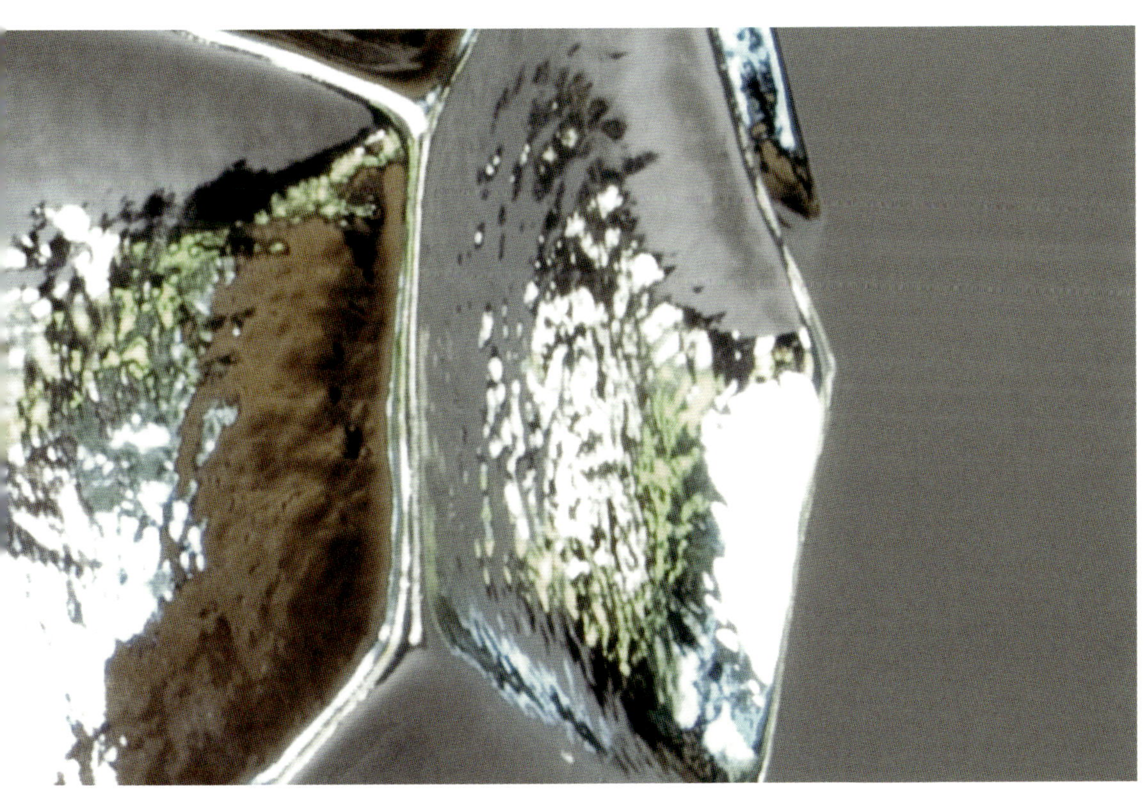

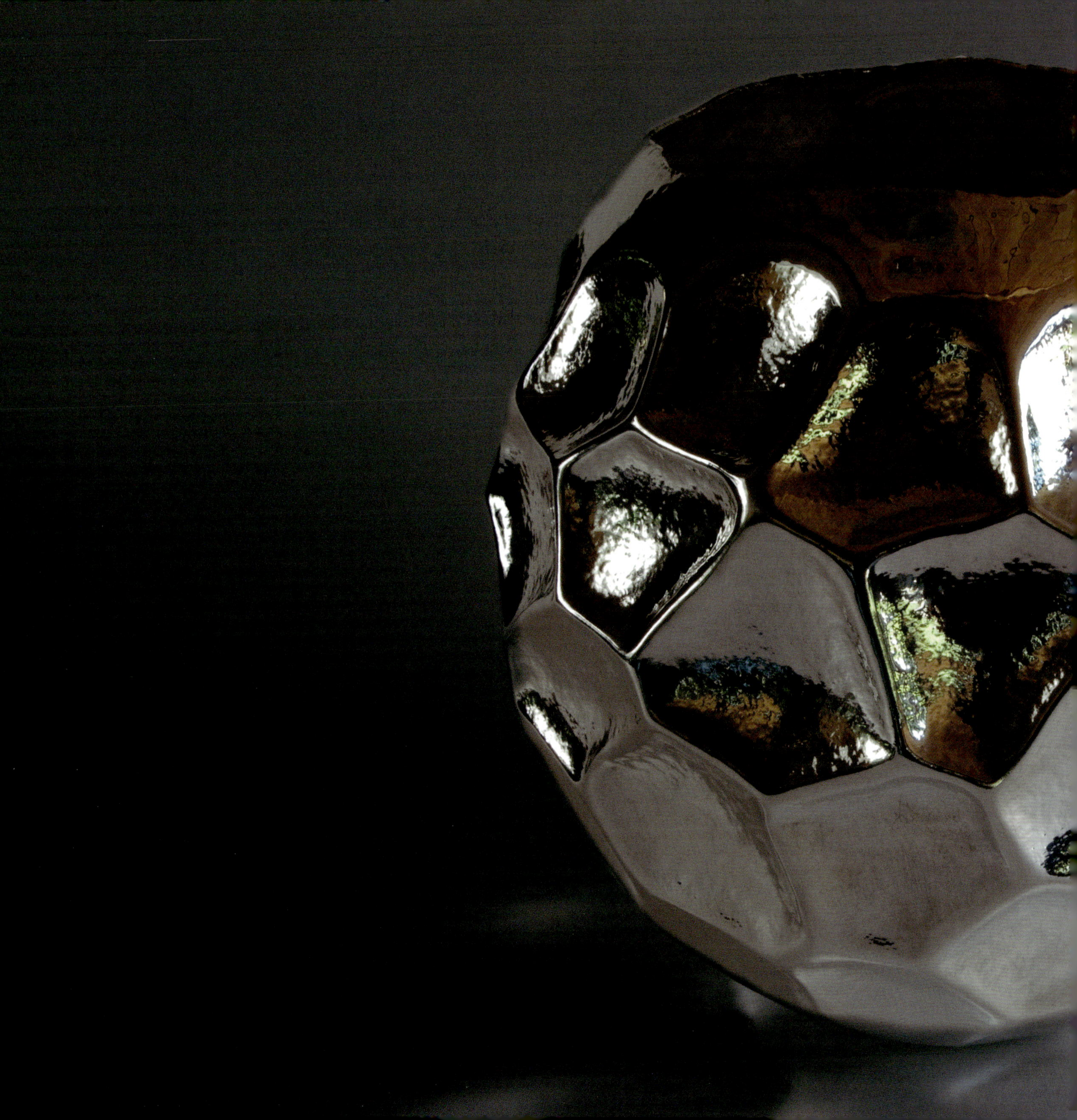

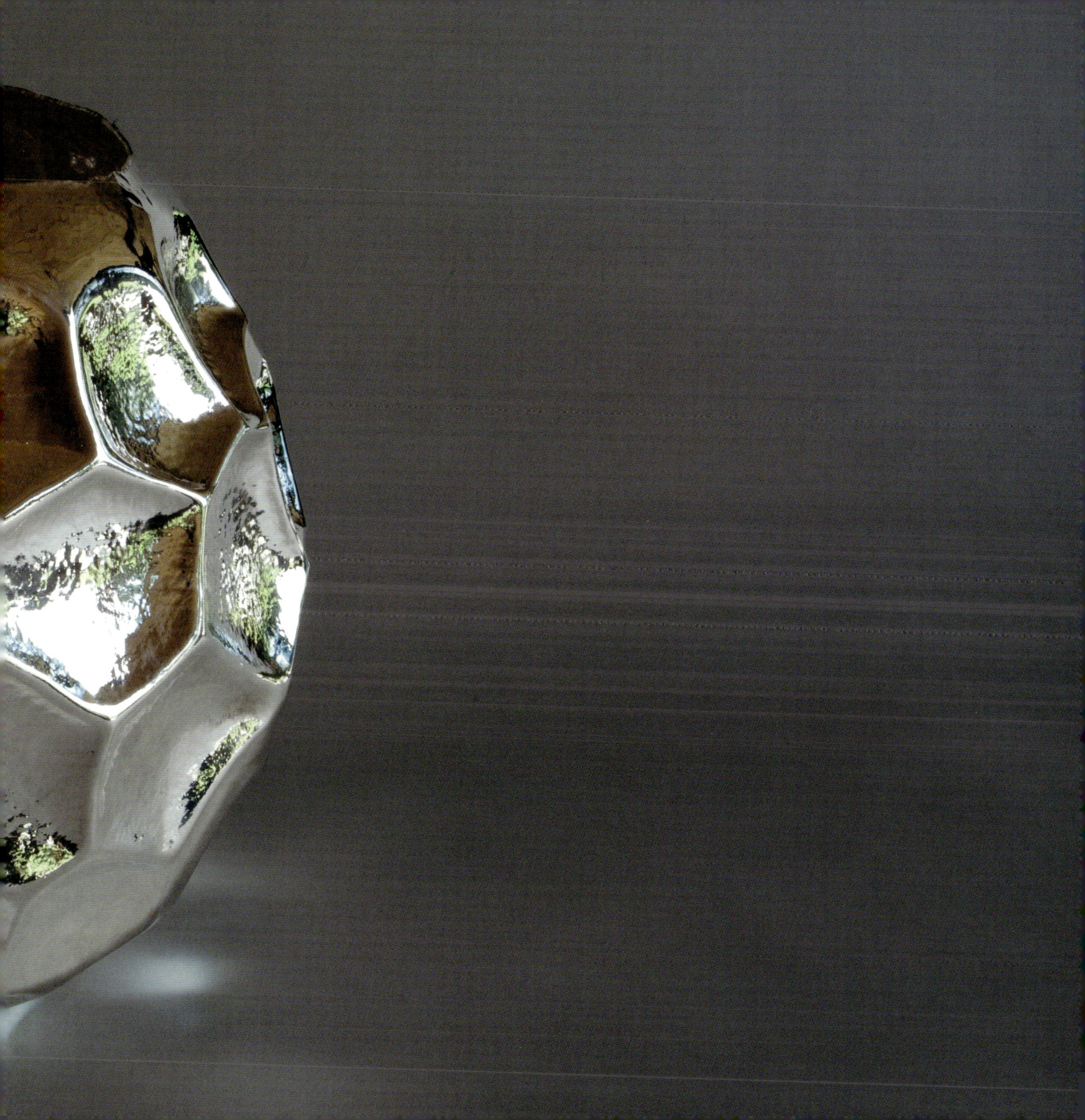

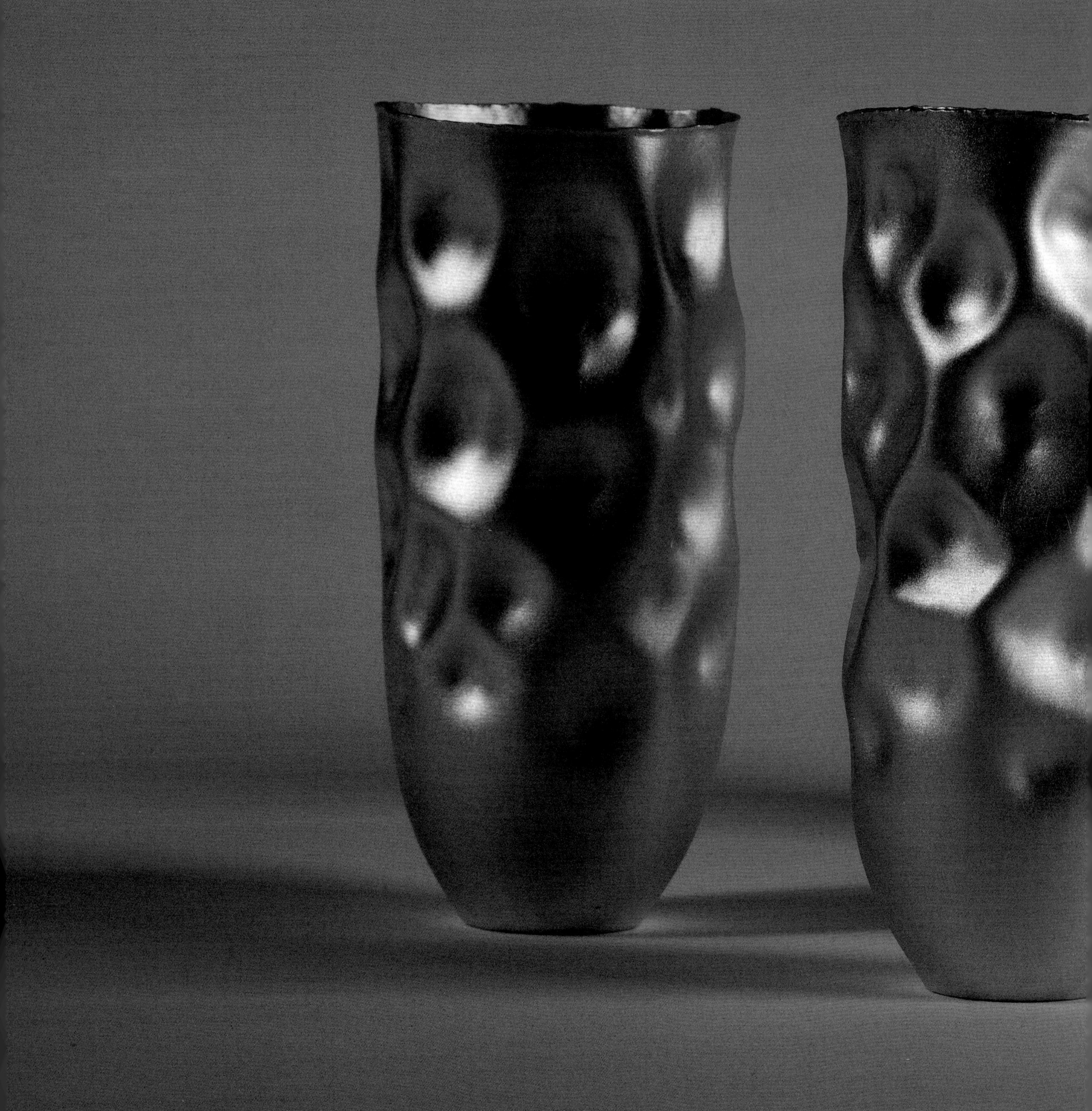

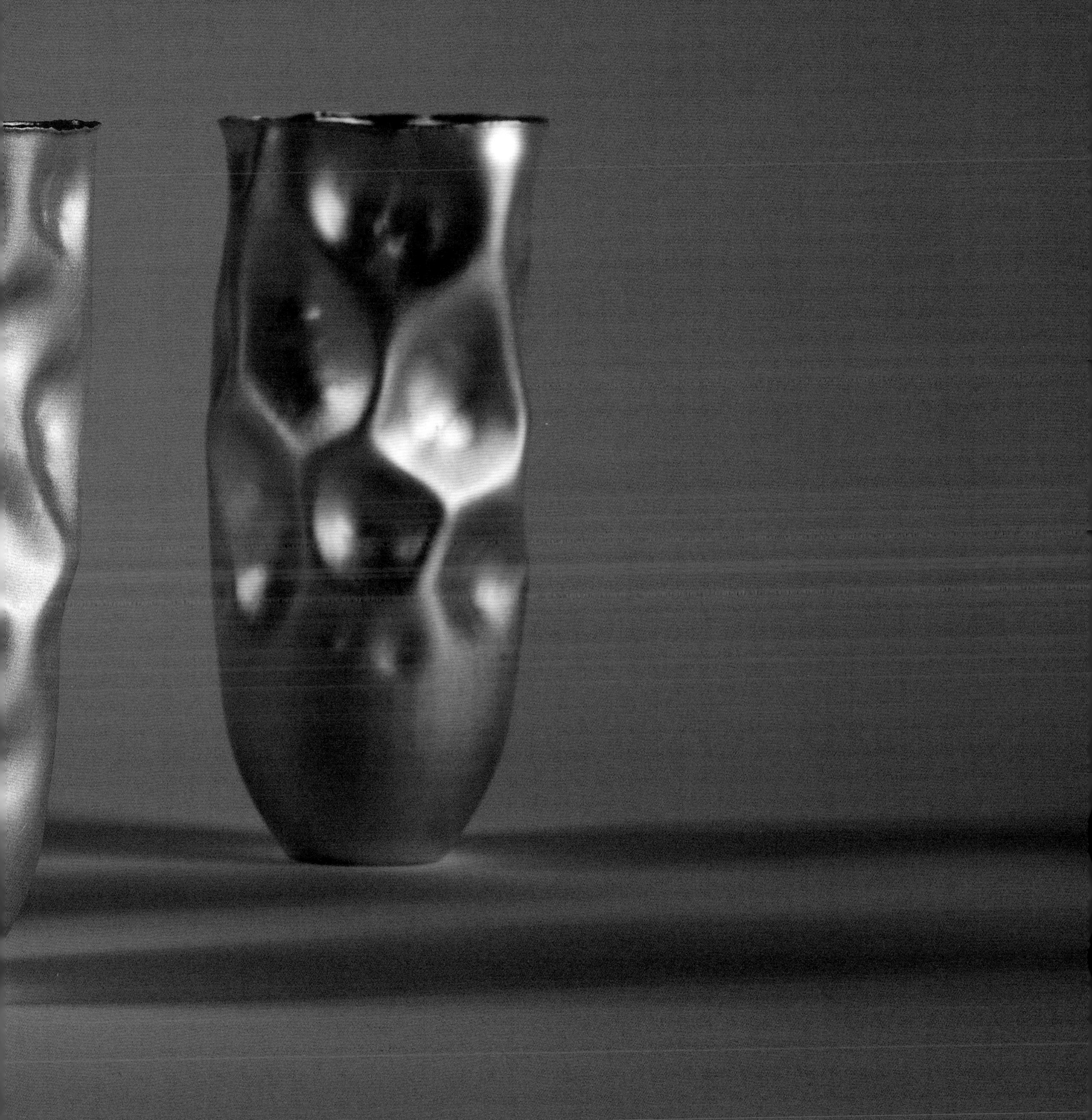

53

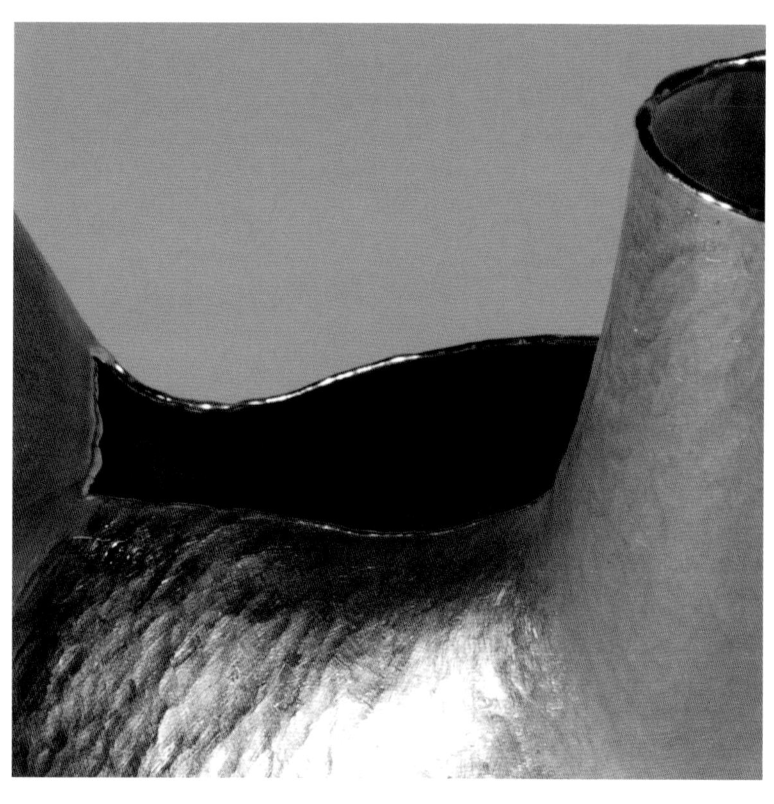

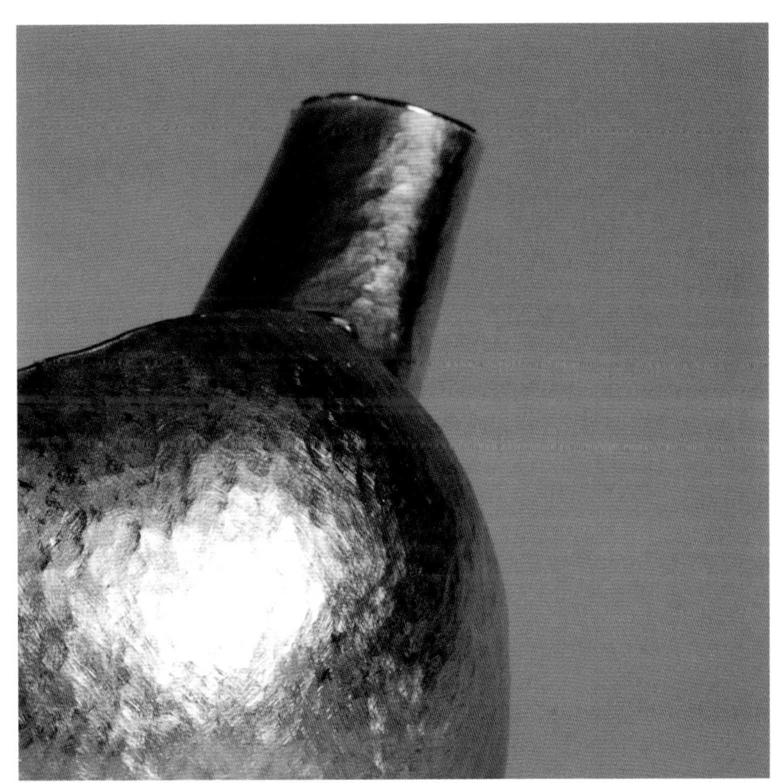

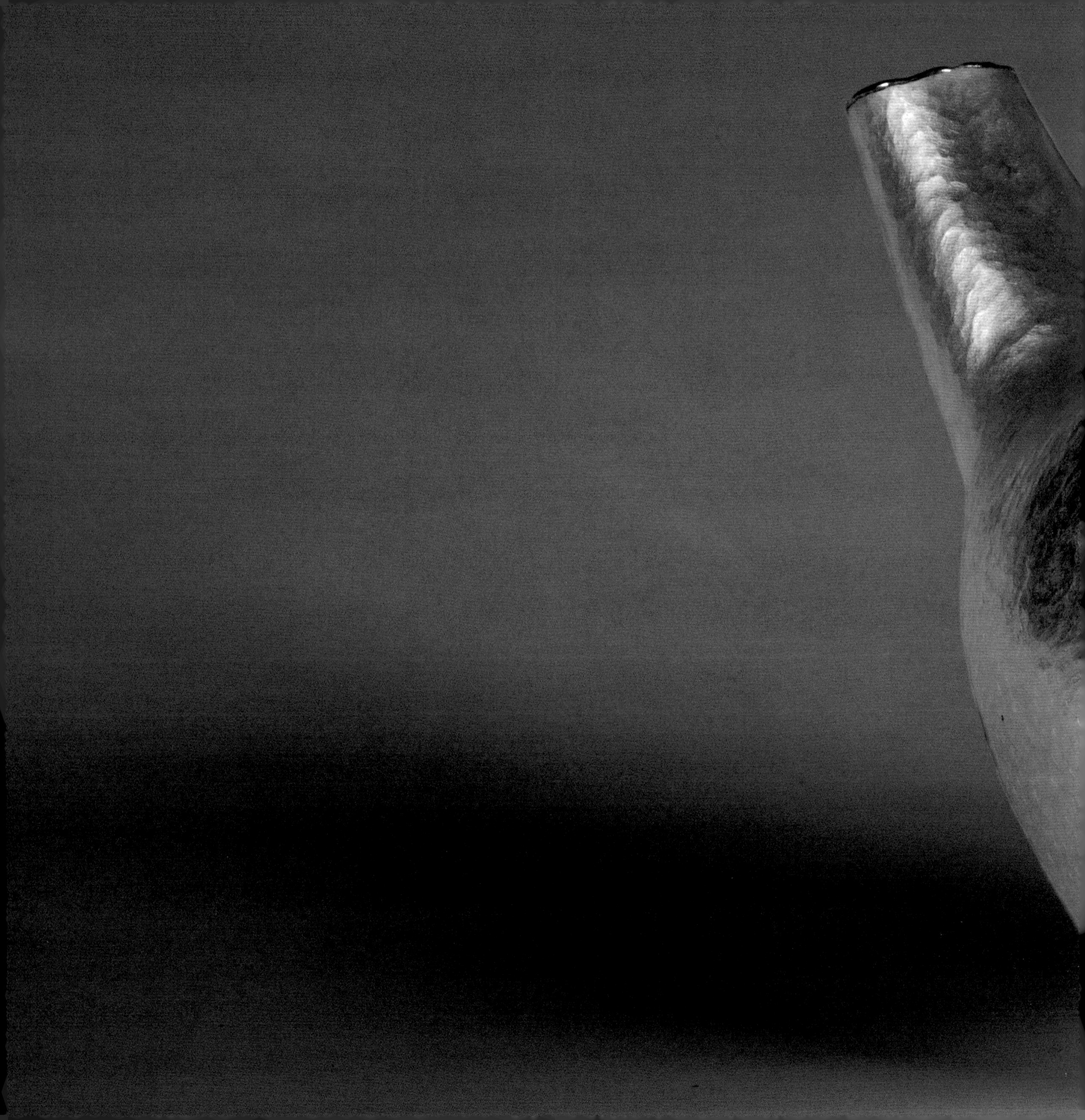

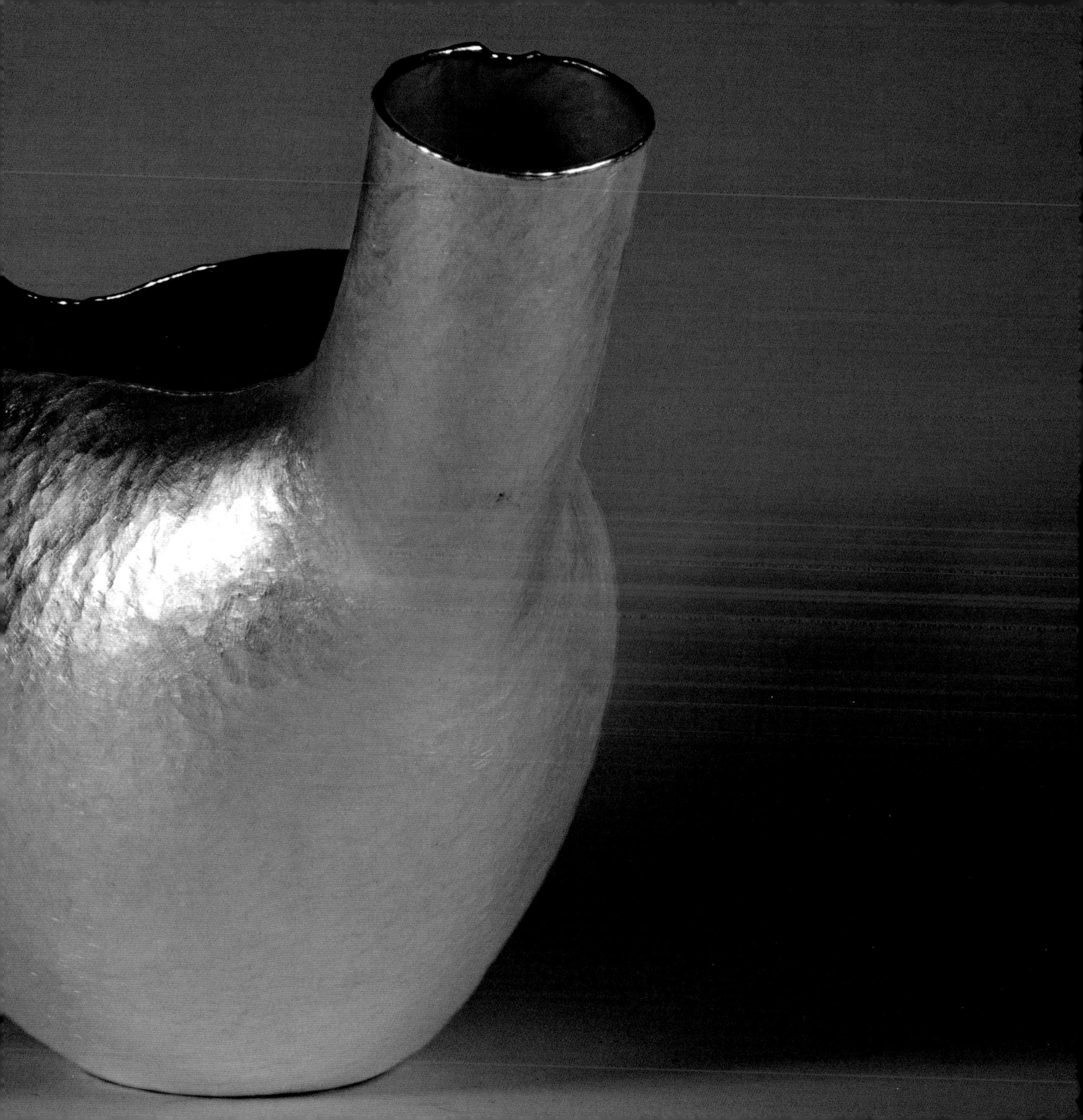

57

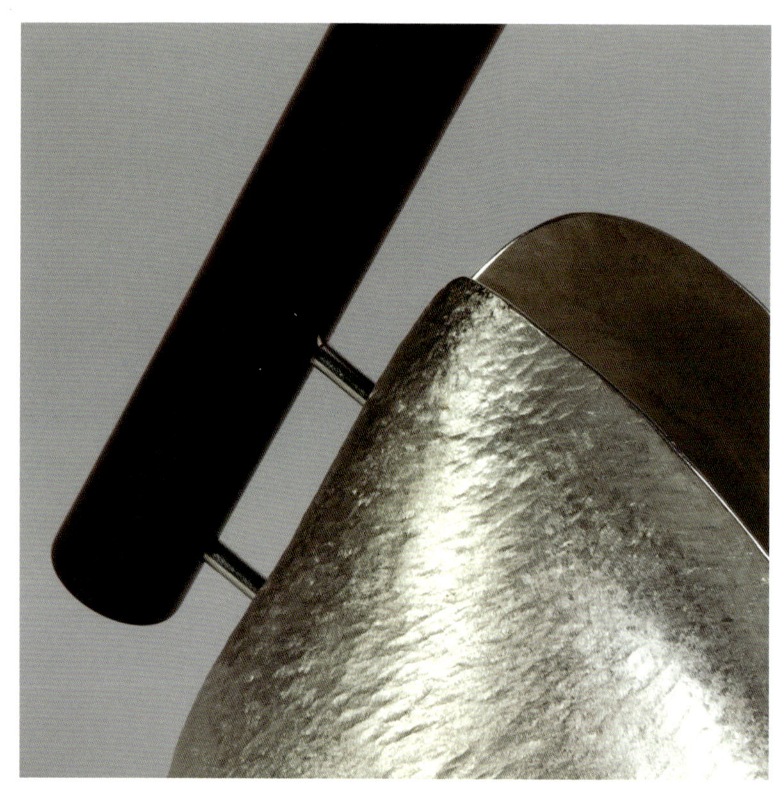

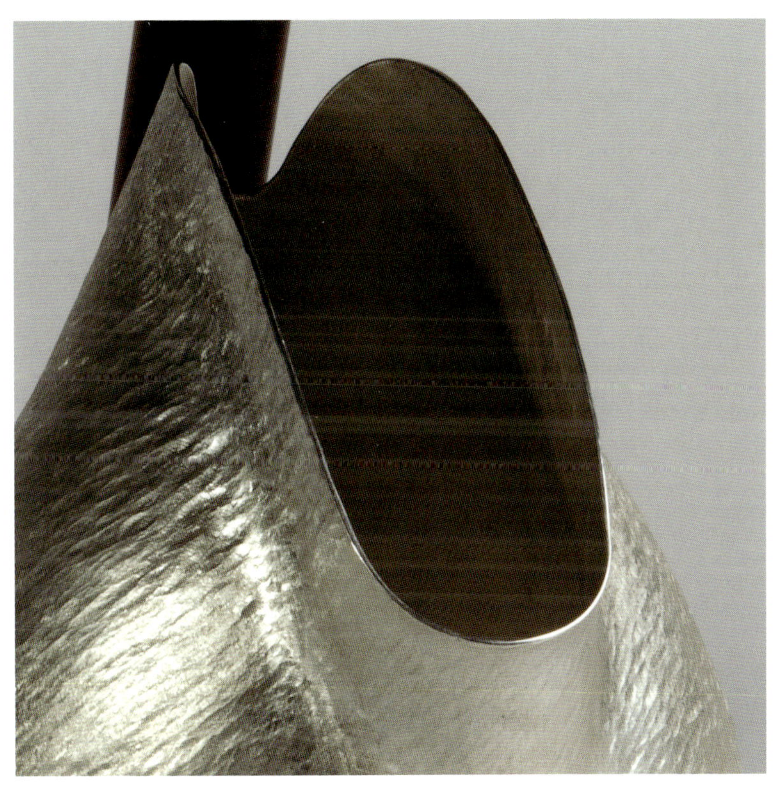

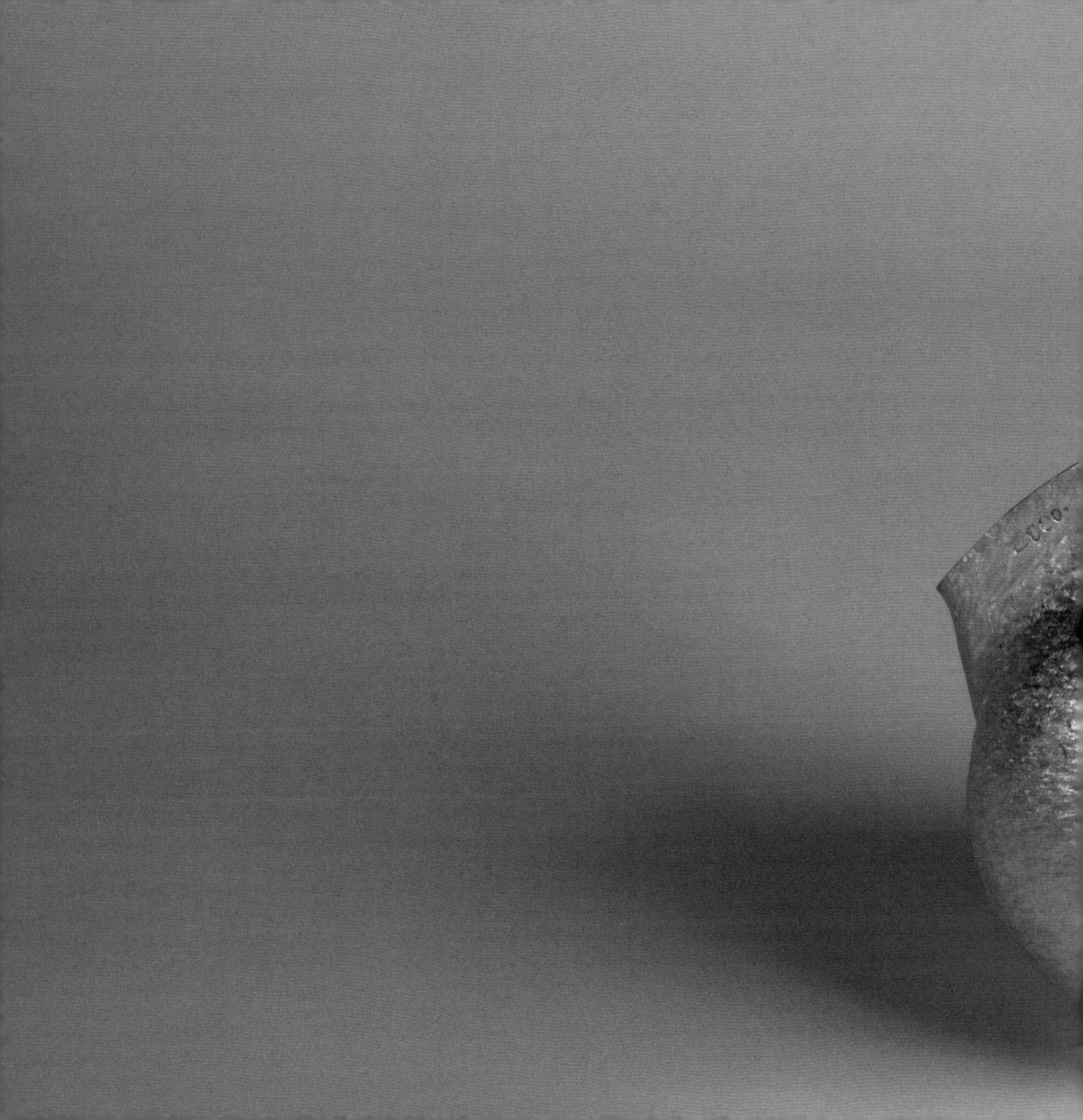

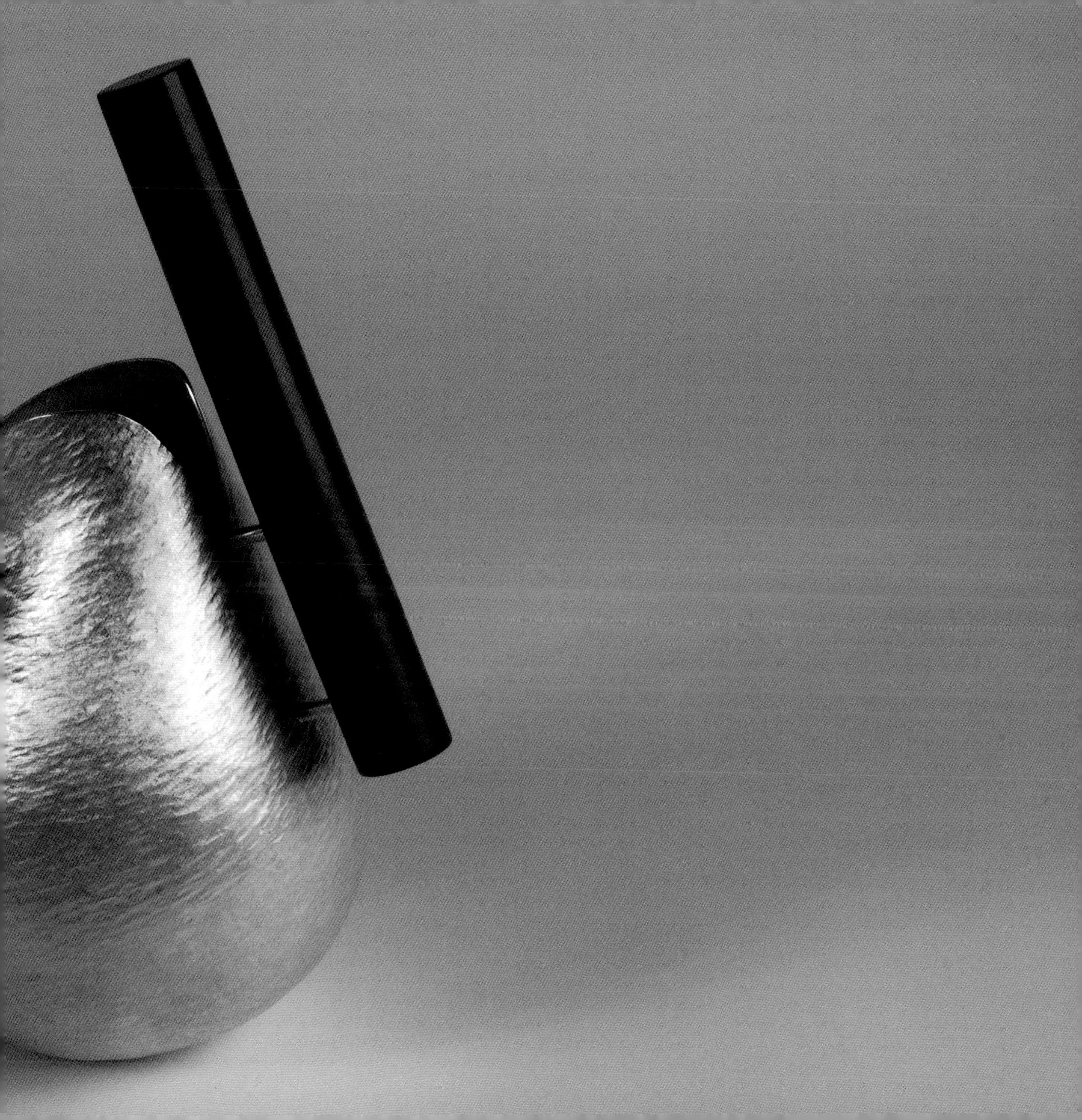

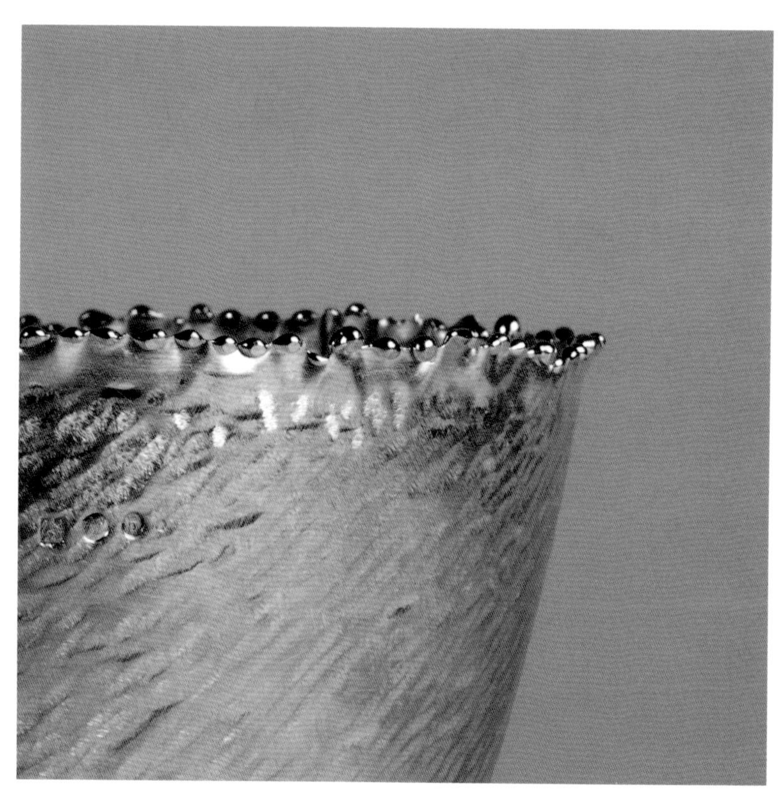

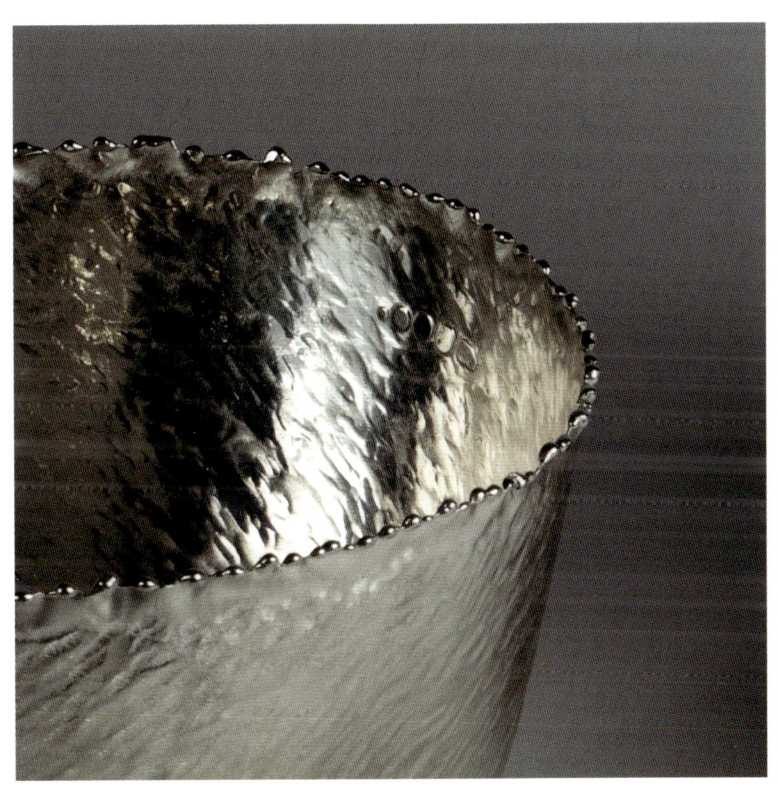

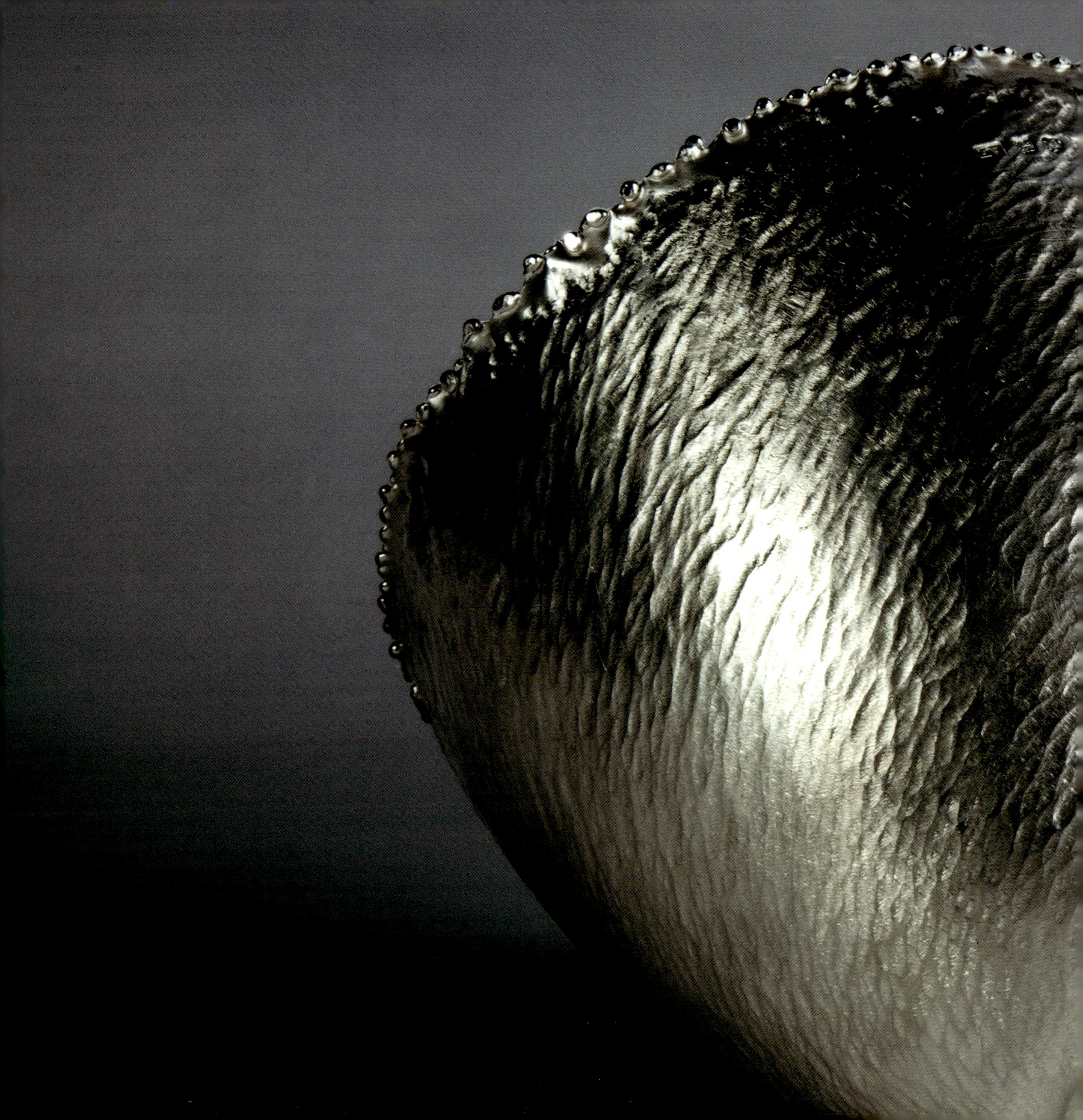

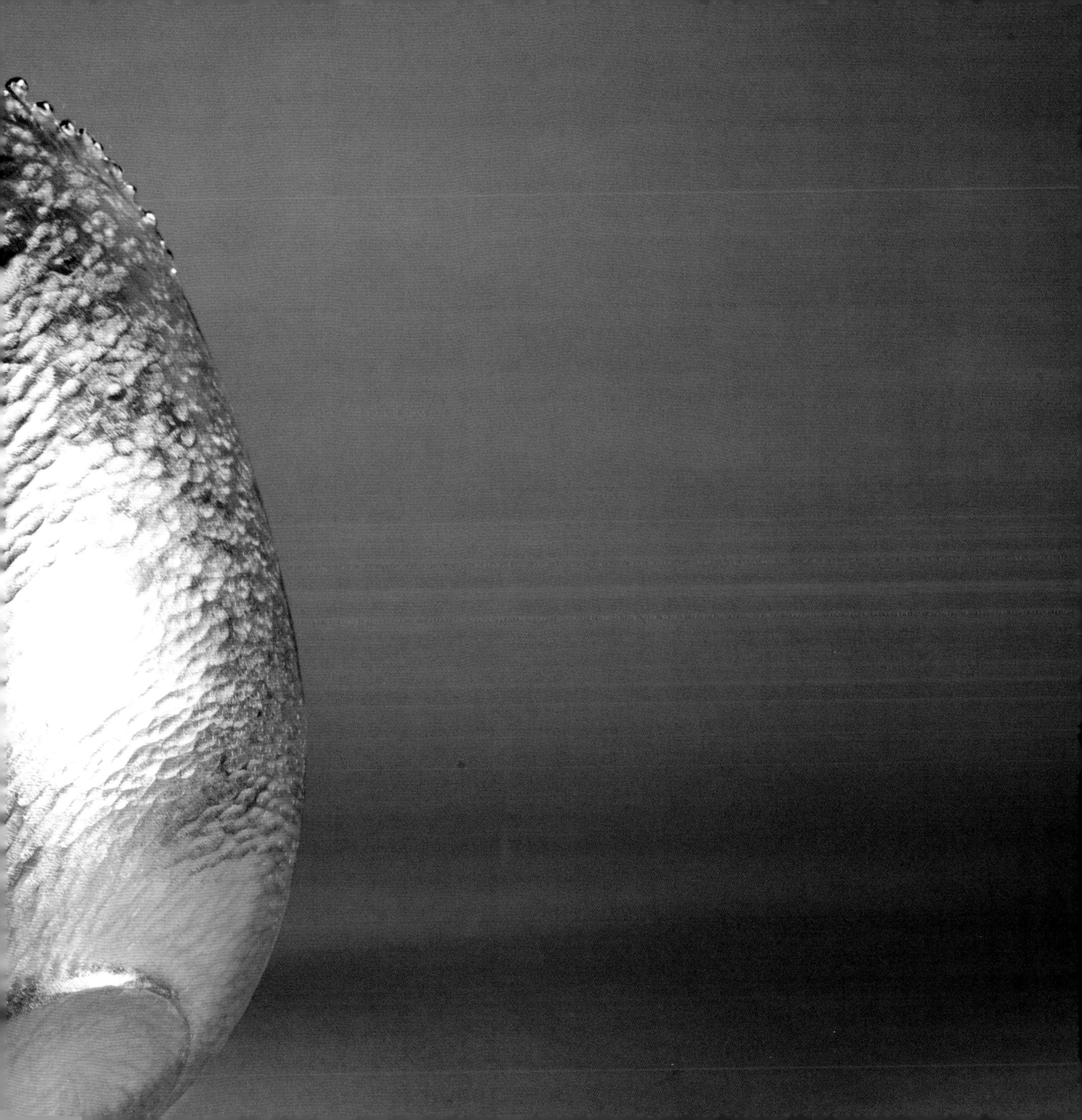

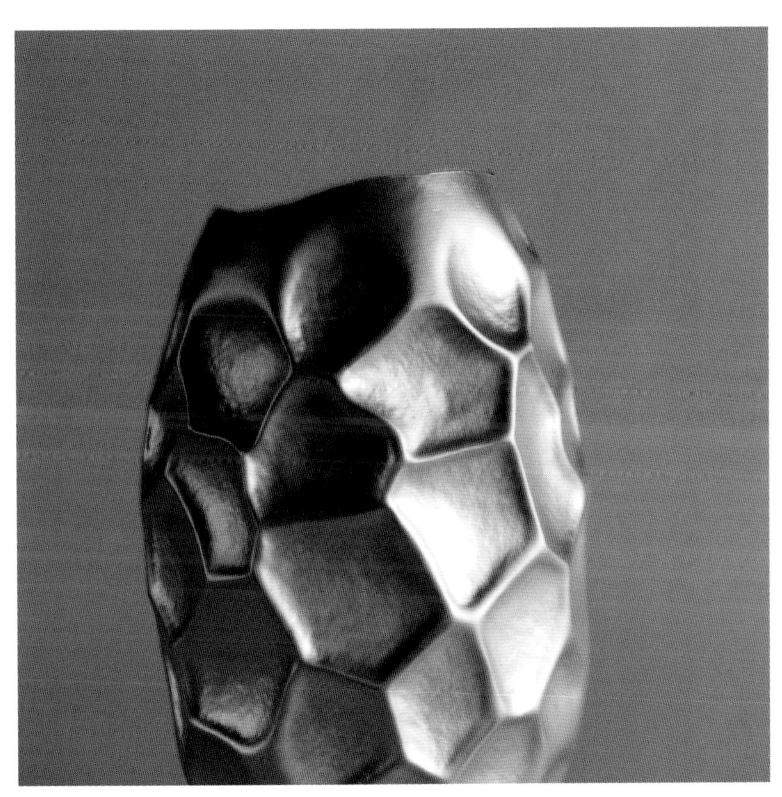

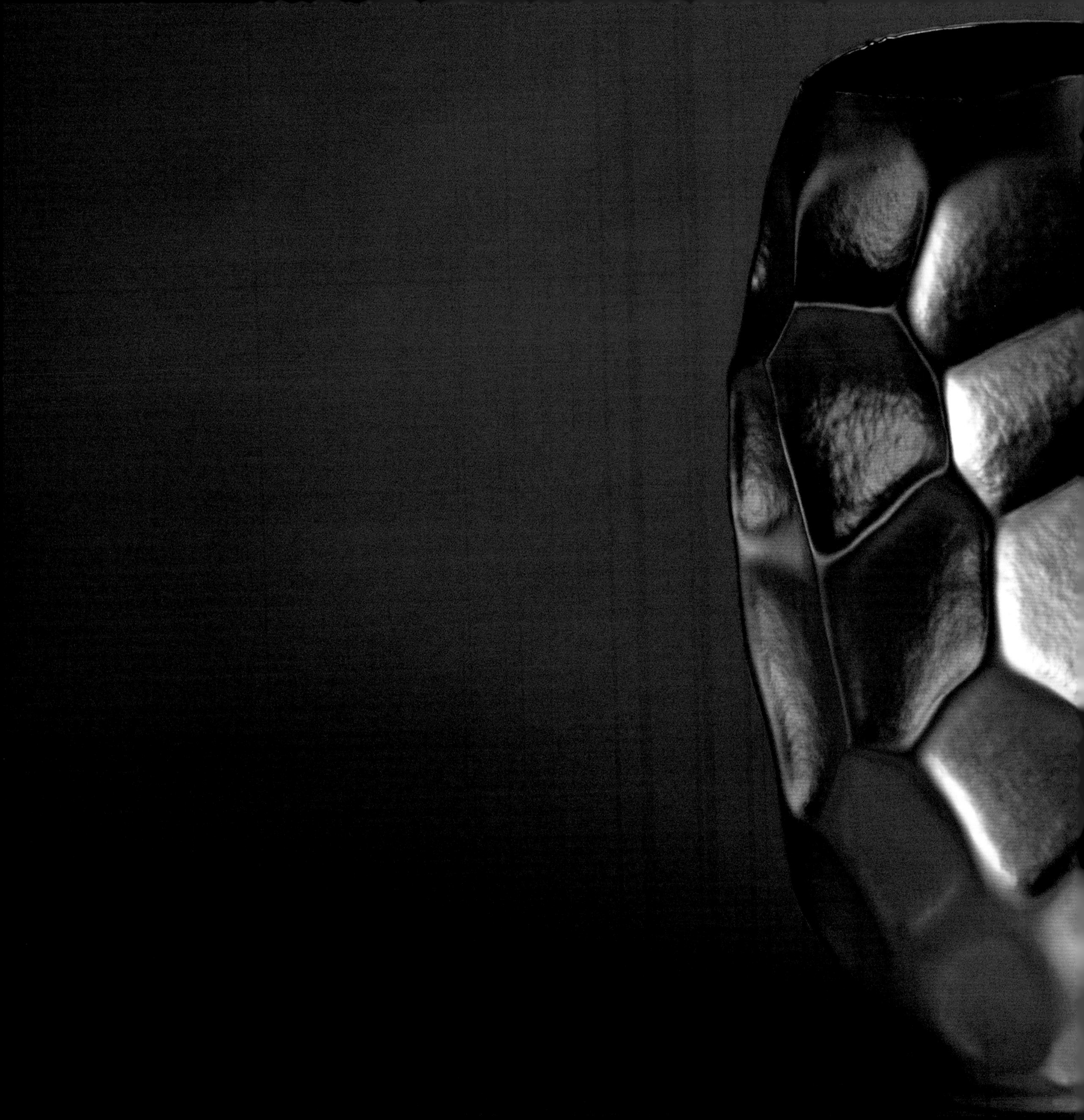

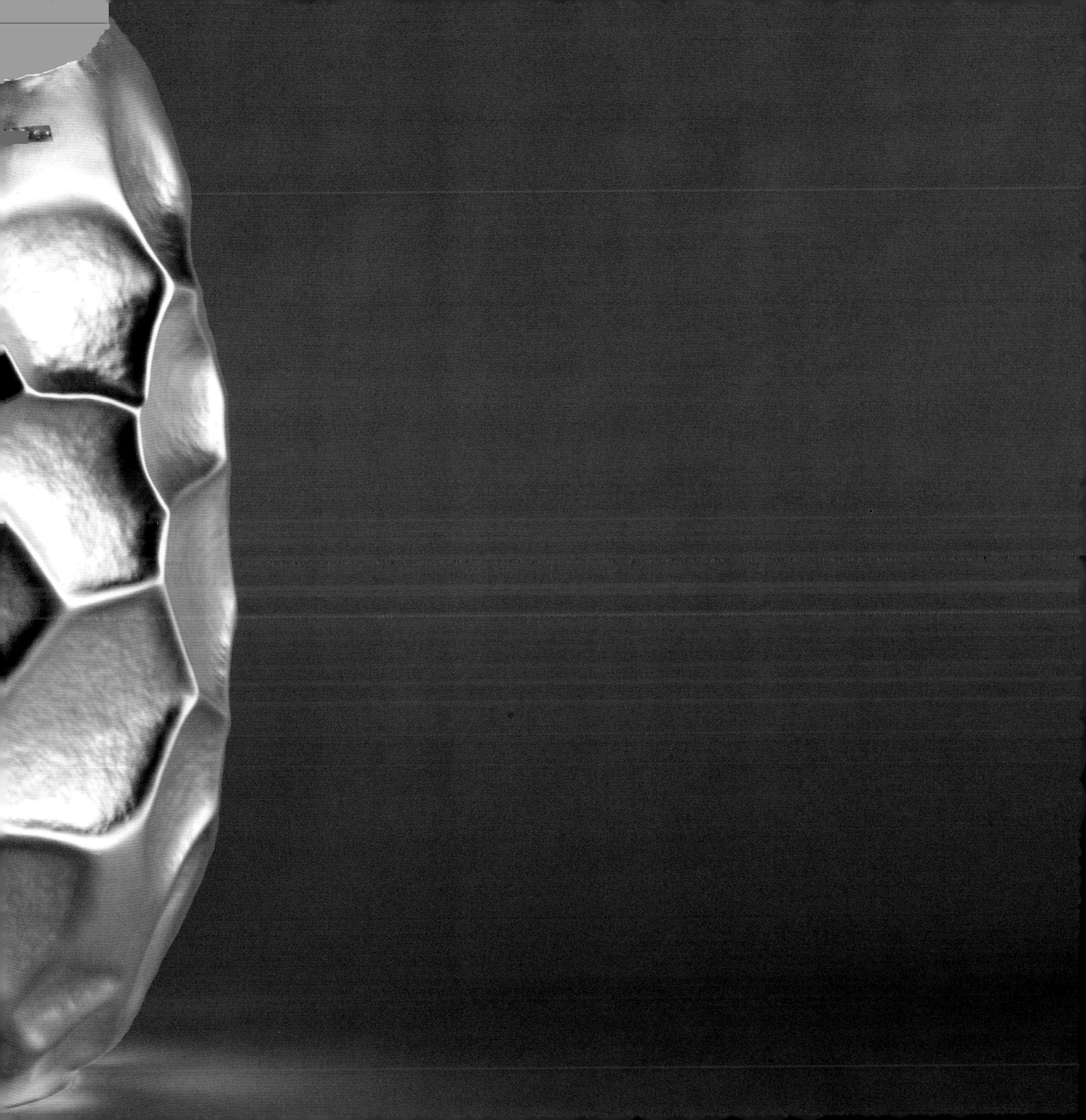

Vaders en zonen

Rob en Jaap Thalen hebben een allesbehalve typische vader-zoon relatie. Het is een relatie waar alles steunt op liefde en vertrouwen, ettelijke keren beproefd, maar door de jaren heen onwrikbaar gebleven.

Het viel me al op, de eerste keer dat ik ze ontmoette, iets meer dan twee jaar geleden. Toen ik ze samen zag, vroeg ik me meteen af of ze vader en zoon waren, zo sterk lijken ze op elkaar. Het vertrouwen en de behaaglijkheid die ze uitstralen, zijn op zijn minst opmerkelijk te noemen.

De band die een man met zijn vader heeft, zet een stempel op zijn leven. Daarom moet elke volwassen zoon de keuze maken en beslissen of die relatie al dan niet zal bepalen wat hij wordt. Een zoon wil weten en begrijpen wie zijn vader is.

Je vader bepaalt wie je bent. Het ouderschap is de moeilijkste, uitdagende en meest lonende job die je ooit zal hebben. Een heel goede vader schept voor zijn kinderen een stevig kader, waarbinnen ze zorg en een leidraad vinden. Dat zijn de prioriteiten waarin moet worden geïnvesteerd.

Weet Jaap dat zijn vader van hem houdt? Ongetwijfeld!
Ik weet niet veel over hun leven samen. Ik weet alleen dat Jaaps ouders scheidden toen hij nog een kind was en dat hij door zijn vader werd grootgebracht, naar het schijnt met heel weinig verkeerde afleiding.
Dag in, dag uit observeerde hij zijn vader urenlang en met eindeloos geduld – een ontzettend creatieve bezigheid.
Jaap is architect van opleiding. De creativiteit zat hem natuurlijk al in het bloed. Je talent en vaardigheid samen met je vader kunnen toepassen en samen kunnen creëren, is iets wat slechts weinigen gegeven is.

Ze concentreren hun energie en passie al jaren op zilverwerk. Deze haast verloren en verwaarloosde kunstvorm lijkt vandaag onstuimig en dynamisch te willen terugkeren.

Rob en Jaap hebben niet bepaald de gemakkelijkste weg gekozen. Elk voorwerp heeft zijn eigen karakter en is een toonbeeld van ultiem vakmanschap en toewijding.
En kijk wat ze samen hebben gecreëerd... Hun prachtige, unieke werken zijn ronduit verbluffend.

Vaders en zonen kunnen een doorslaggevende rol spelen in de wederzijdse aanmoediging om zich optimaal te ontwikkelen.

Het beroemdste vader-zoon duo in de wereld van de architectuur is Eliel en Eero Saarinen. De Fin Eliel Saarinen kwam in Chicago terecht naar aanleiding van zijn deelname aan de prijsvraag voor het ontwerp van de Chicago Tribune Tower, die in 1921 plaatsvond. Eero zat als klein kind urenlang onder zijn vaders tekentafel en ontwierp van jongsaf meubilair voor veel van zijn vaders gebouwen in Cranbrook. Na zijn studies architectuur aan de Universiteit van Yale, keerde Eero in 1936 terug naar Cranbrook om er les te geven en er met zijn vader aan de slag te gaan.
Dit verhaal over de samenwerking tussen vader en zoon, krijgt vandaag een nieuw hoofdstuk: Rob and Jaap Thalen, een opmerkelijk duo.

George A. Larson, architect, Chicago / New York

Pères et fils

Rob et Jaap Thalen sont une exception à la règle des relations entre père et fils. Leur relation repose sur l'amour et la confiance dont ils se témoignent mutuellement depuis des années. Je l'ai remarqué dès que nous nous sommes rencontrés il y a deux ans. Je les ai vus ensemble, me demandant s'ils étaient effectivement père et fils. La ressemblance était évidente. Ils dégageaient une confiance et une tranquillité qui ne trompent pas.

Le rapport qu'un homme entretient avec son père façonne sa vie et chaque homme doit choisir dans quelle mesure sa relation avec son père influencera ou non son existence. Un fils veut savoir et comprendre qui est vraiment son père.

Votre père détermine qui vous êtes. Être parent est la mission la plus difficile, la plus périlleuse, mais aussi la plus gratifiante qu'un homme ait à accomplir au cours de sa vie. Tout bon père doit avant tout veiller à élever et à éduquer ses enfants. Telles sont ses priorités, ce en quoi il doit s'investir.

Jaap a-t-il conscience de l'amour que lui porte son père ? Sans aucun doute ! Je ne connais pas bien leur vie, hormis

le fait que les parents de Jaap ont divorcé alors qu'il était encore très jeune et qu'il a été élevé par son père, apparemment de façon assez stricte.
Travailler avec son père, vous mettre quotidiennement sous son autorité pour accomplir ensemble un acte créatif est une chose incroyable. Jaap est architecte de formation et bien sûr, sa créativité est un don inné. Pouvoir utiliser ce don avec son père pour créer ensemble quelque chose est une chance que peu de gens ont.

Depuis quelques années, ils concentrent leur énergie et leur passion à l'argenterie. Cette forme d'expression artistique pratiquement disparue et oubliée connaît aujourd'hui un nouvel élan, un nouveau dynamisme.

Ni Rob, ni Jaap n'ont choisi la solution de facilité. Chaque objet a son propre caractère et dégage un savoir-faire d'artisan et un engagement sans bornes. Regardez ce qu'ils ont réalisé ensemble. J'admire ces créations uniques.

Les pères et les fils ont cette fantastique capacité de pouvoir s'aider mutuellement à retirer le meilleur d'eux-mêmes.

Eliel et Eero Saarinen font partie des duos père-fils les plus célèbres du monde de l'architecture. Eliel Saarinen, un architecte finlandais, est venu à Chicago en 1921 pour participer au célèbre concours organisé dans le cadre de la construction de la Tribune Tower à Chicago. Eero a littéralement grandi sous la table à dessin de son père et très tôt, il a dessiné des meubles pour bon nombre des bâtiments de la main de son père à Cranbrook. Après avoir étudié l'architecture à l'Université de Yale, Eero est alors retourné à Cranbrook en 1936 pour enseigner et travailler avec son père.

Cette belle histoire de collaboration entre père et fils se perpétue aujourd'hui par celle de Rob et Jaap Thalen, qui forment un duo remarquable.

George A. Larson, architecte, Chicago / New York

Väter und Söhne

Rob und Jaap Thalen haben alles andere als eine typische Vater-Sohn-Beziehung. Es ist eine Beziehung, in der alles auf Liebe und Vertrauen beruht, die etliche Male auf die Probe gestellt wurde, aber über die Jahre unerschütterlich geblieben ist.

Das ist mir bereits aufgefallen, als ich sie das erste Mal vor etwas mehr als zwei Jahren getroffen habe. Als ich sie zusammen sah, habe ich mich sofort gefragt, ob sie Vater und Sohn seien, da sie sich so sehr ähnlich sehen. Das Vertrauen und die Behaglichkeit, die sie ausstrahlen, sind wenigstens als bemerkenswert zu bezeichnen.

Die Bindung, die ein Mann mit seinem Vater hat, prägt sein Leben. Deshalb muss jeder erwachsene Sohn die Wahl treffen und beschließen, ob die Beziehung bestimmen soll, was er tut oder nicht.
Ein Sohn will wissen und verstehen, wer sein Vater ist.

Sein Vater bestimmt, wer er ist. Die Elternschaft ist die schwierigste, anspruchsvollste und lohnendste Aufgabe, die man je haben wird. Ein vollkommener Vater schafft für seine Kinder einen soliden Rahmen, in dem sie Fürsorge und

Anleitung finden. Dies sind die Prioritäten, in die investiert werden muss.

Weiß Jaap, dass sein Vater ihn liebt? Zweifelsohne! Ich weiß nicht viel über ihr gemeinsames Leben. Ich weiß nur, dass sich Jaaps Eltern scheiden lassen haben, als er noch ein Kind war, und dass er von seinem Vater aufgezogen wurde, und dies scheinbar mit sehr wenig Ablenkung.
Tag ein, Tag aus hat er seinen Vater stundenlang mit endloser Geduld beobachtet – eine unglaublich kreative Beschäftigung. Jaap ist Architekt von Beruf. Die Kreativität hatte er natürlich bereits im Blut. Sein Talent und seine Fähigkeiten gemeinsam mit seinem Vater nutzen und gemeinsam etwas schaffen zu können, ist etwas, was nur Wenigen gegeben ist.

Sie konzentrieren ihre Energie und Leidenschaft bereits seit Jahren auf Silberarbeiten. Dies fast verlorene und vernachlässigte Kunstform scheint heute heftig und dynamisch zurückkehren zu wollen.

Rob und Jaap haben nicht gerade den einfachsten Weg gewählt. Jedes Objekt hat seinen eigenen Charakter und ist ein Vorbild höchster Handwerkskunst und Hingabe.
Und schauen Sie, was sie gemeinsam geschaffen haben... Ihre wunderschönen, einzigartigen Werke sind einfach erstaunlich.

Väter und Söhne können eine entscheidende Rolle bei der gegenseitigen Ermutigung spielen, um sich optimal zu entwickeln.

Das berühmteste Vater-Sohn-Duo in der Welt der Architektur sind Eliel und Eero Saarinen. Den Finnen Eliel Saarinen verschlug es aufgrund seiner Teilnahme am Wettbewerb für den Chicago Tribune Tower, der 1921 stattgefunden hat, nach Chicago. Eero saß als kleines Kind stundenlang unter dem Reißbrett seines Vaters und entwarf seit der Kindheit Möbel für viele Gebäude seines Vaters in Cranbrook. Nach dem Studium der Architektur an der Yale University kehrte Eero 1936 wieder nach Cranbrook zurück, um dort zu unterrichten und mit seinem Vater zu arbeiten.

Ich lade den Leser jetzt ein, ein neues Kapitel der Geschichte über die Zusammenarbeit zwischen Vater und Sohn kennenzulernen: Rob und Jaap Thalen, ein bemerkenswertes Duo.

George A. Larson, Architekt, Chicago / New York

About fathers and sons

Rob and Jaap Thalen are an exception to the rule of father son relationships.
I think it is about love and trust proven over and over, consistent through many years.

I find it remarkable from the first time we met over two years ago. I saw them together – wondering whether they were father and son – the resemblance is remarkable. They seem to exude a confidence and comfortableness that is unmistakable.

The connection a man has with his father shapes his life, which is why every adult son must choose if that relationship will or won't define him.
A son wants to know and understand who his father is.

Your father determines who you are. Parenting is the most difficult, challenging and rewarding job you will ever have. Every good father must build on a framework of providing nurturing and guiding. These are priorities to invest in.

Does Jaap know his father loves him? Without a doubt!

I don't know a great deal about their life together other than Jaap's parents were divorced early on in his life and he grew up with his father, apparently with very few distractions. Working with his father, the patience in daily observing the skill of shared design authority is a tremendously creative act. Jaap is an architect by education and of course the creative skill is a gift one is born with, then using that skill with your father and creating together is something that must take a gift that few have. Since a number of years they focused their energy and passion on silverware. This almost lost and neglected art form gains a new impetus and dynamism.

Neither Rob nor Jaap chooses the easy path. Each object has its own character and exudes the ultimate in craftsmanship and commitment.
Look at what they have created together, I marvel at the beautiful and unique creations.

Fathers and sons can play a critical role in helping each other become the best they can be.
The most famous father and son duo in the architectural world is Eliel and Eero Saarinen.
The Finnish Eliel Saarinen came to Chicago to develop the building design for the Chicago Tribune Tower competition

of 1921. Eero grew up sitting under his father's drawing table. Early on he designed furniture for many of his father's buildings at Cranbrook. After studying architecture at Yale University Eero returned to Cranbrook in 1936 to teach and go into practice with his father.

This story of collaboration between father and son is carried on today by Rob and Jaap Thalen, a truly remarkable duo.

George A. Larson architect, Chicago / New York

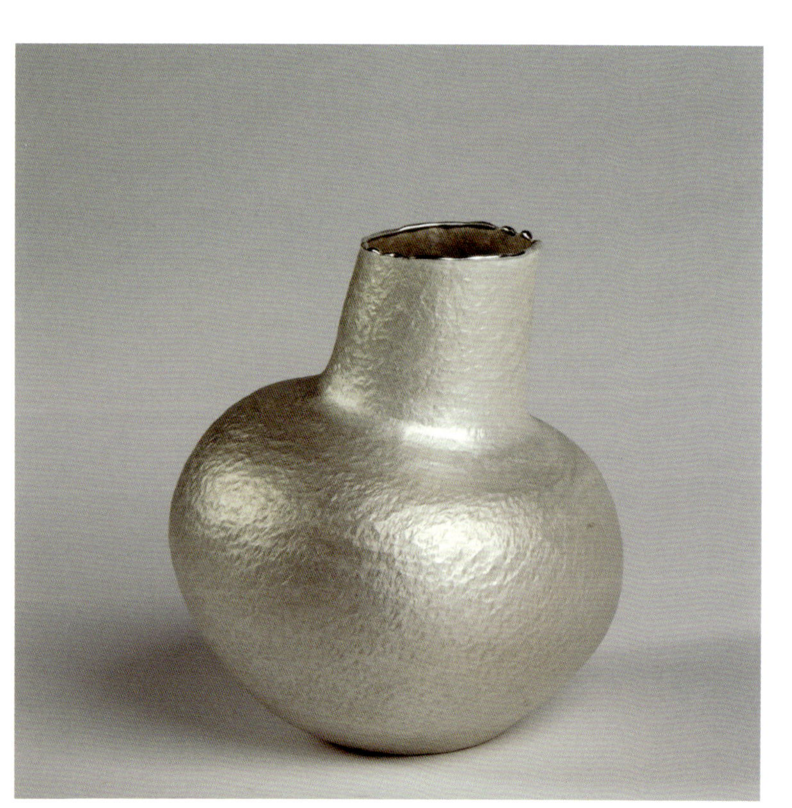

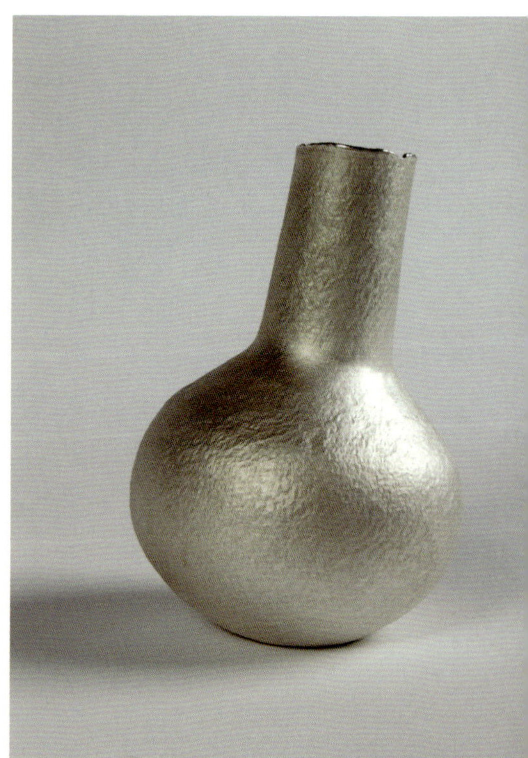

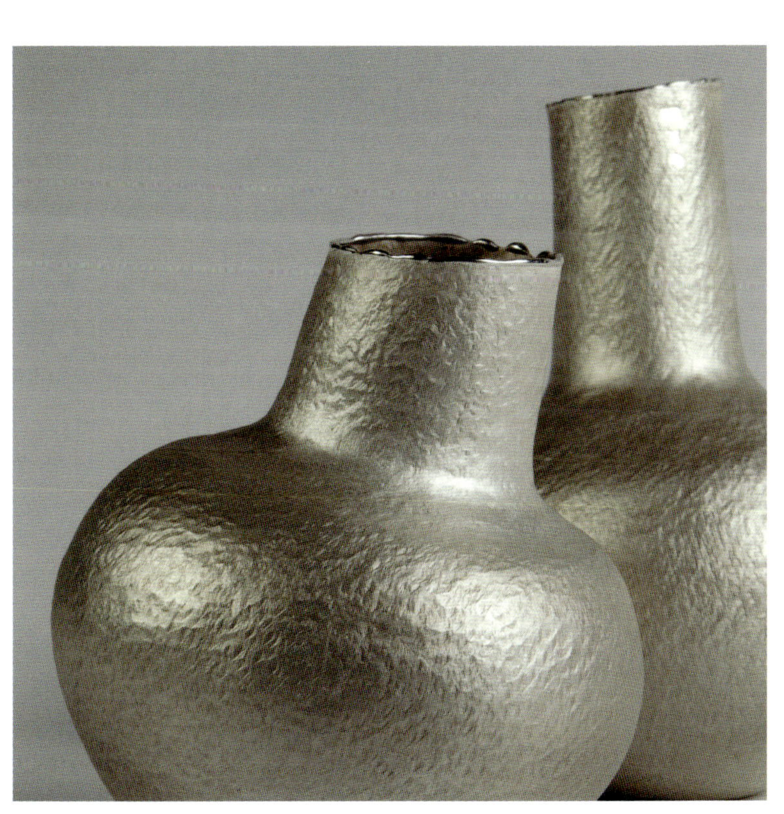

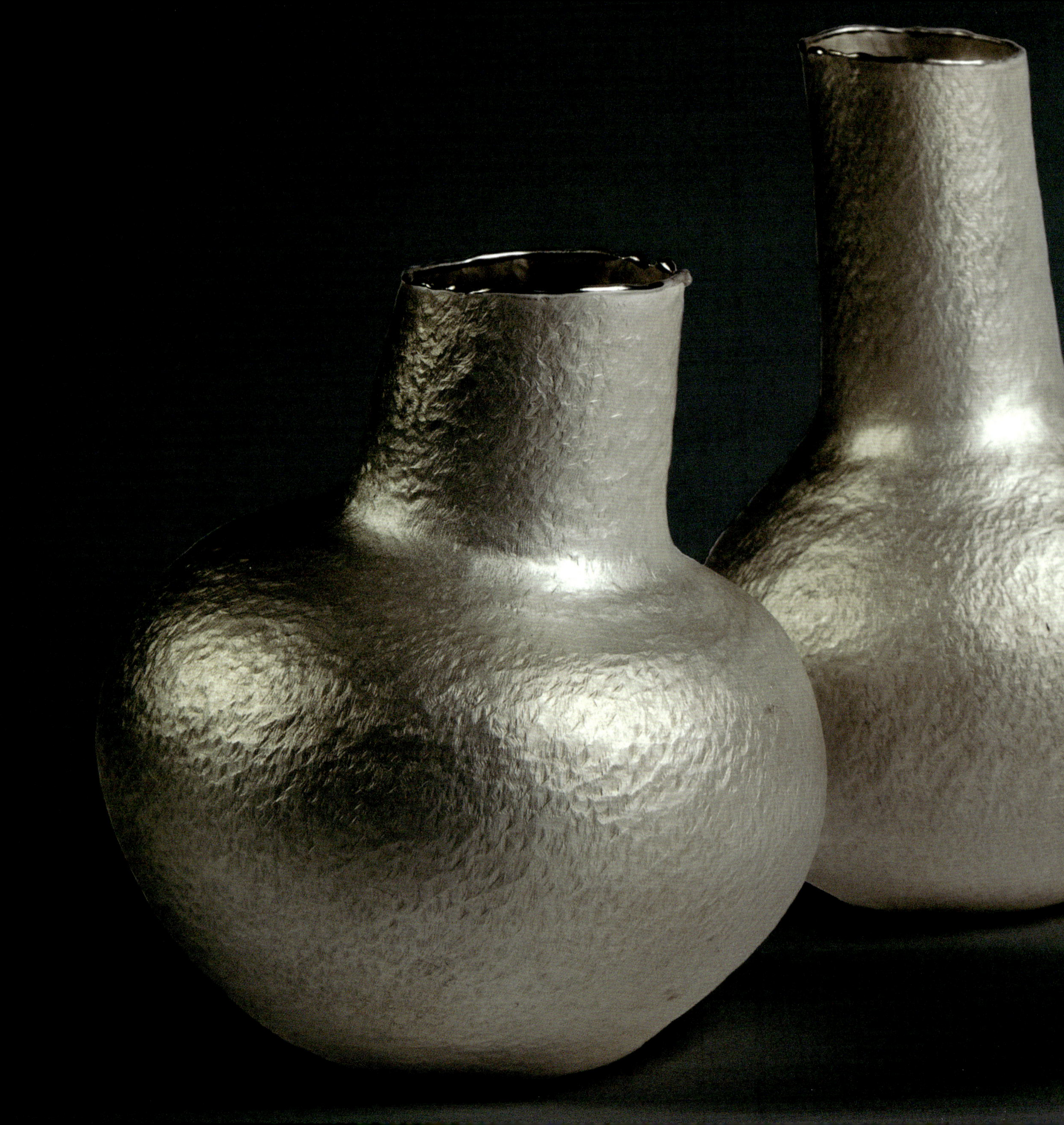

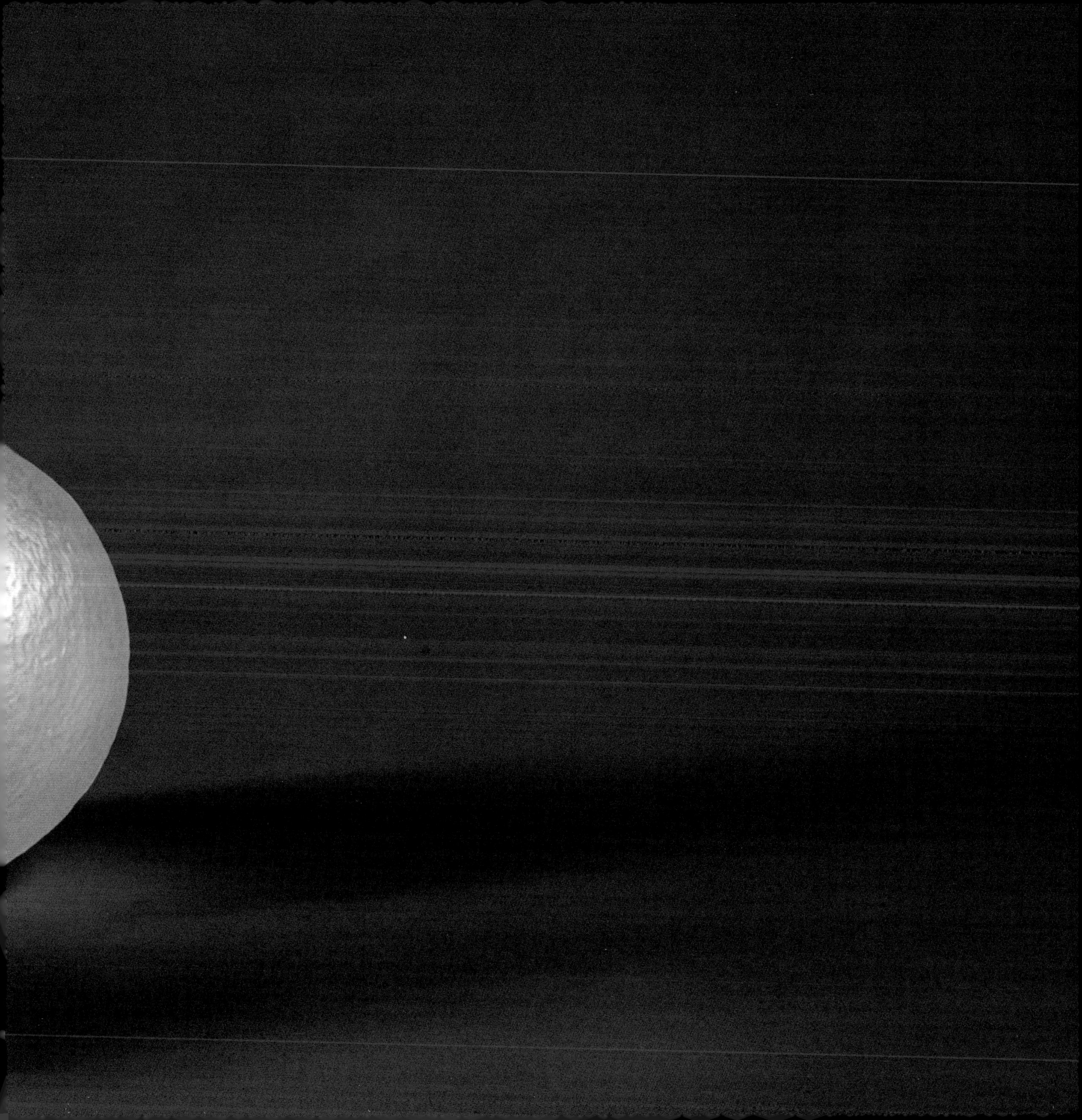

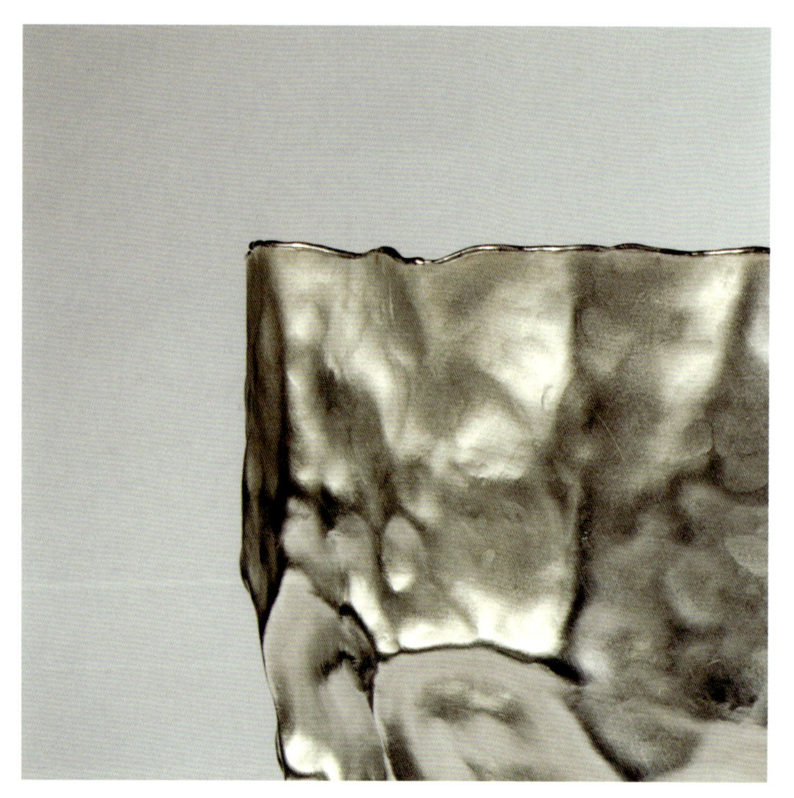

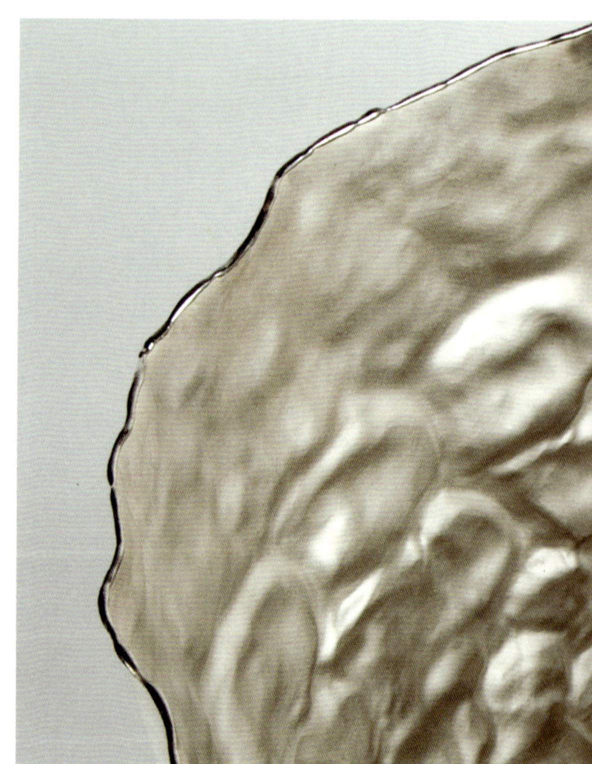

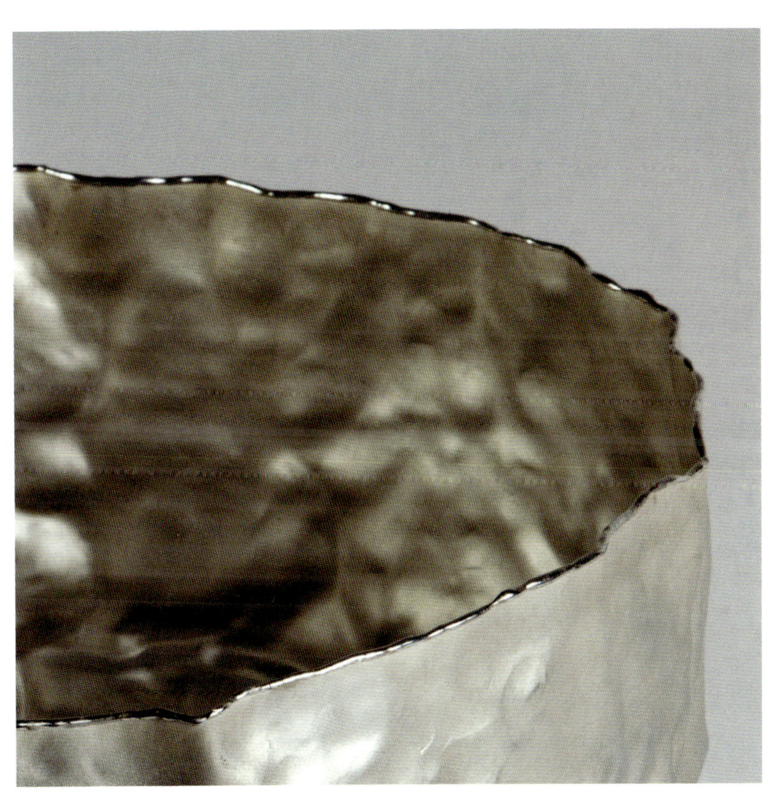

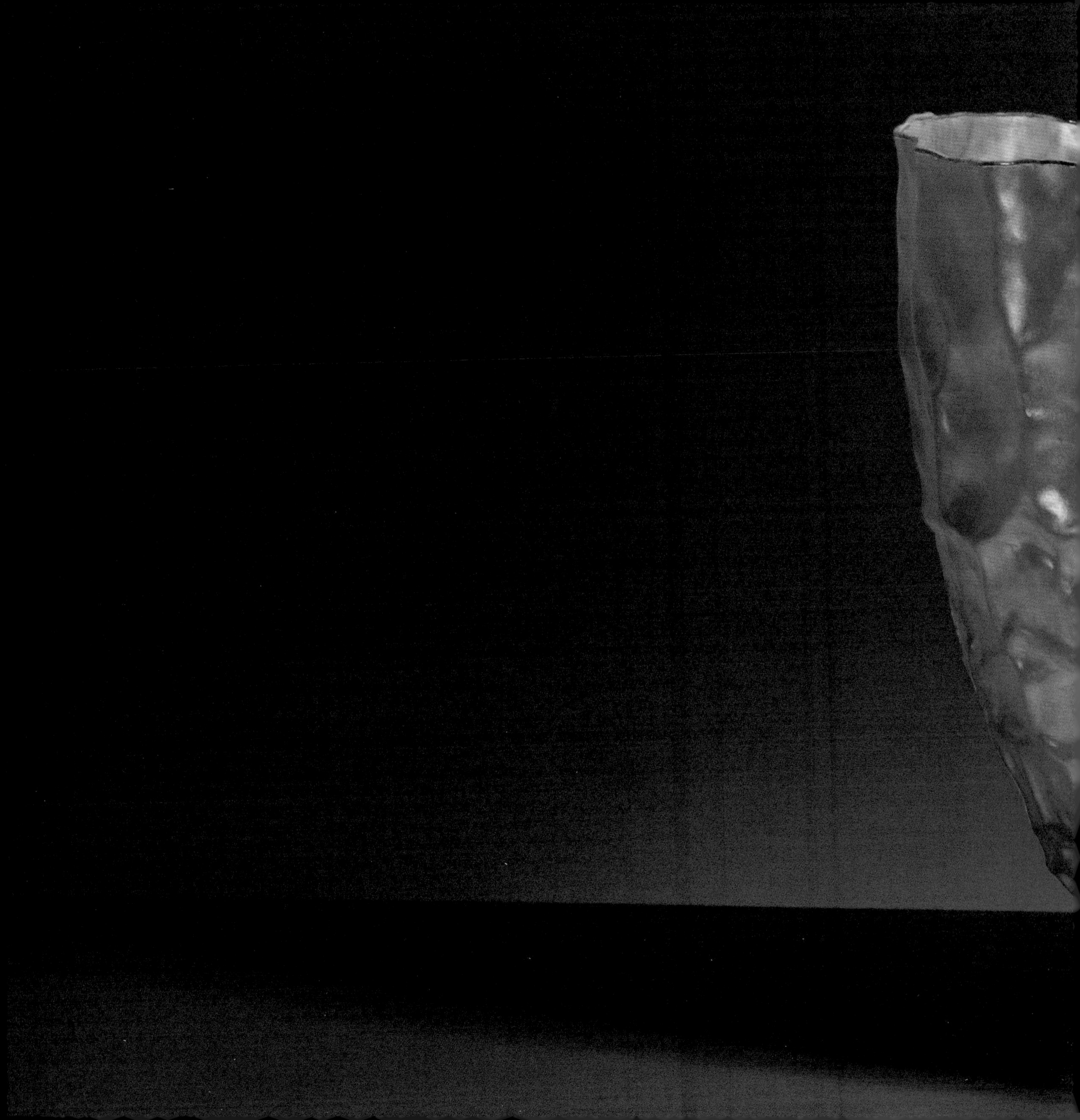

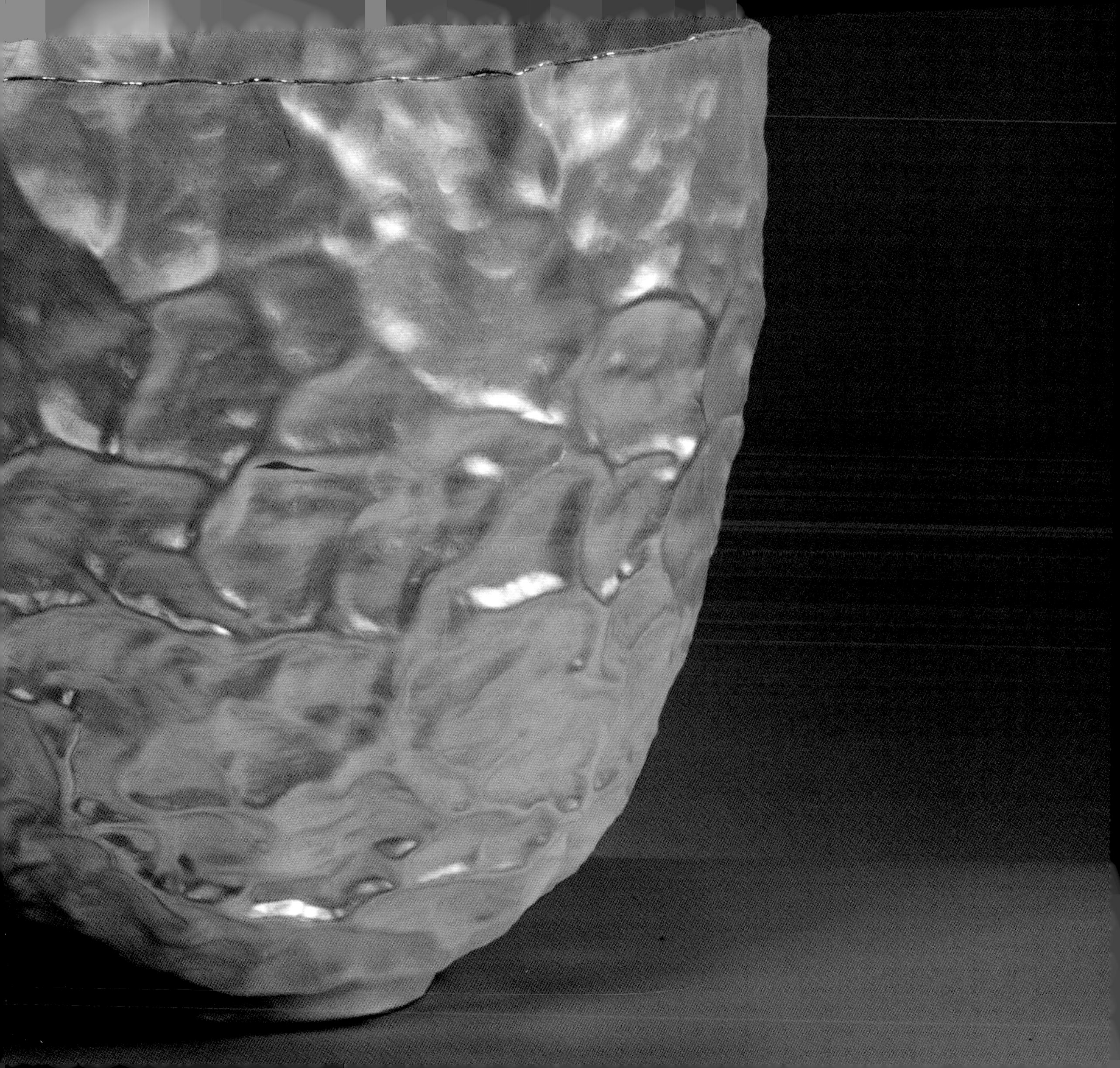

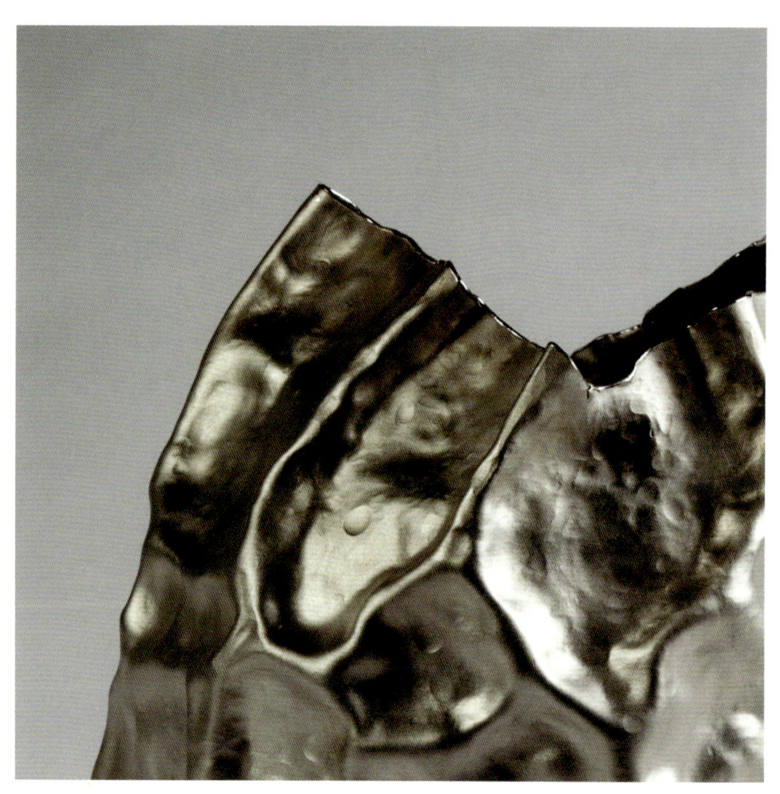

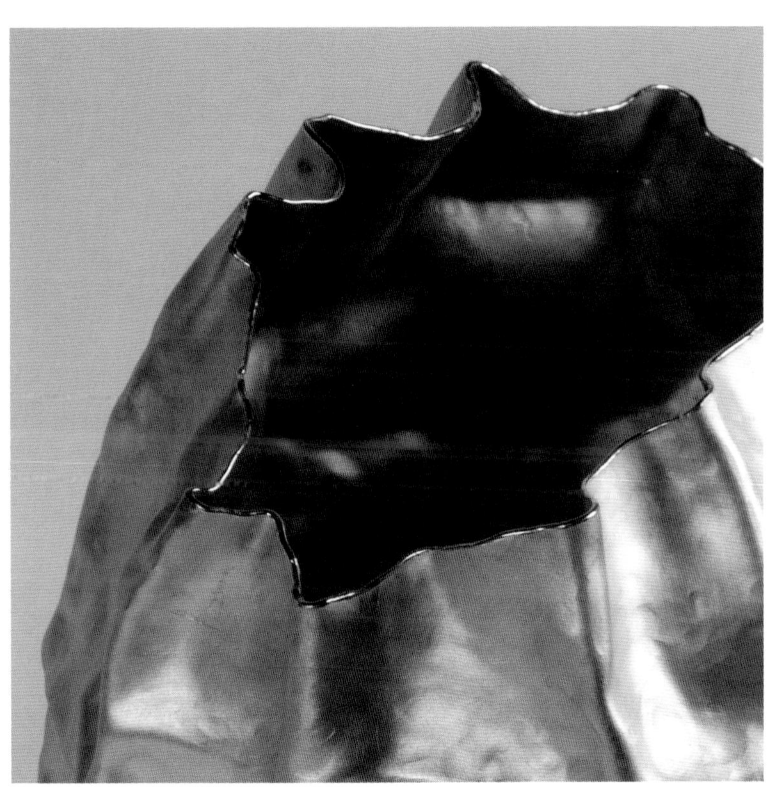

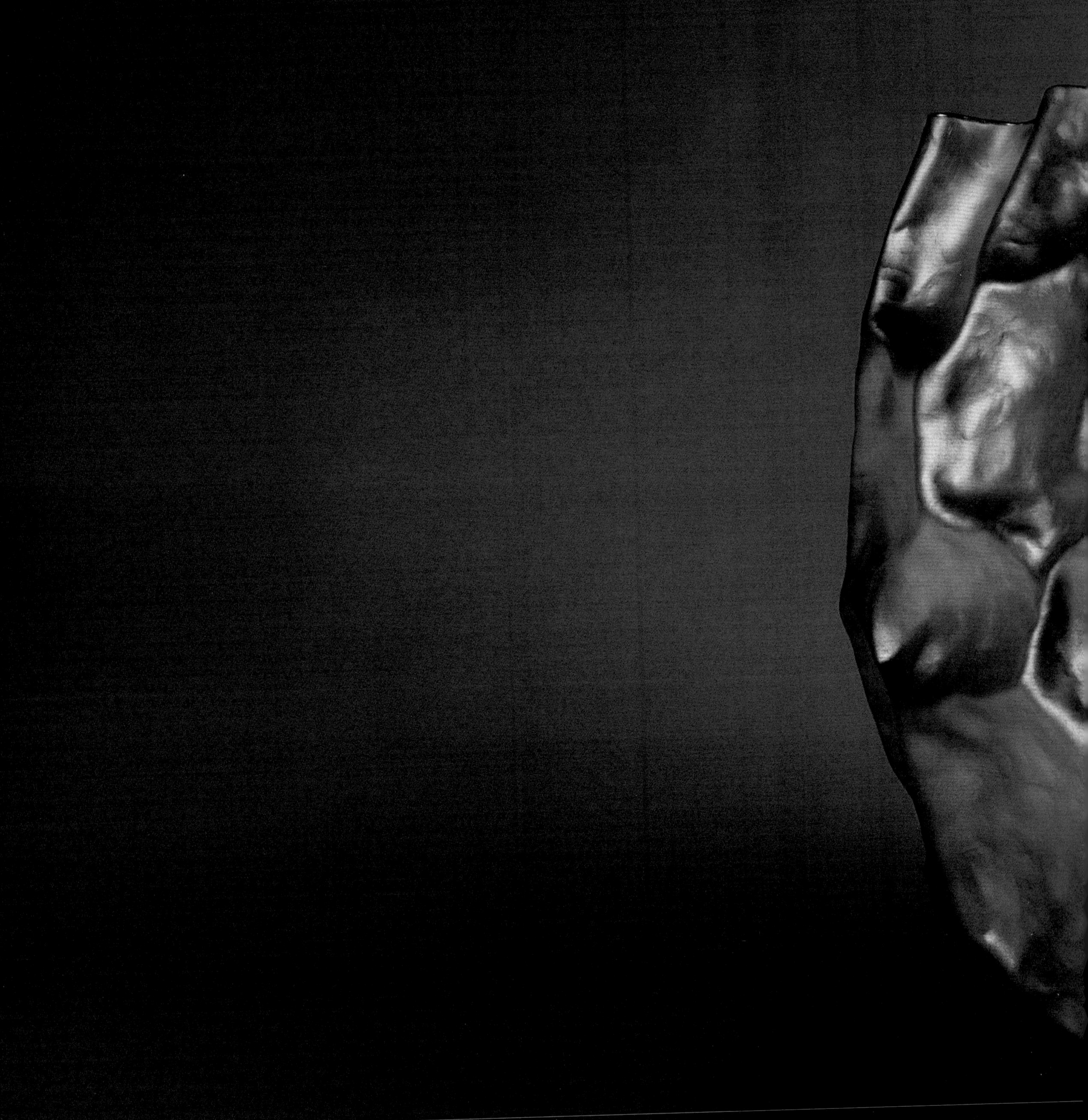

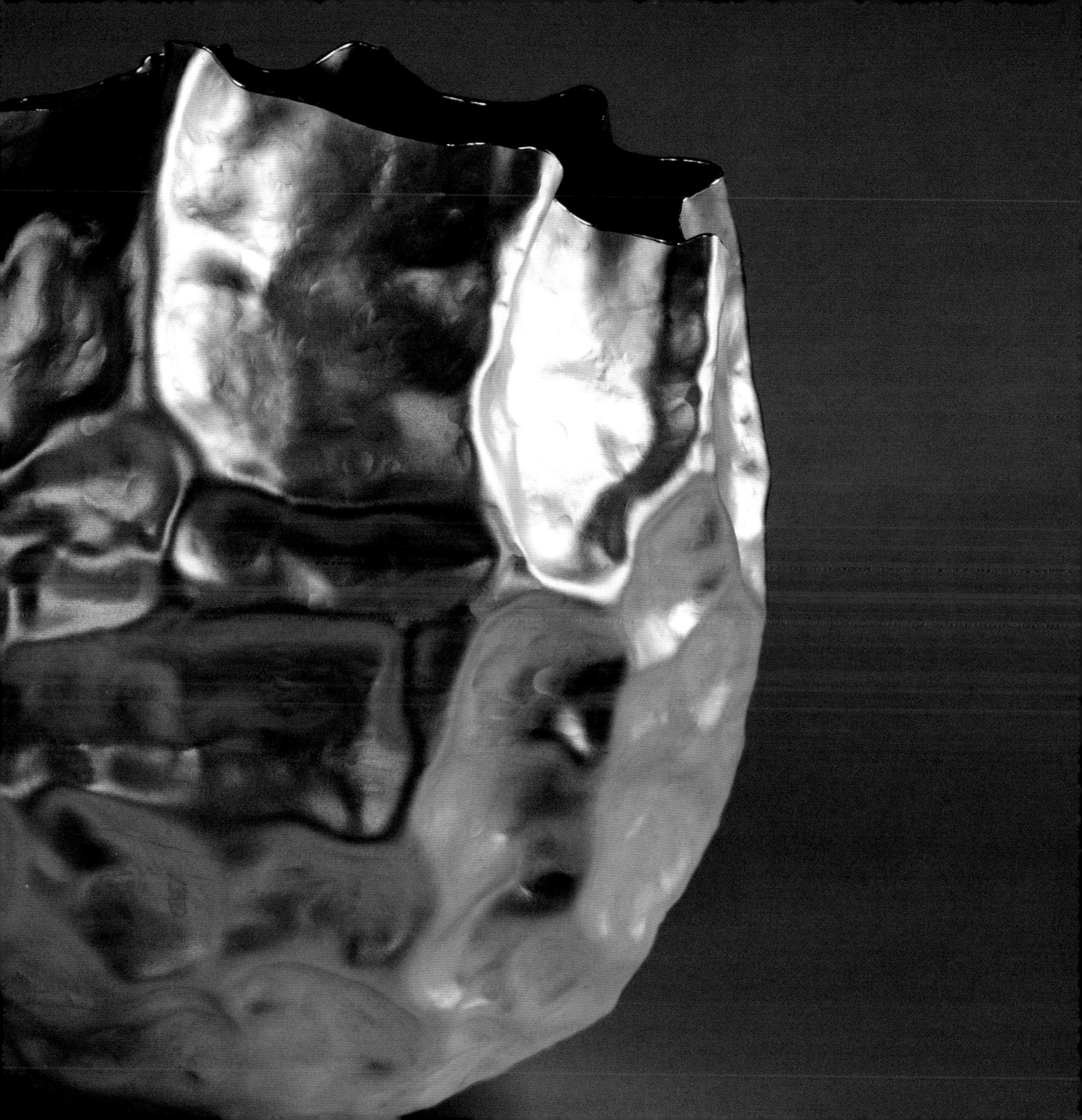

93

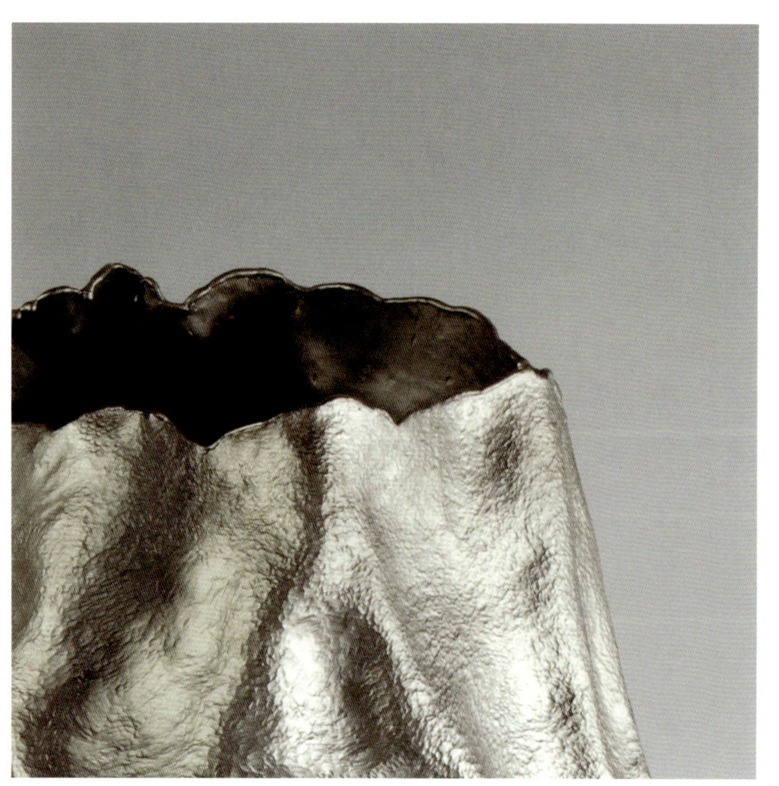

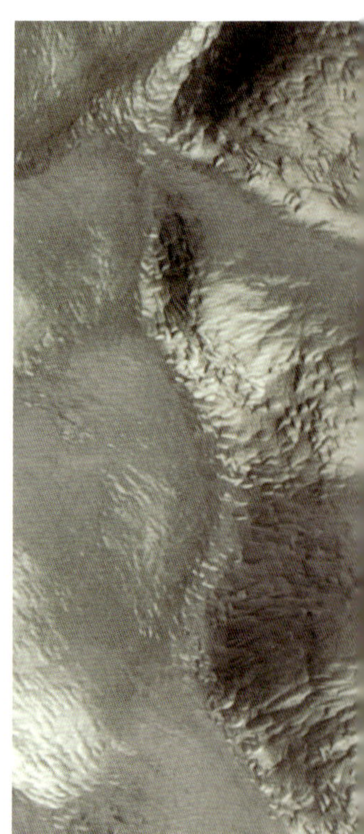

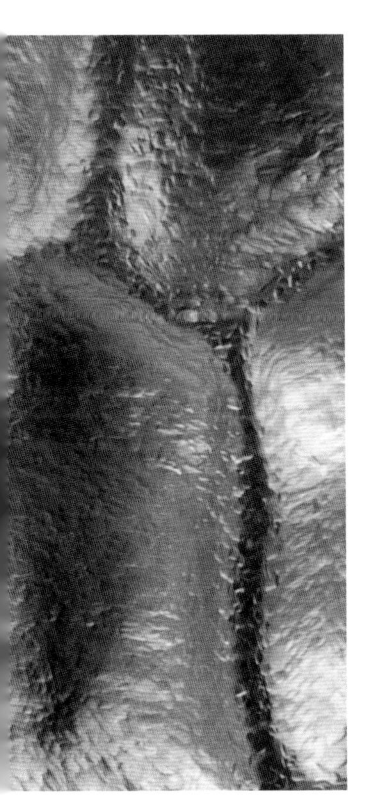

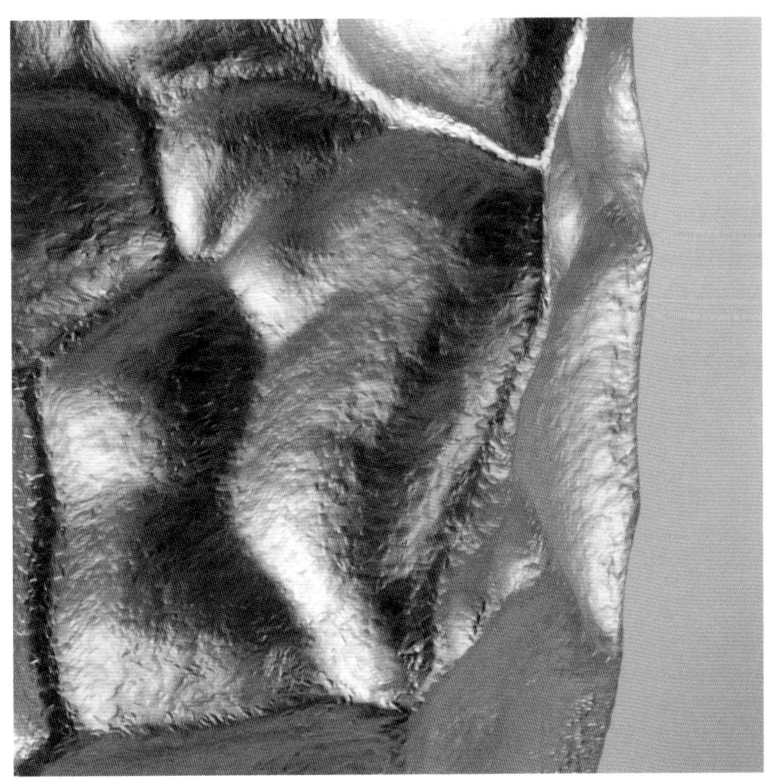

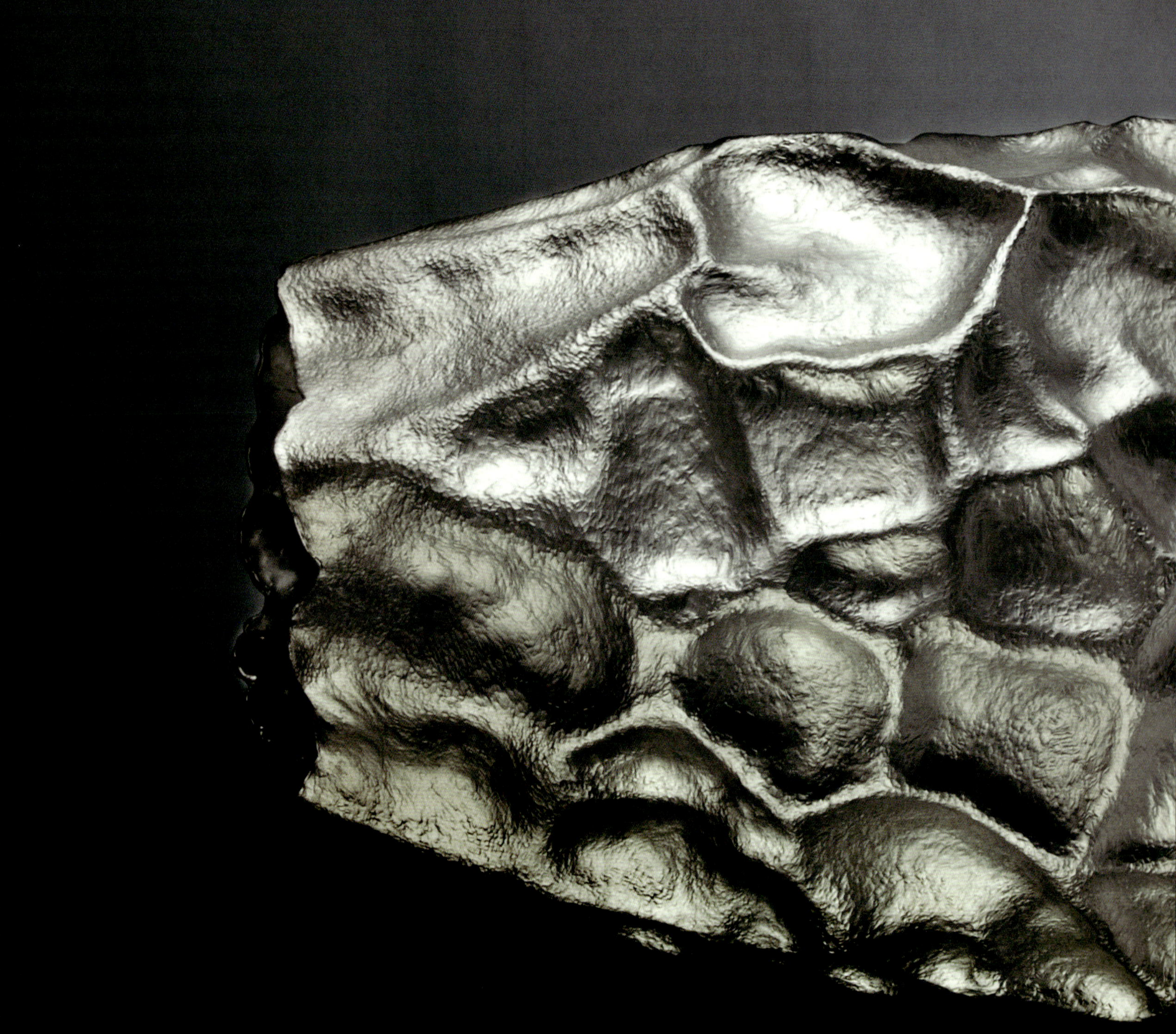

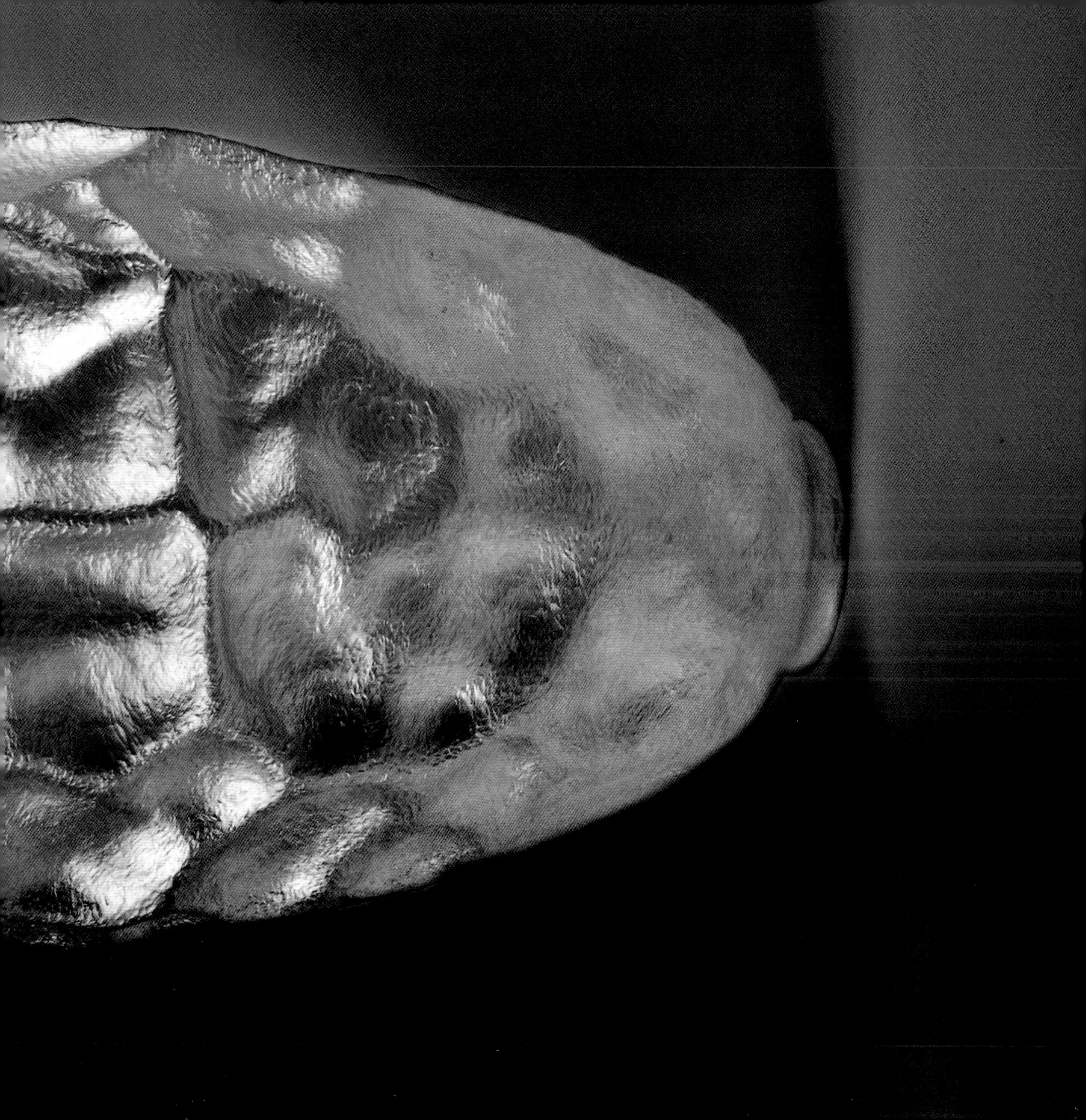

97

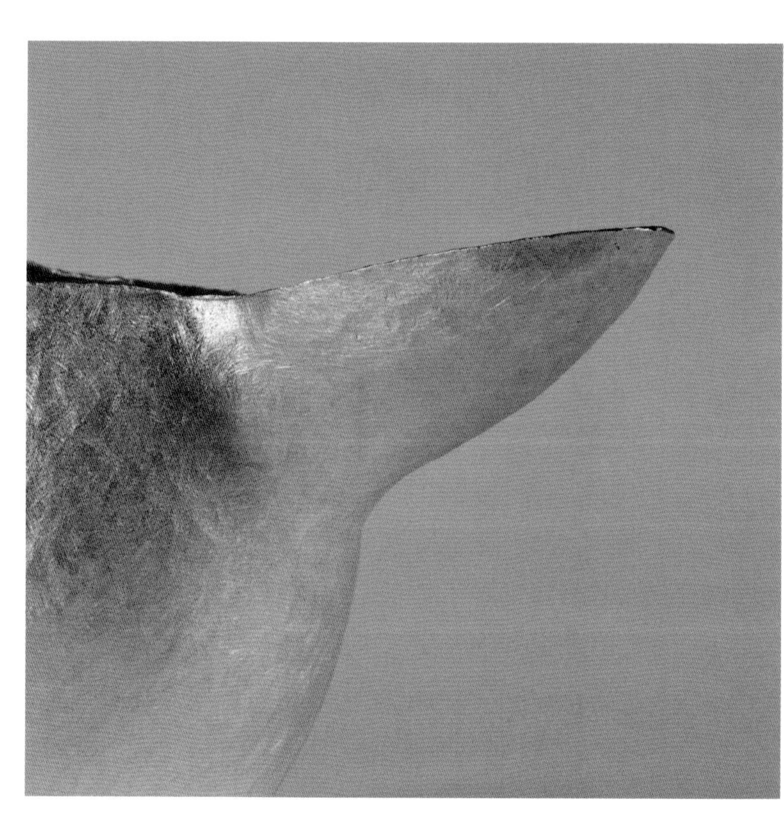

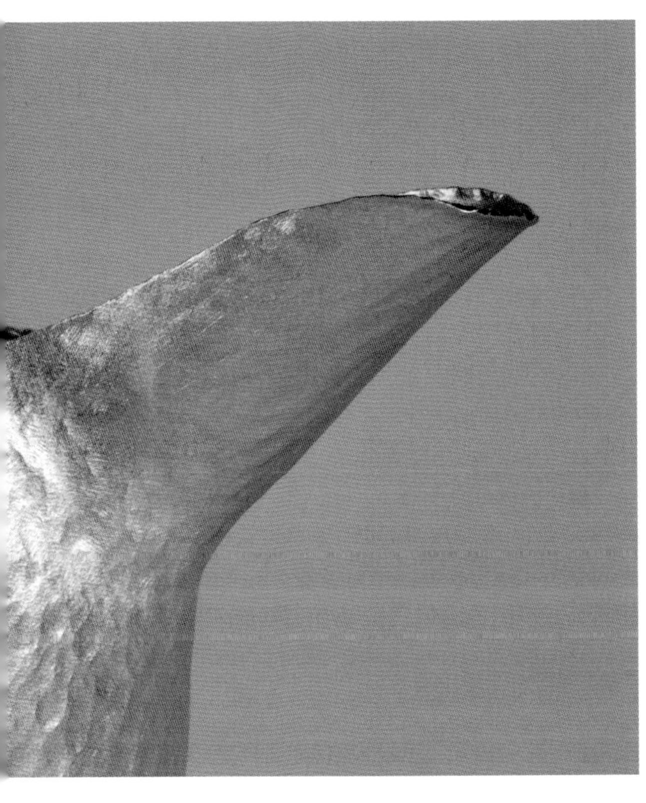

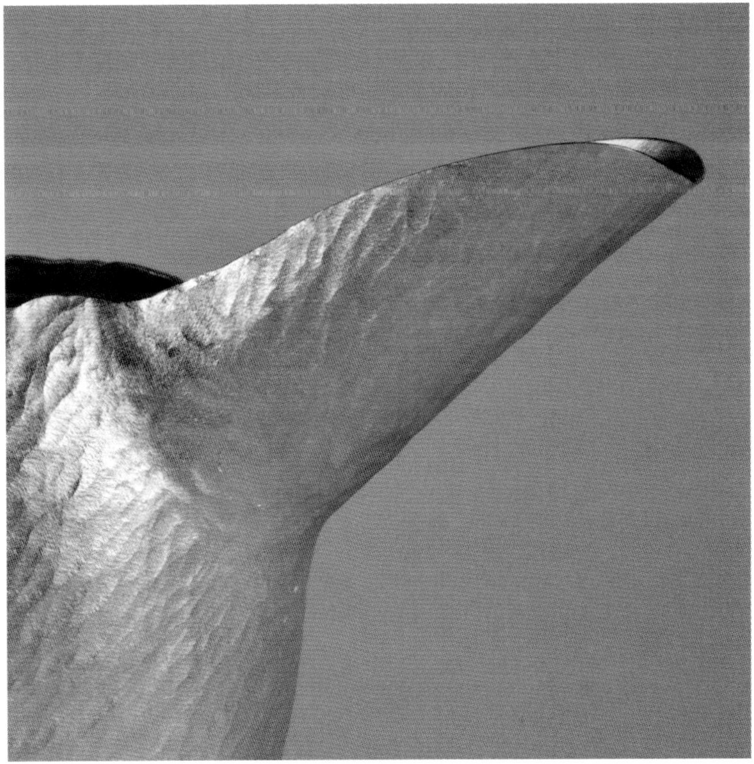

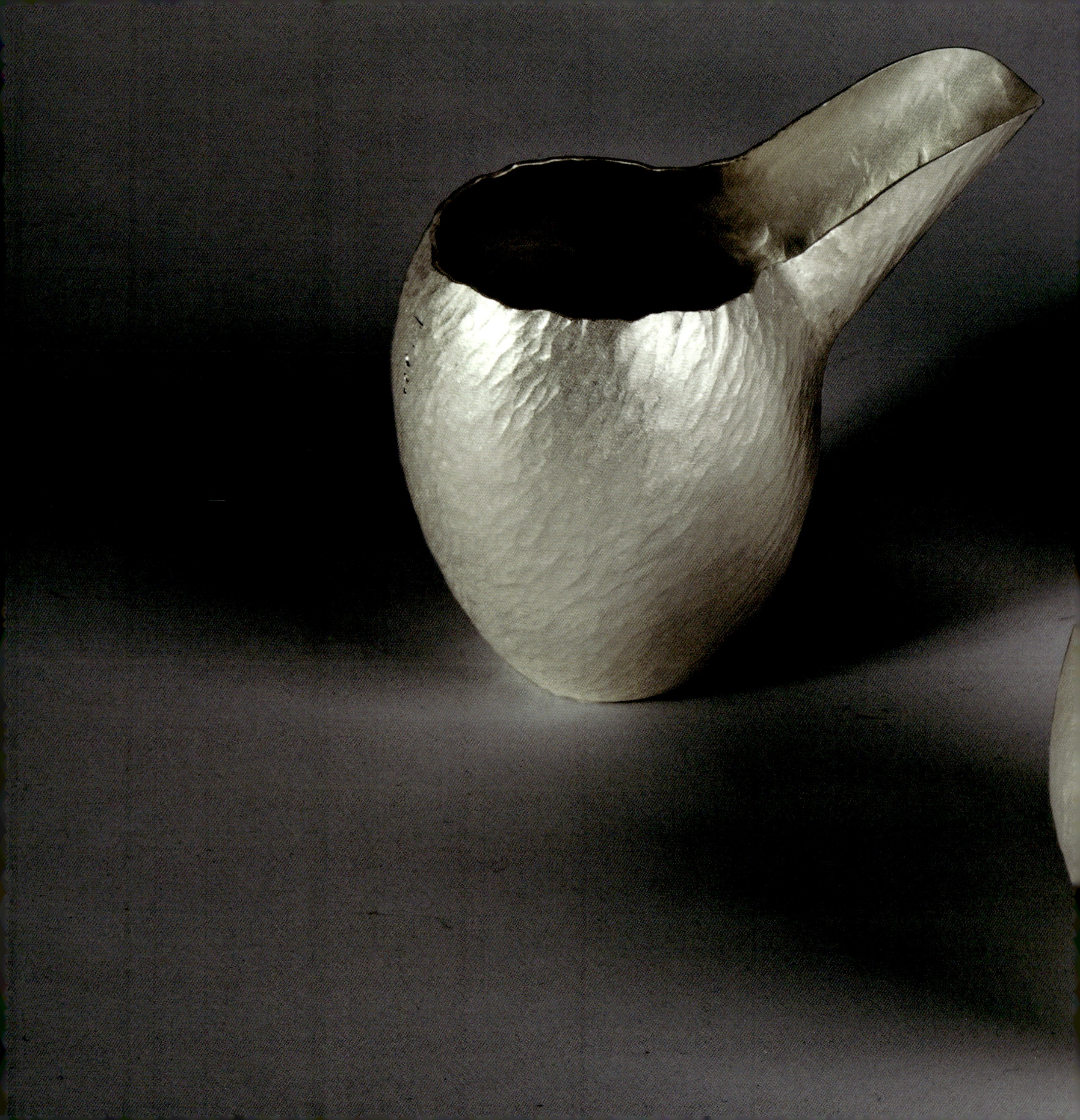

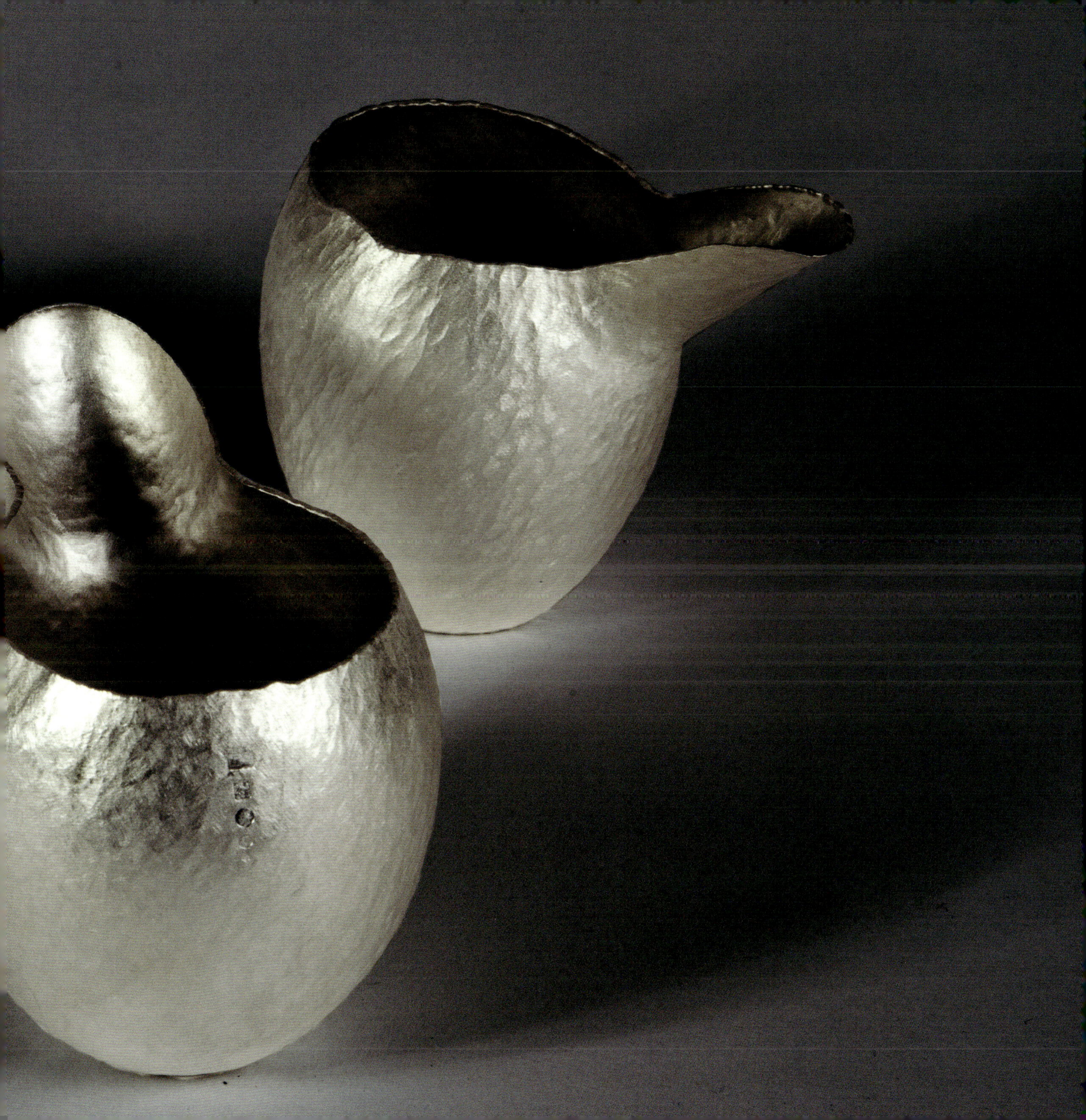

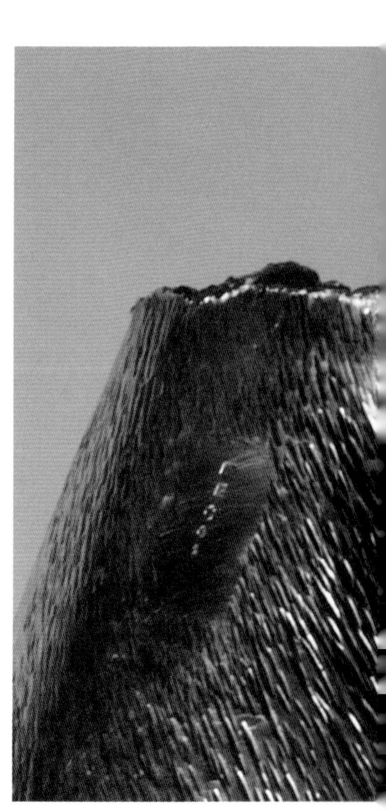

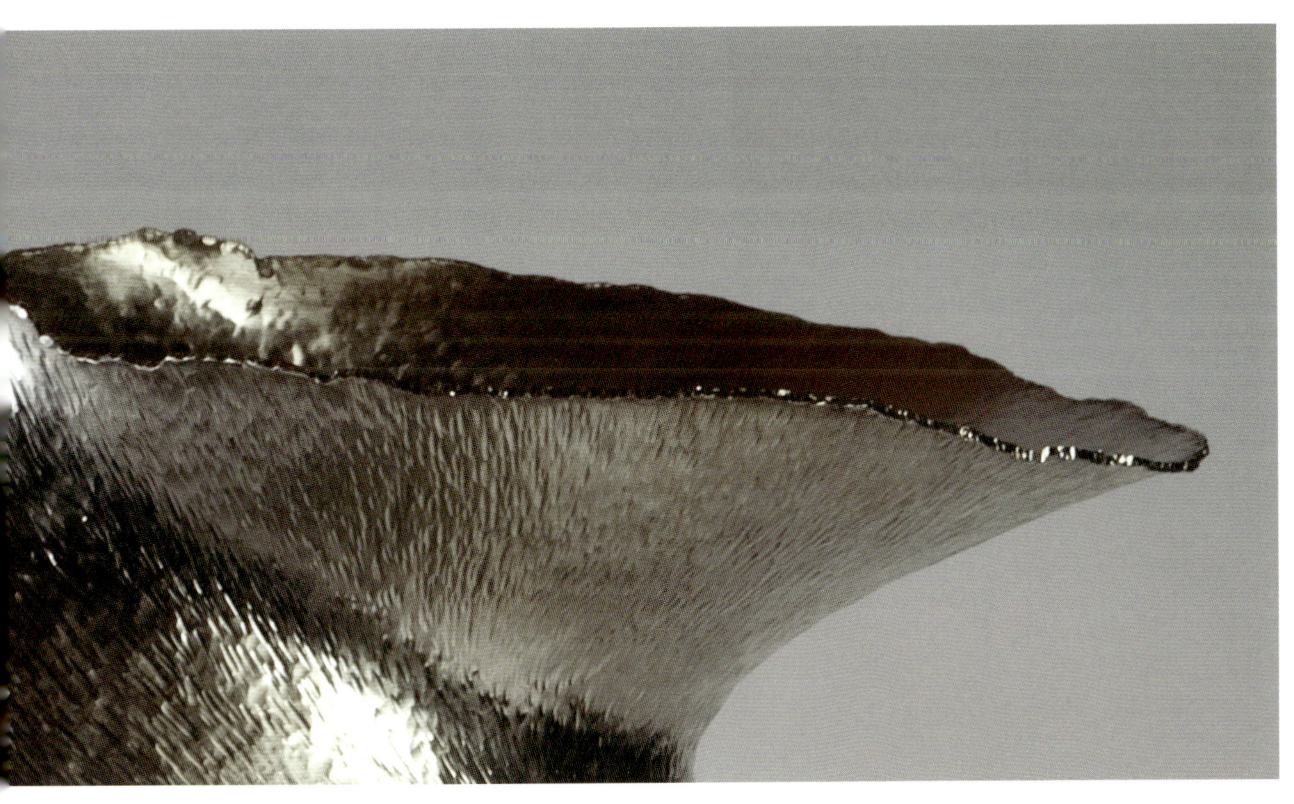

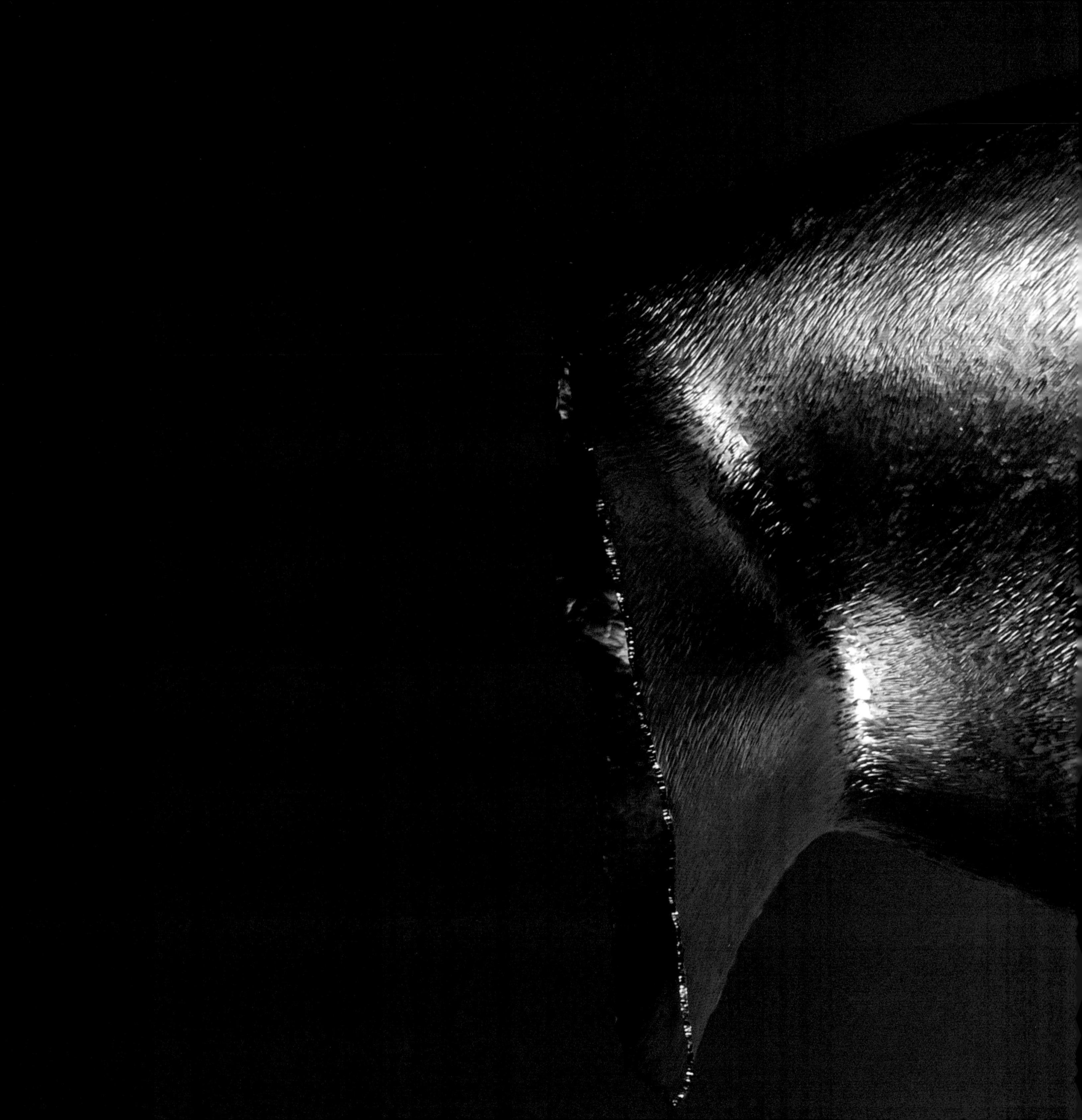

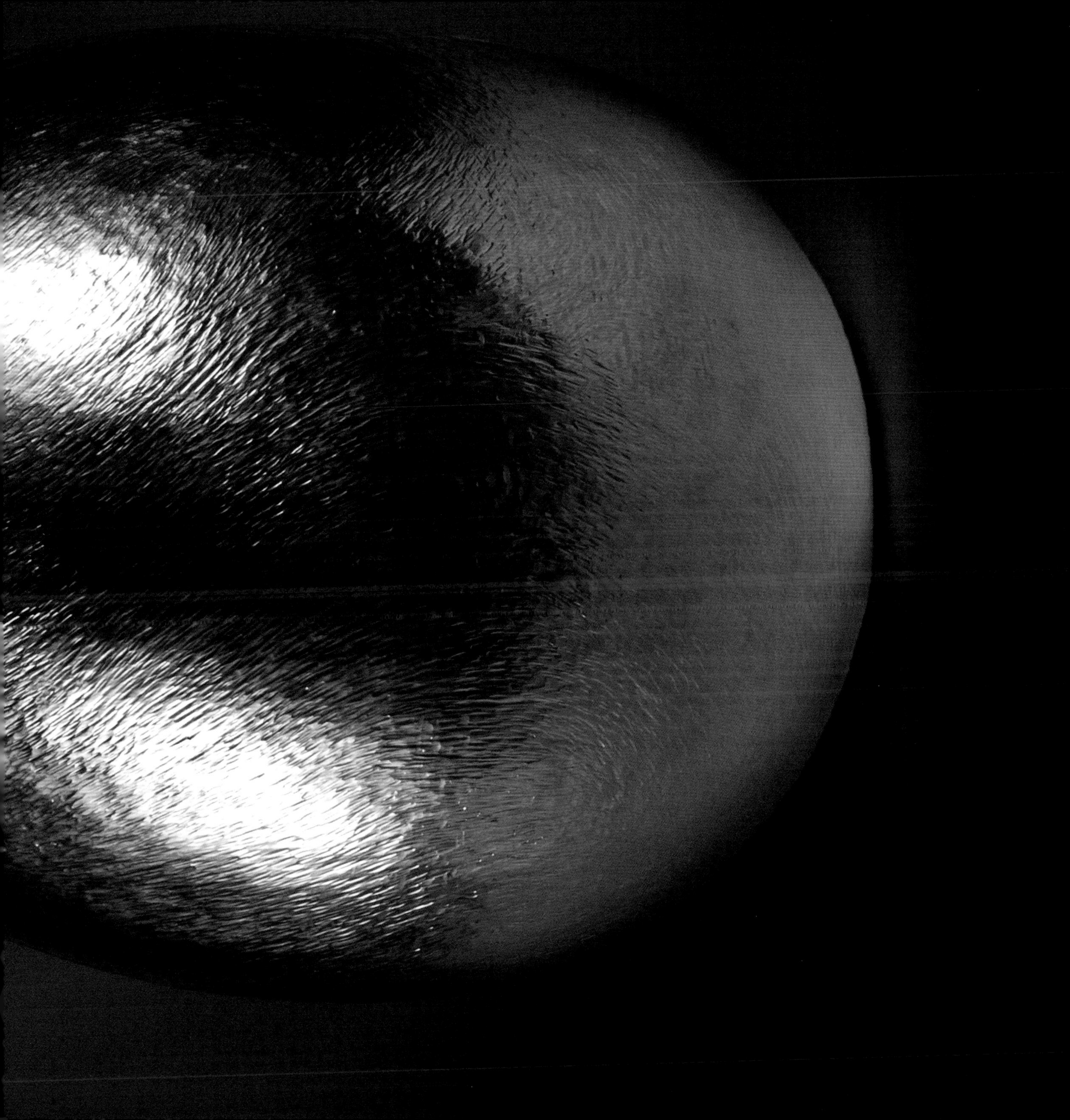

105

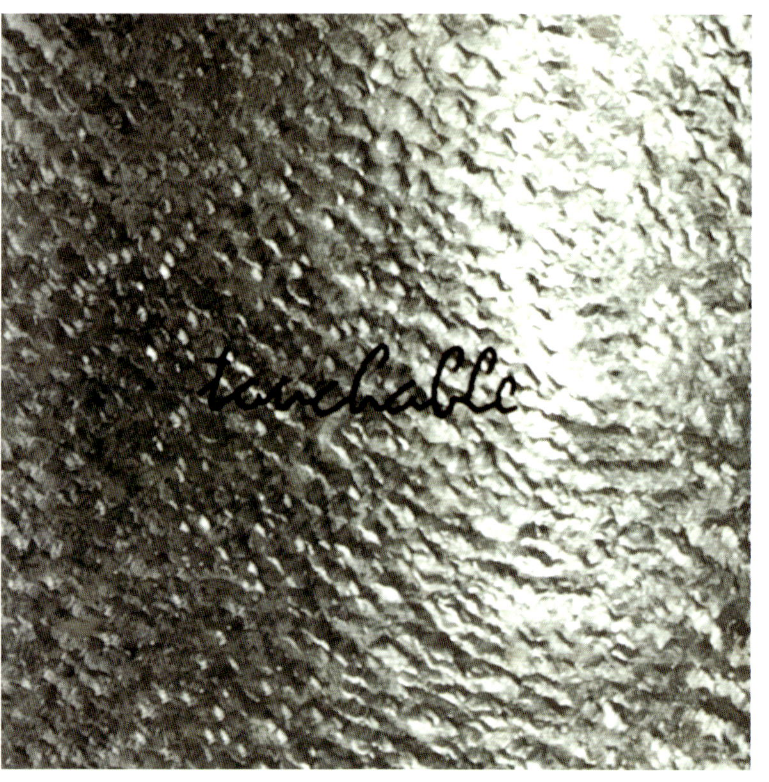

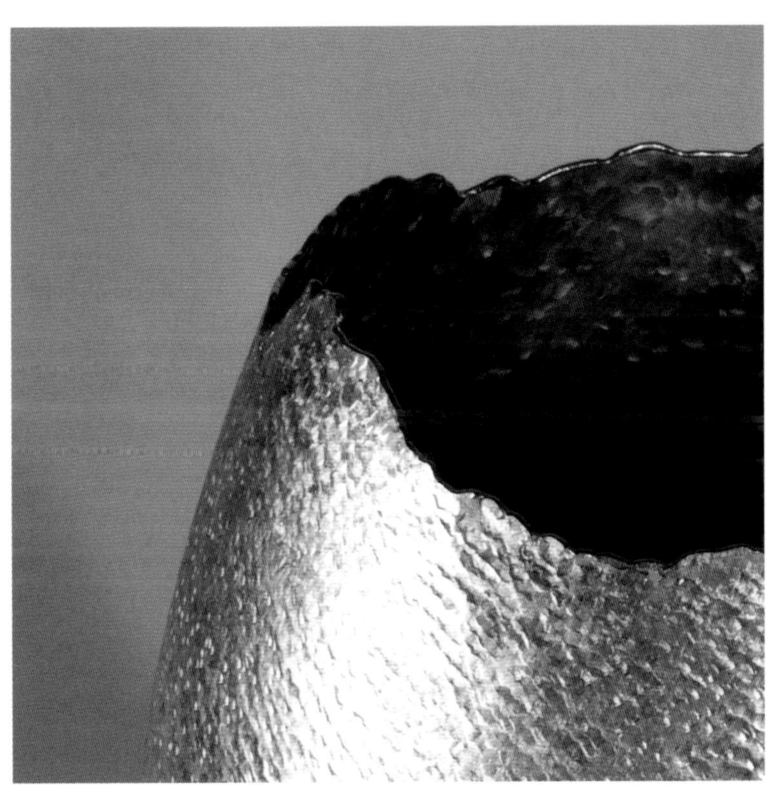

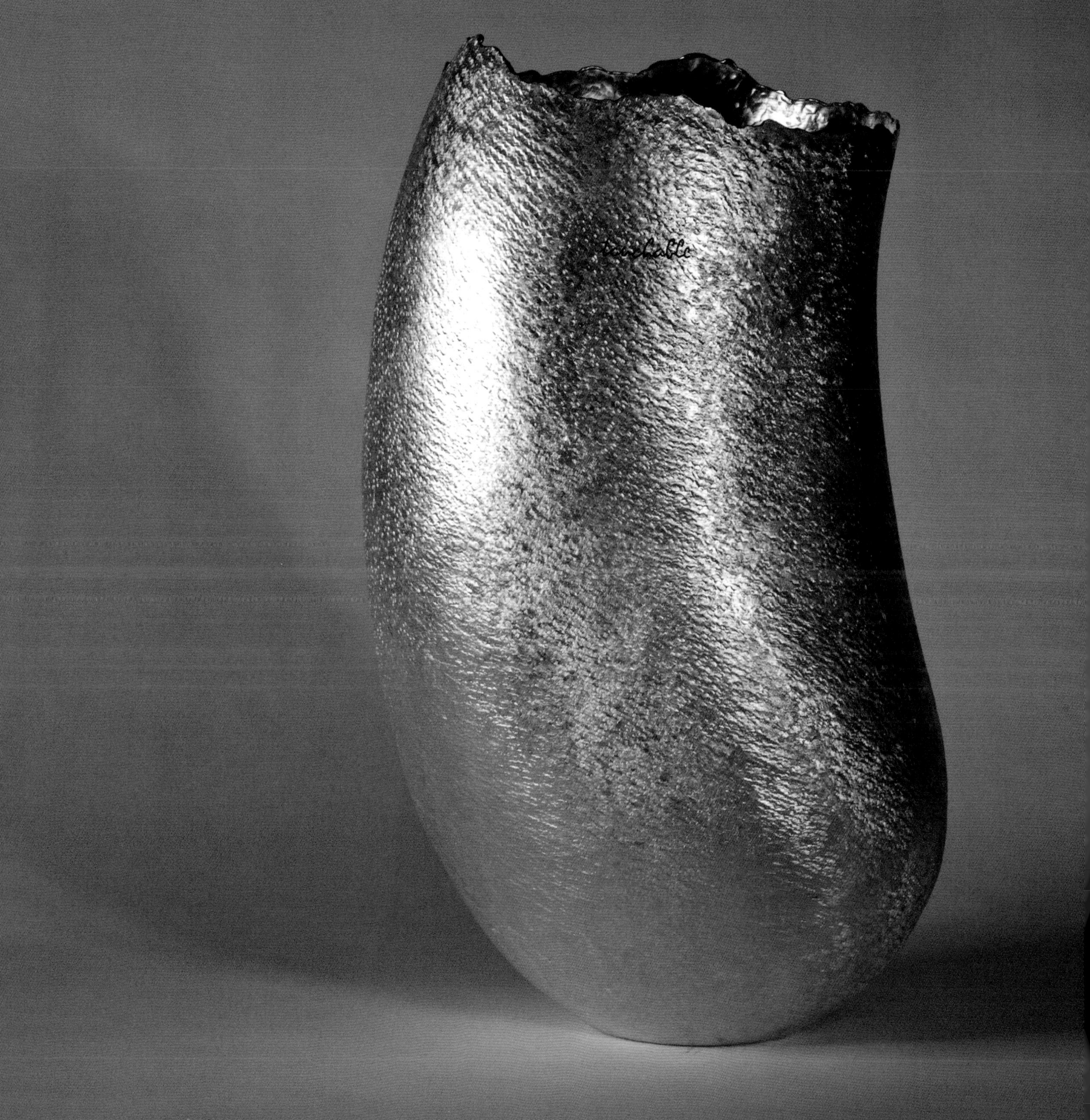

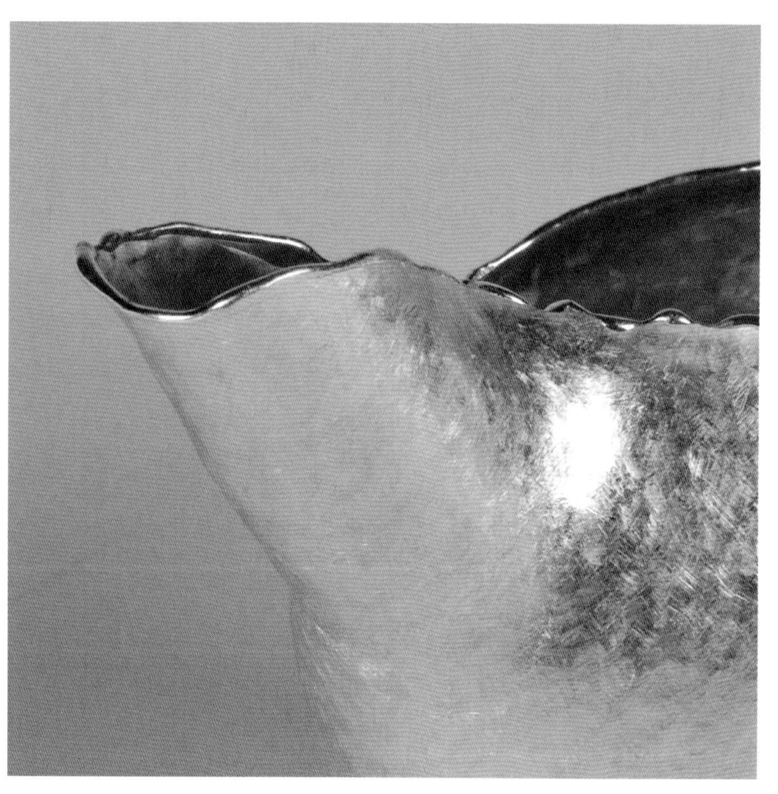

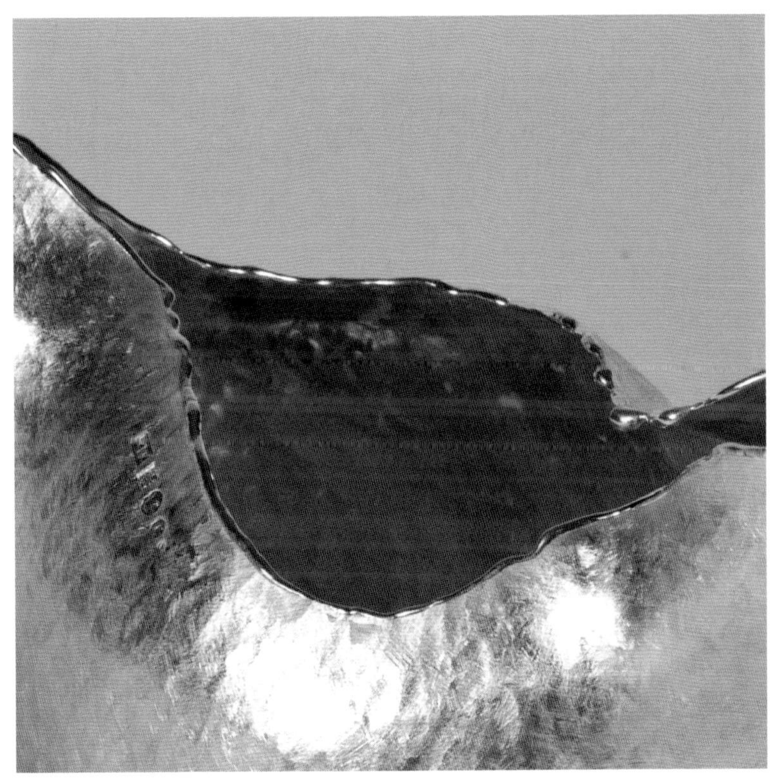

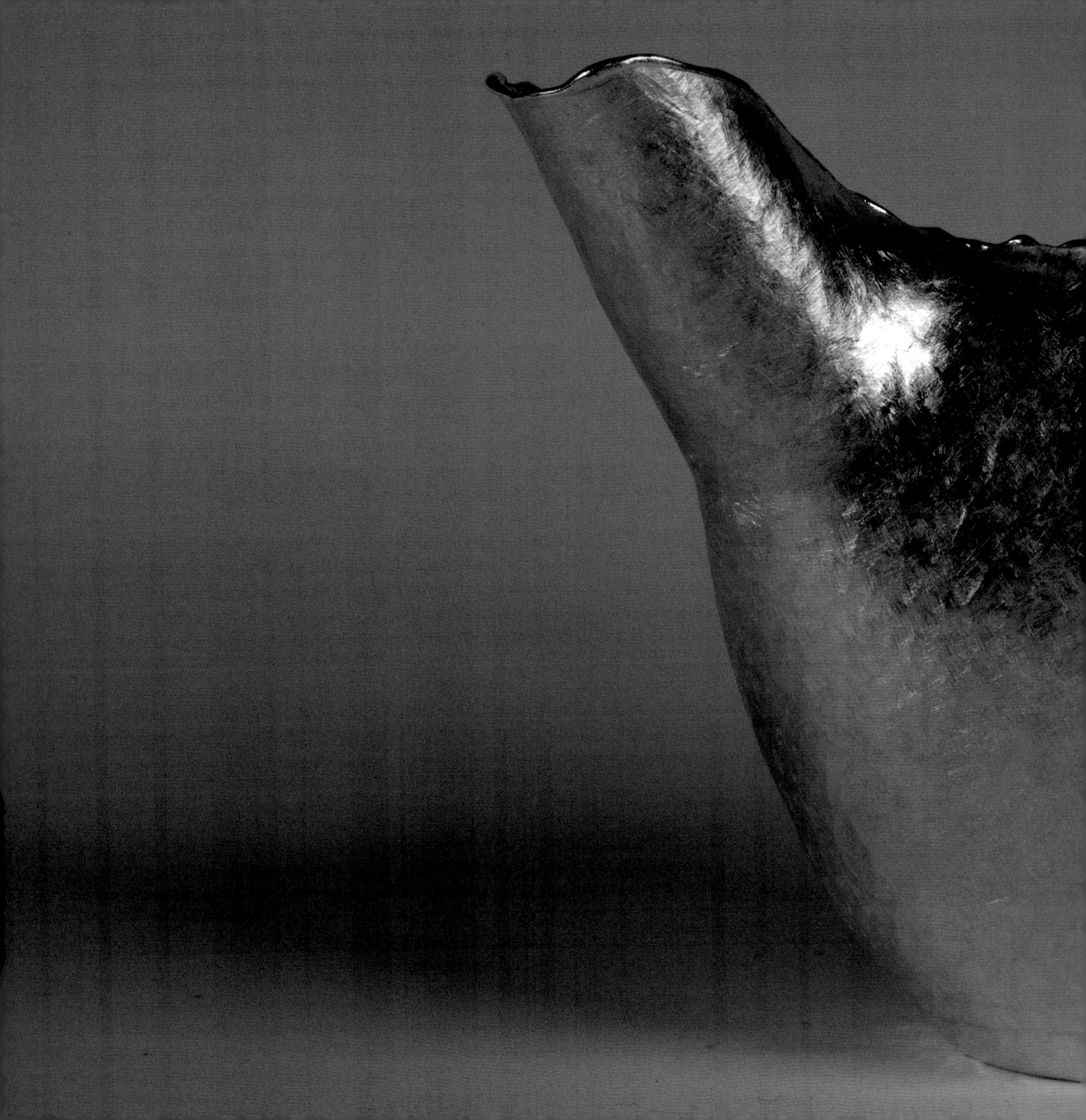

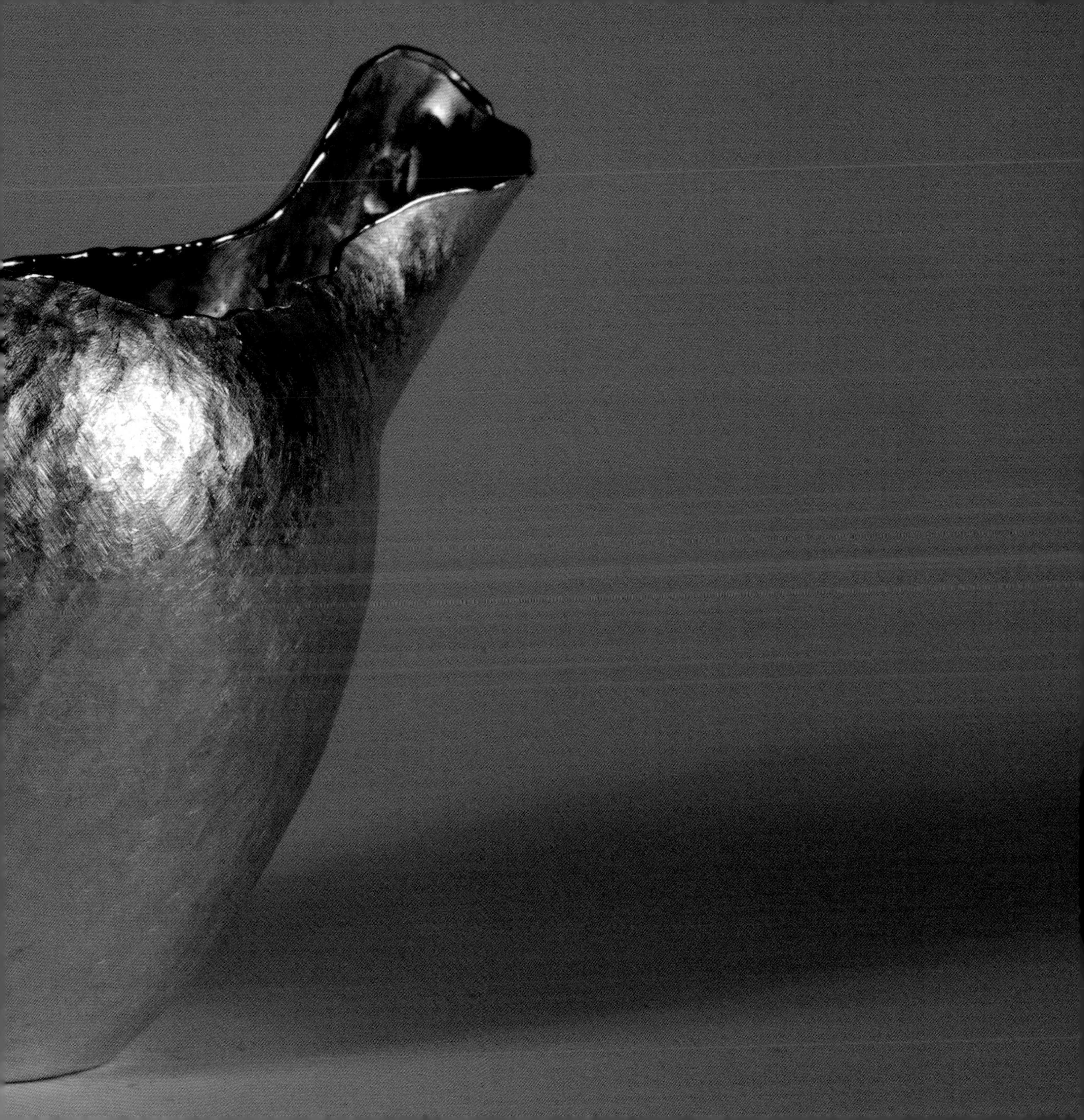

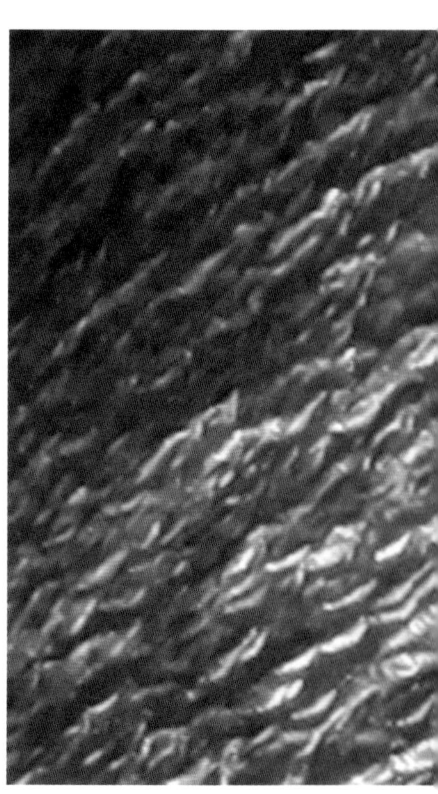

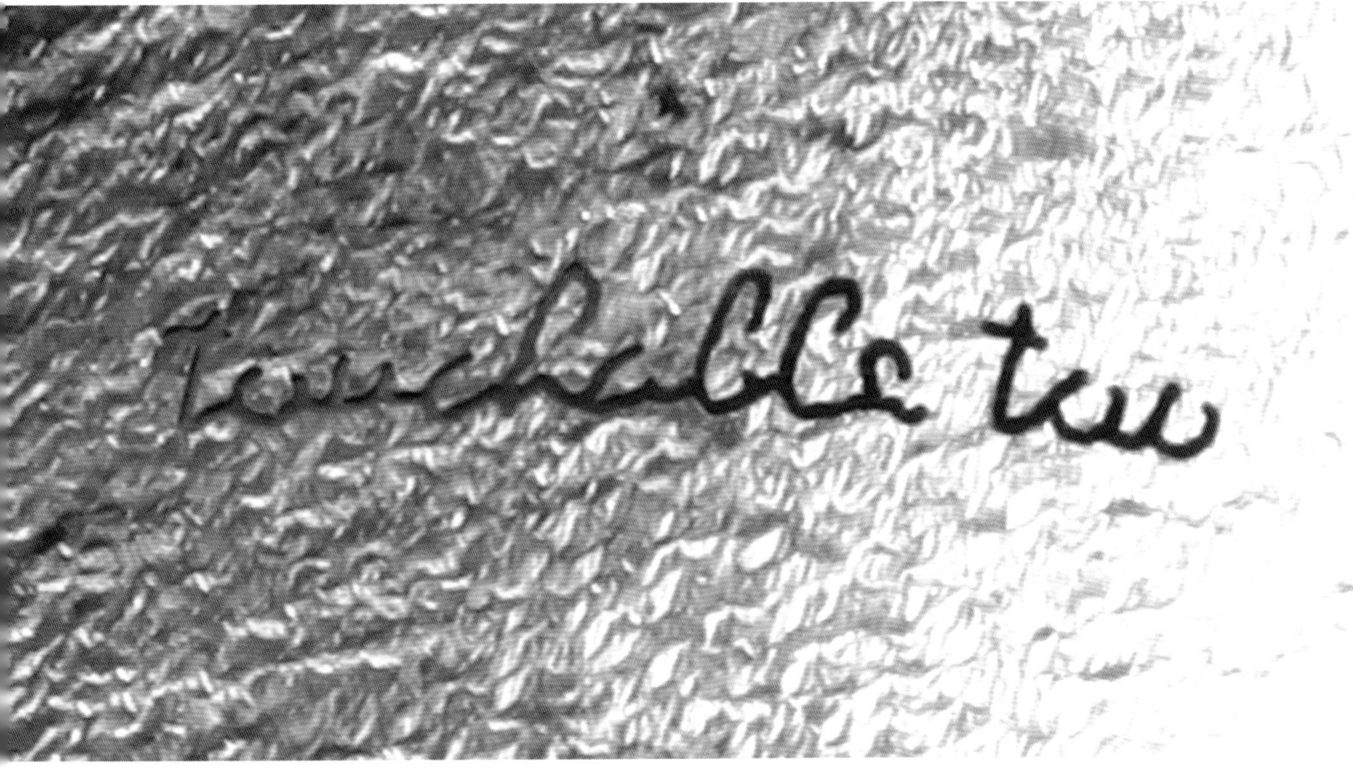

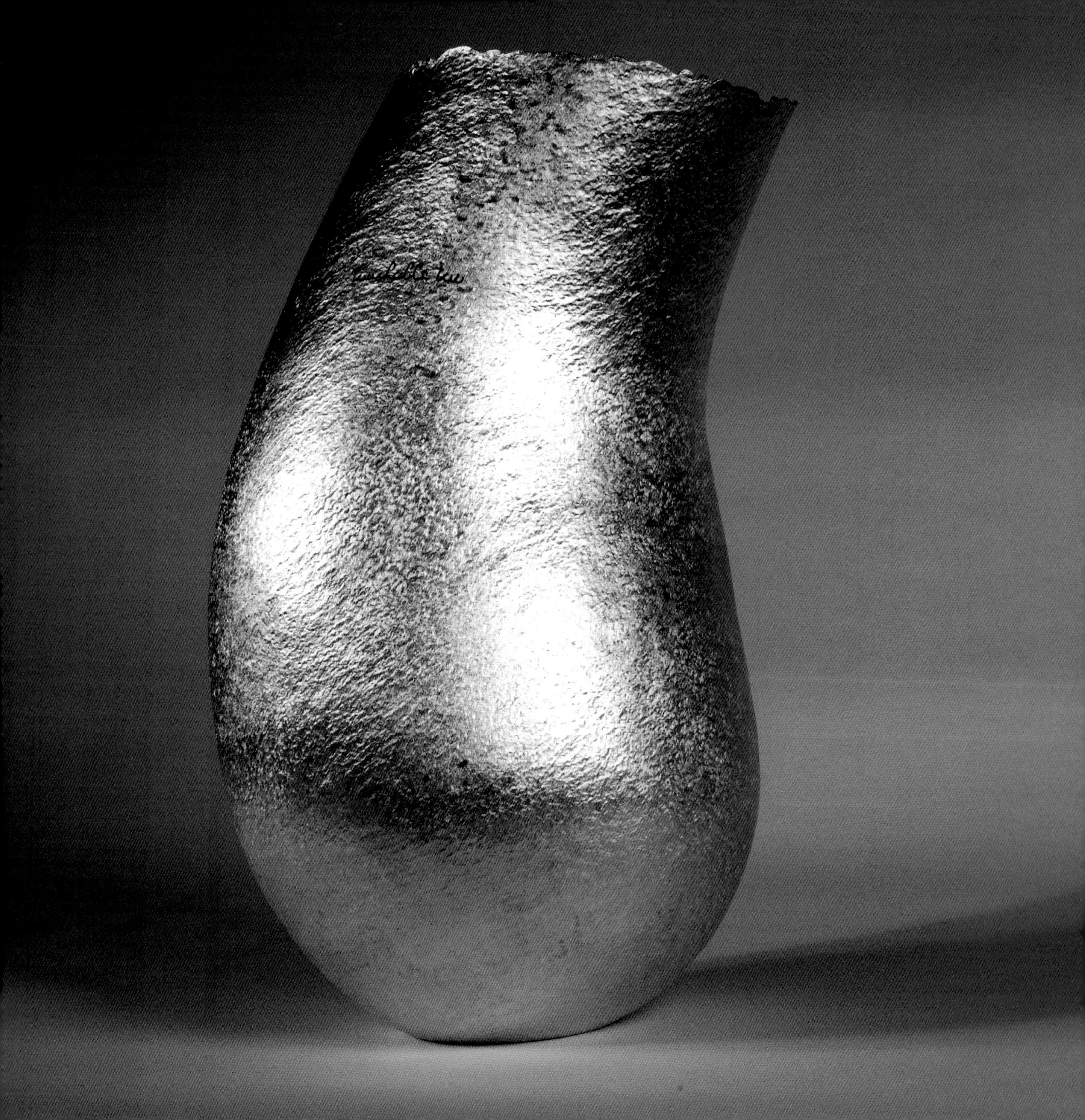

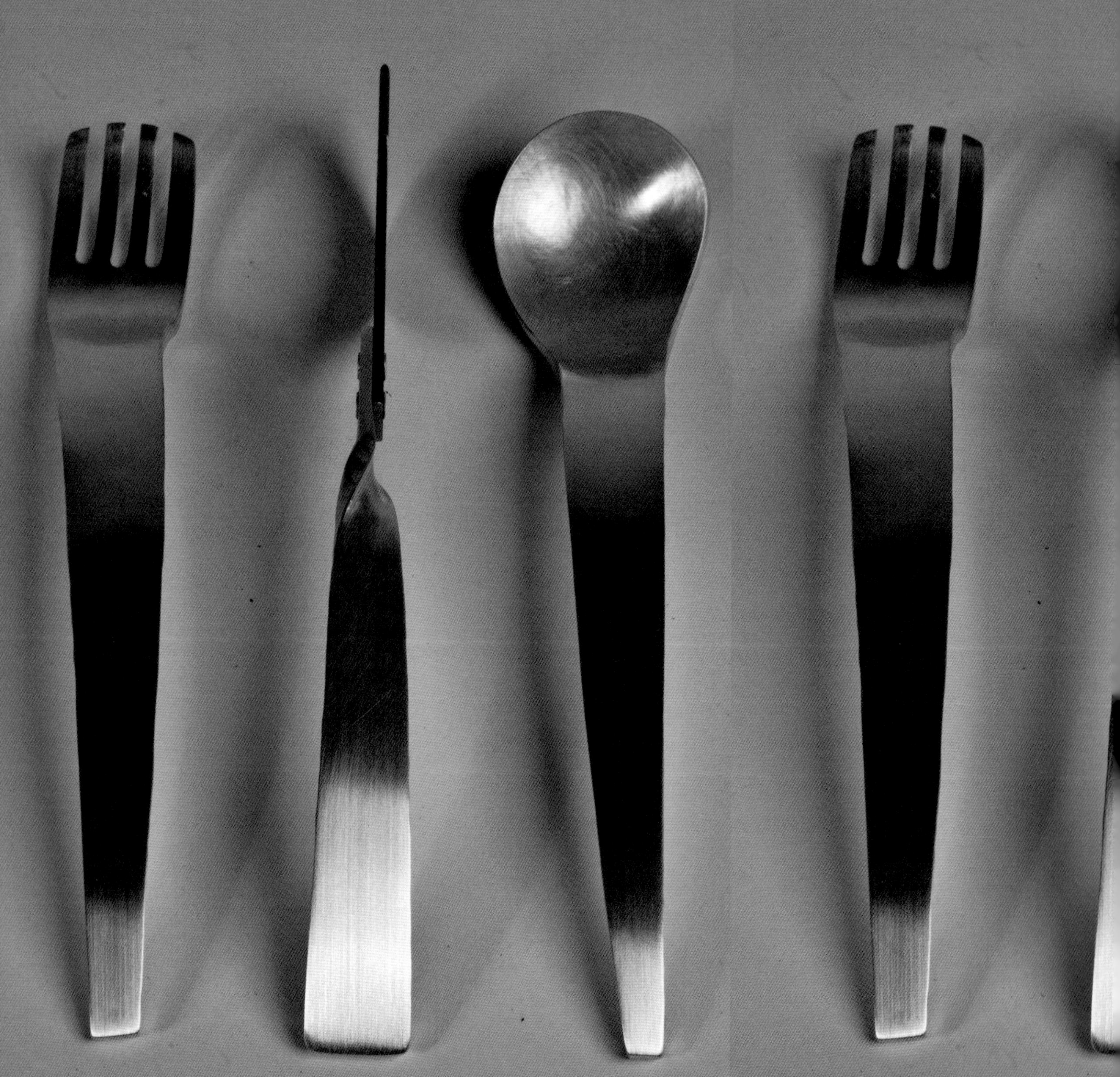

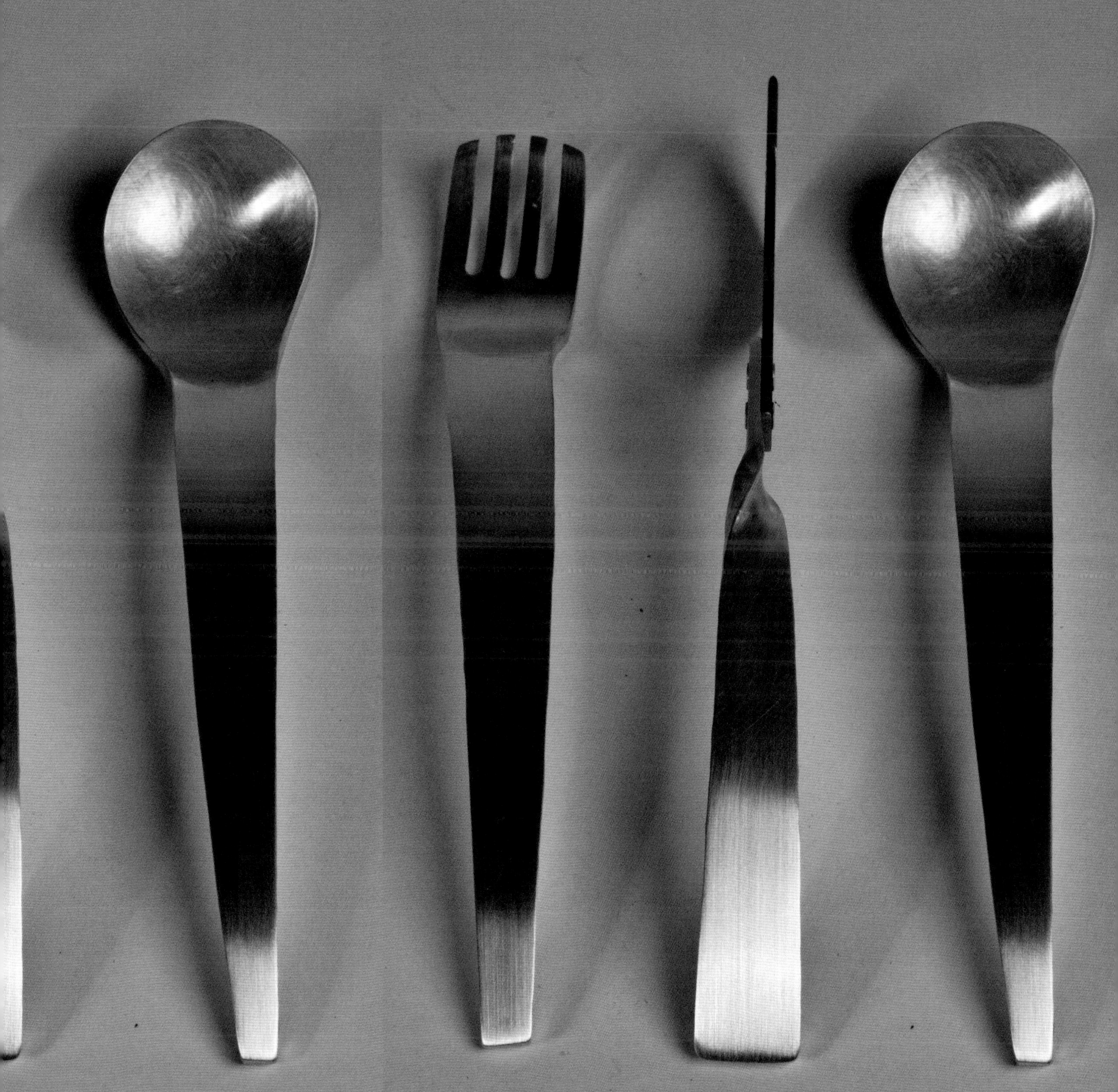

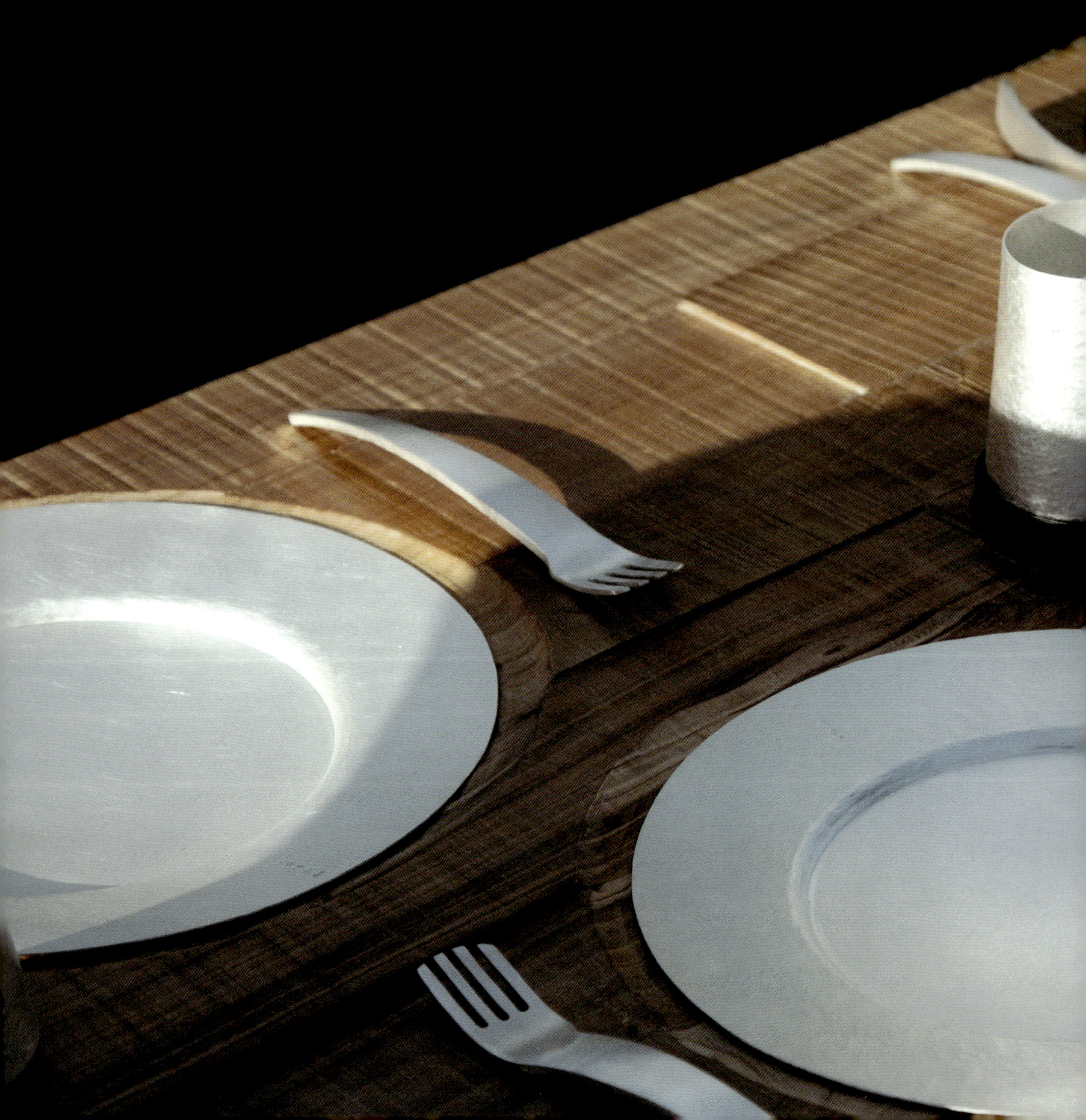

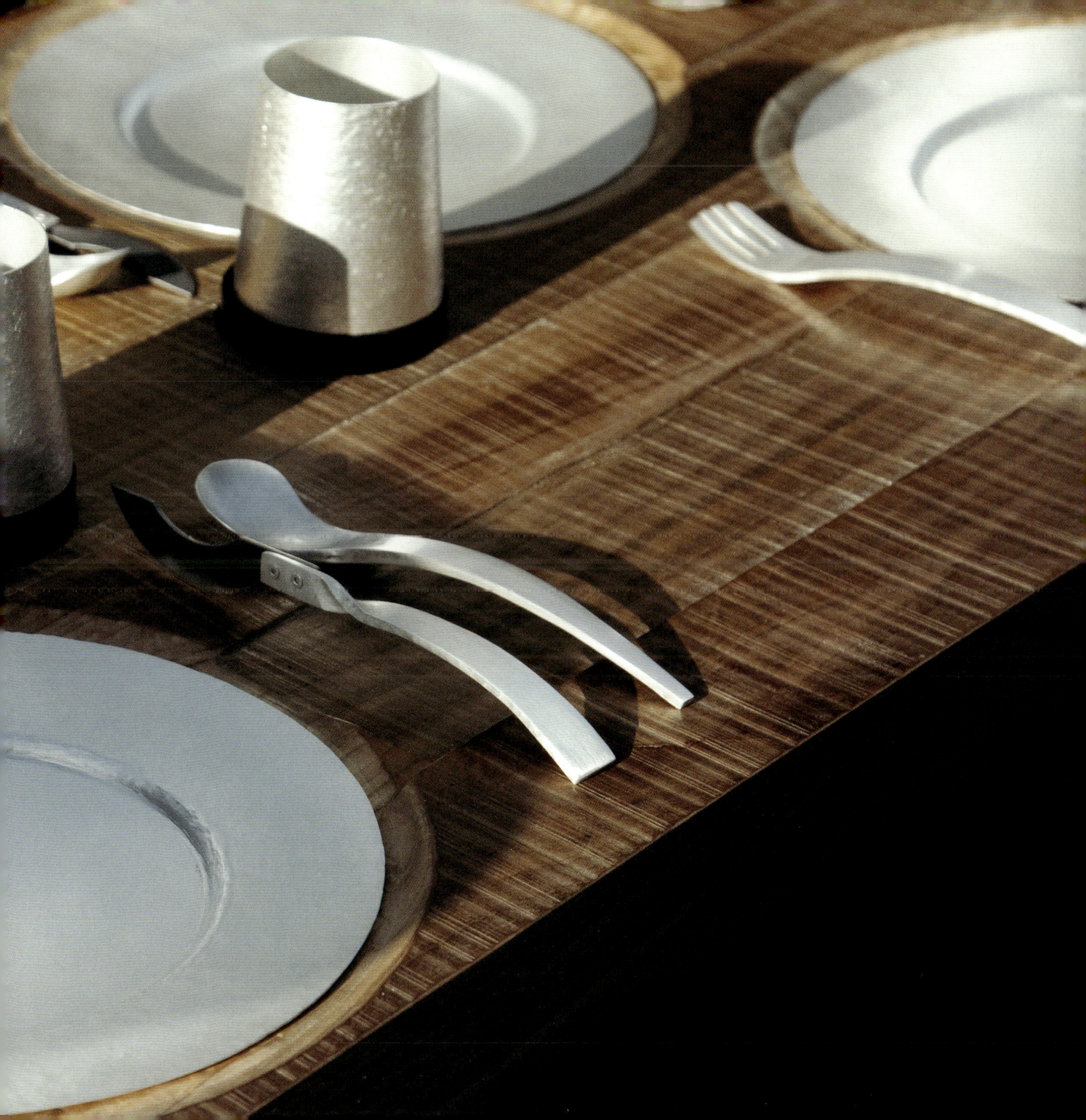

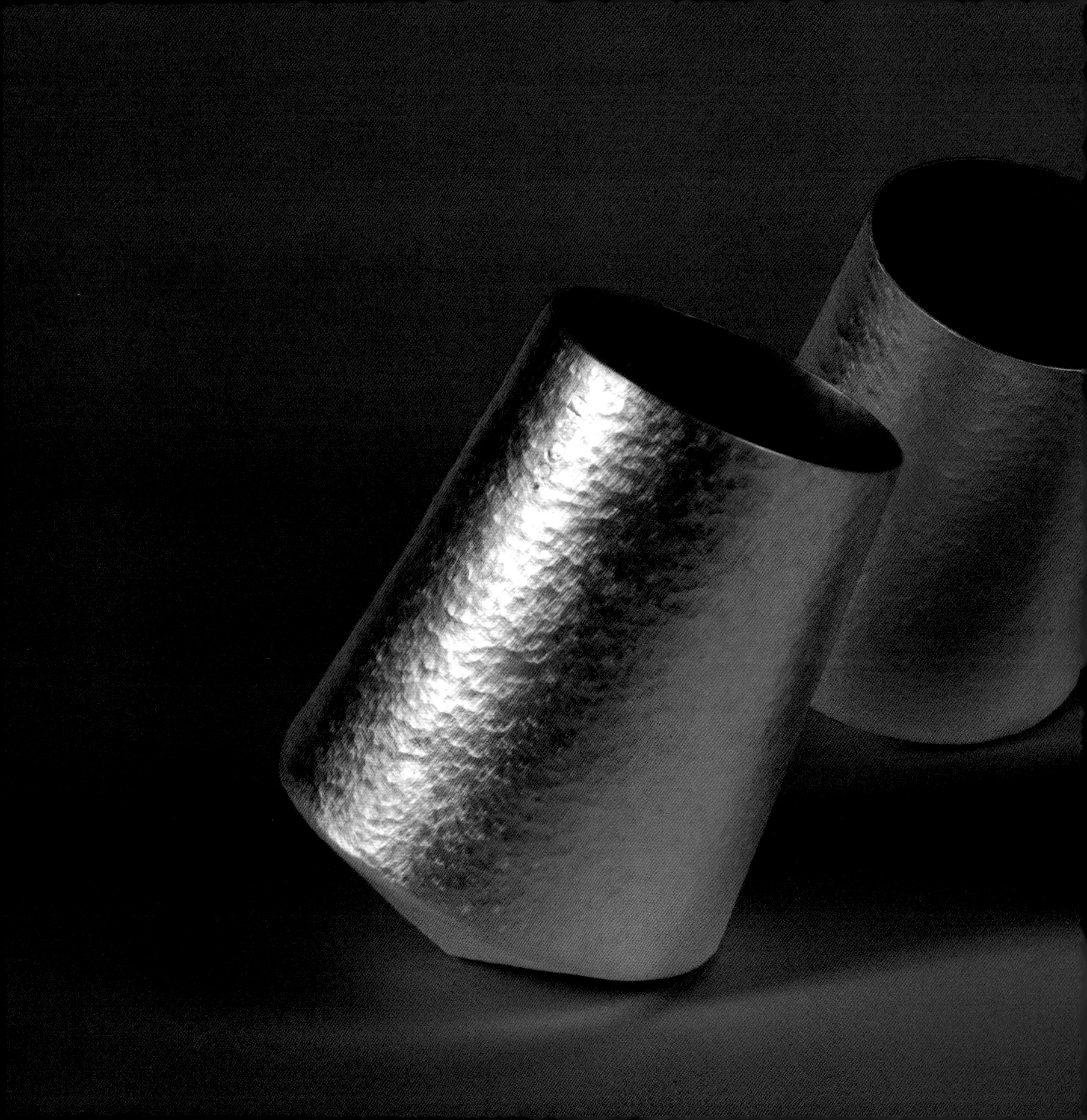

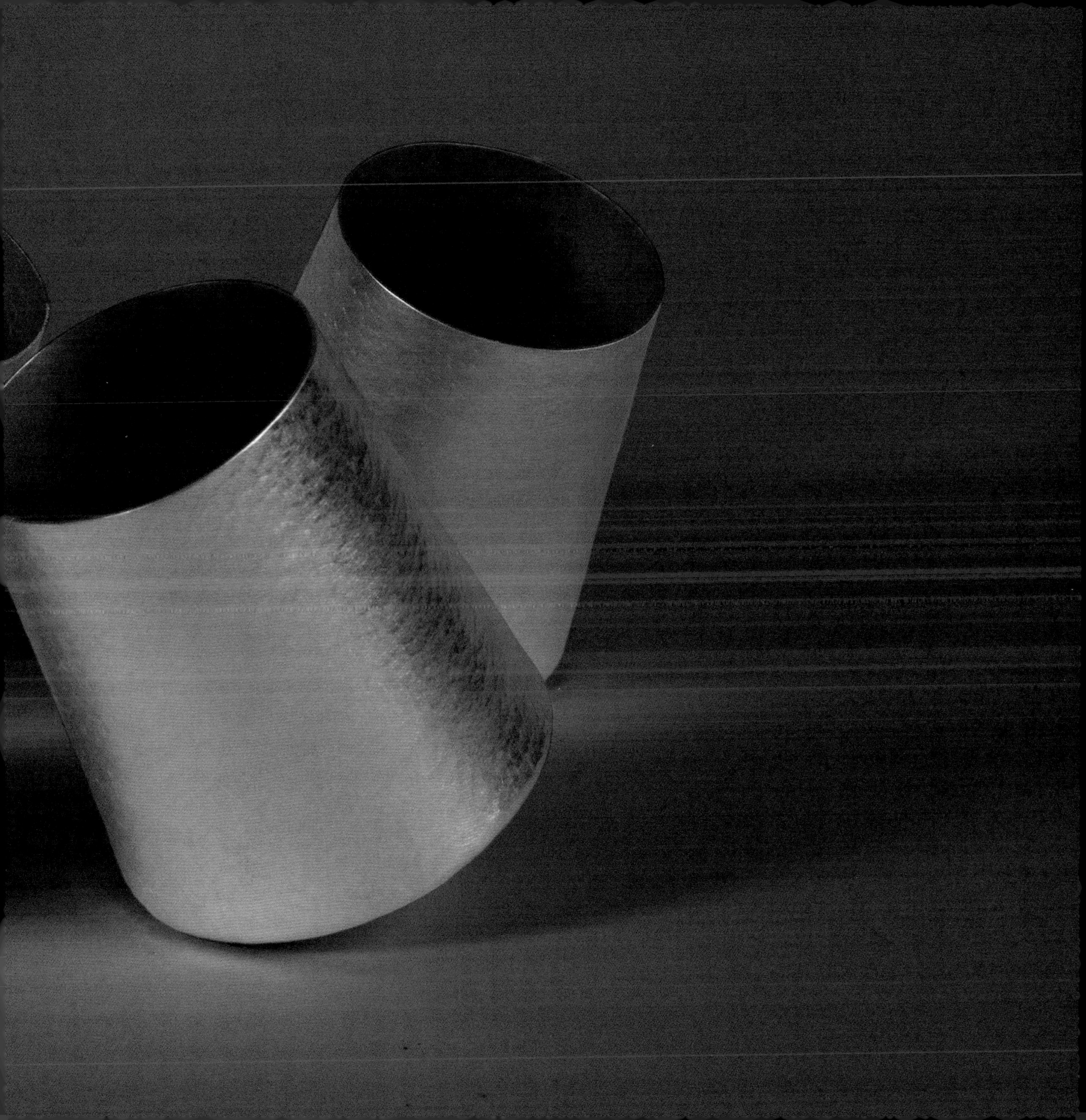

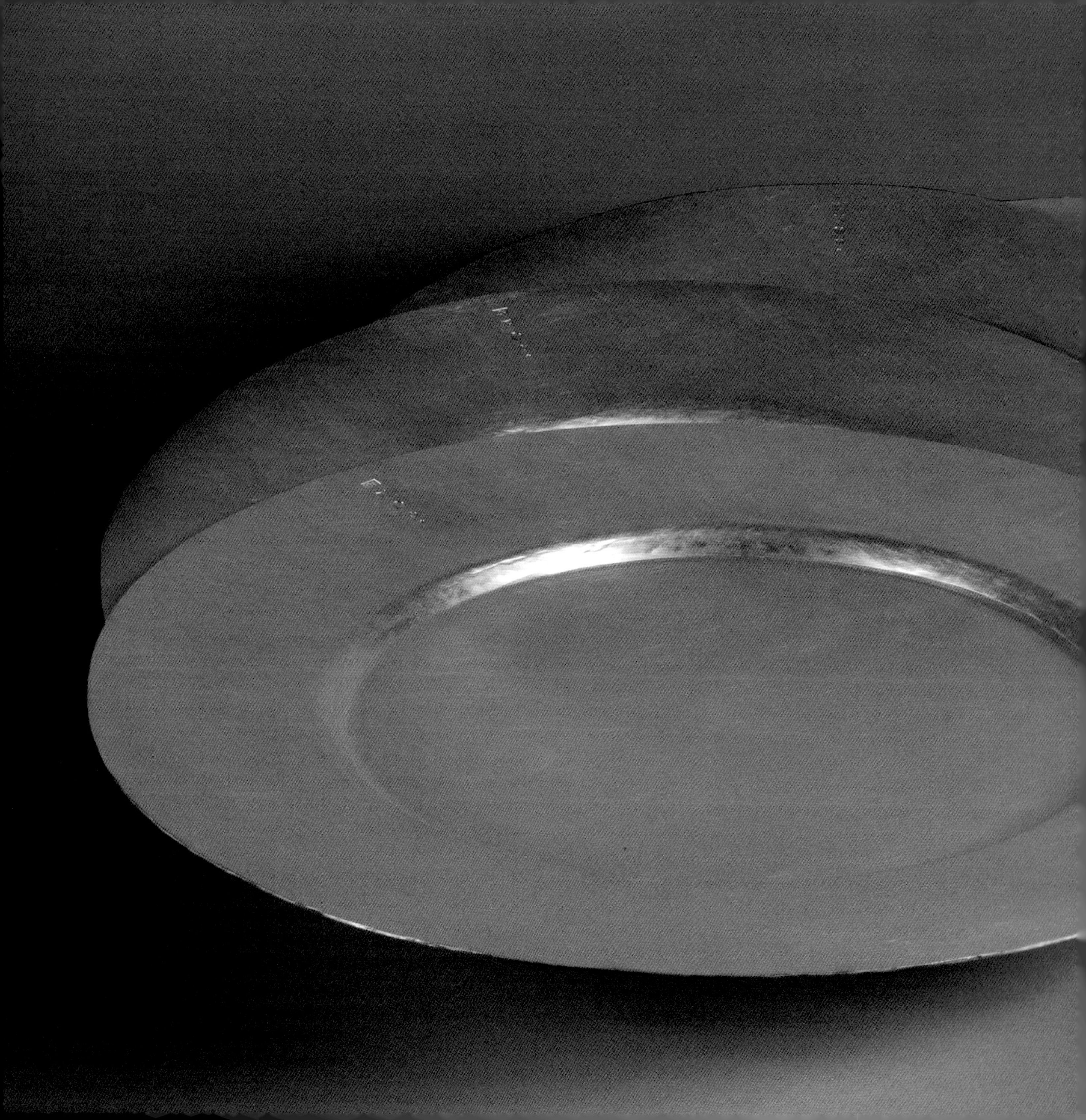

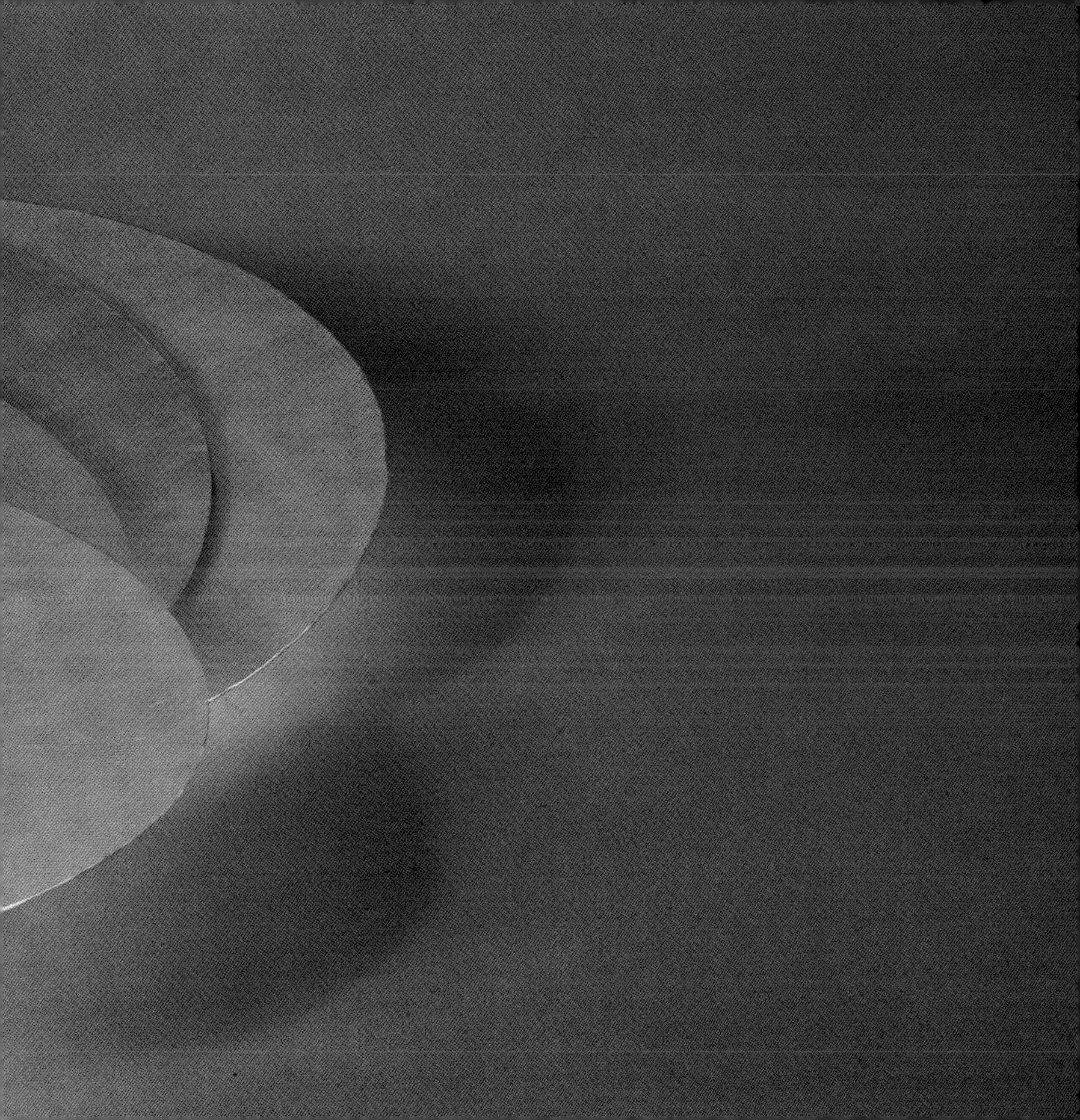

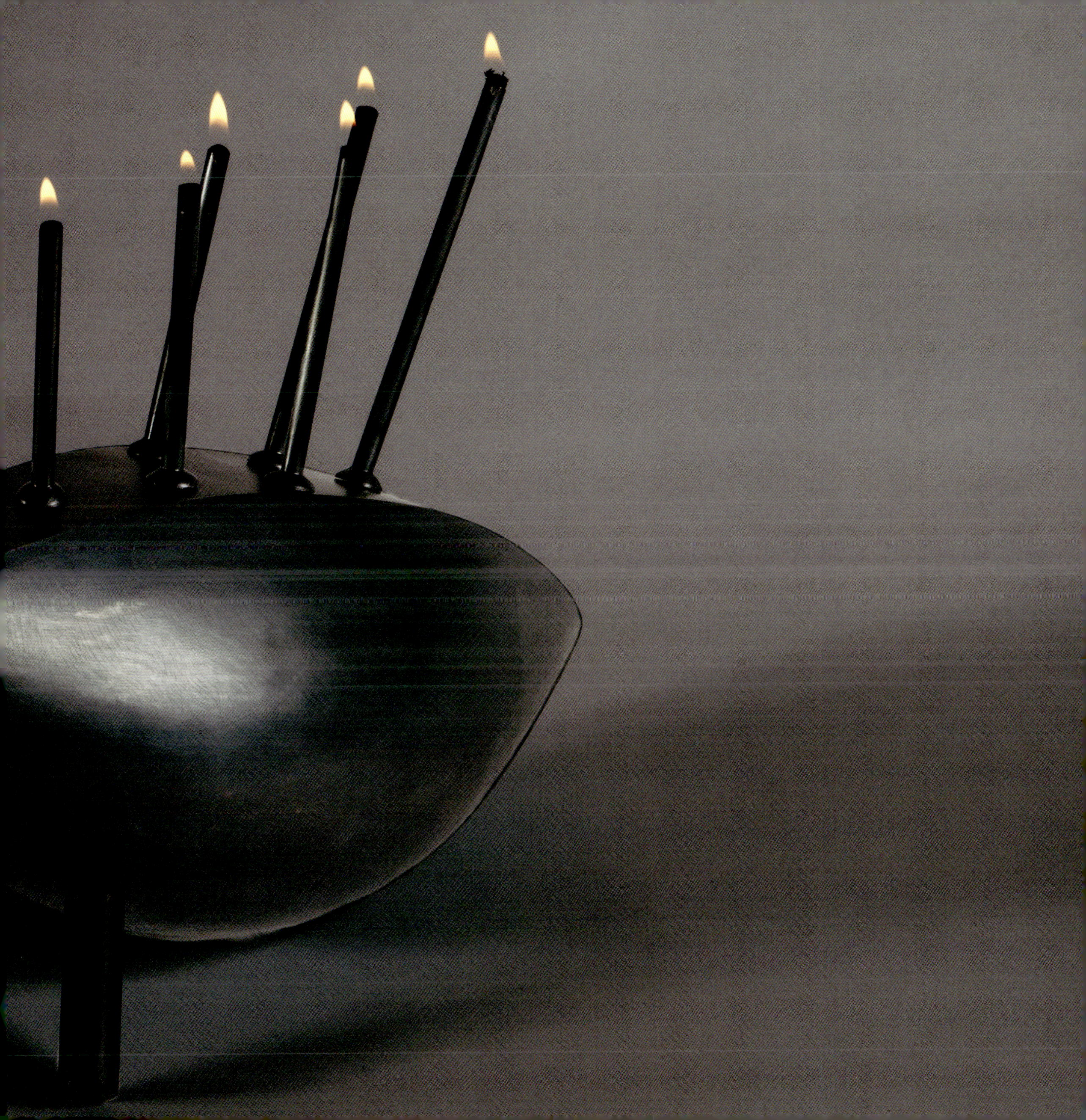

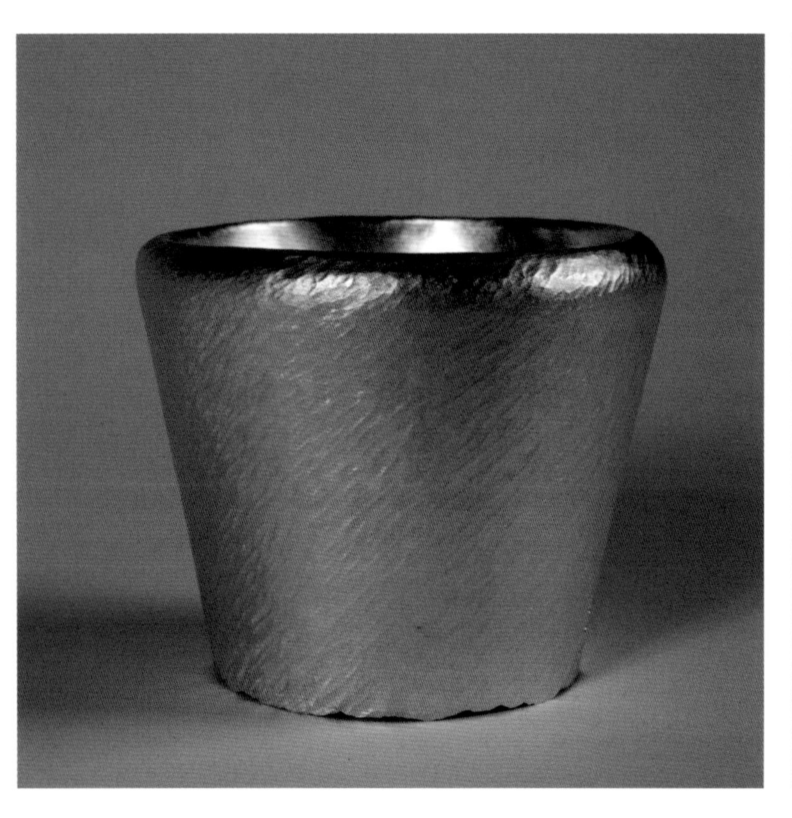

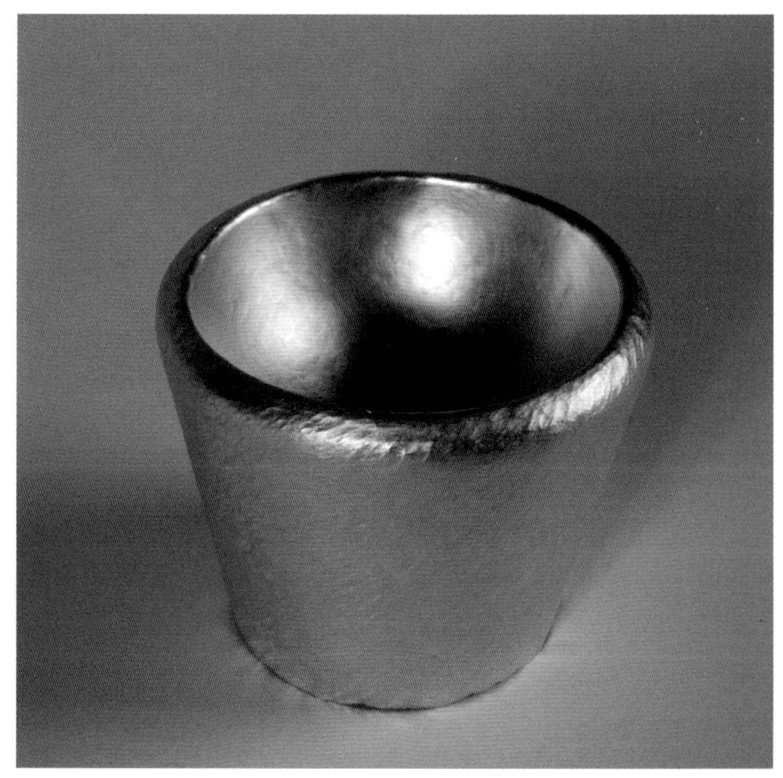

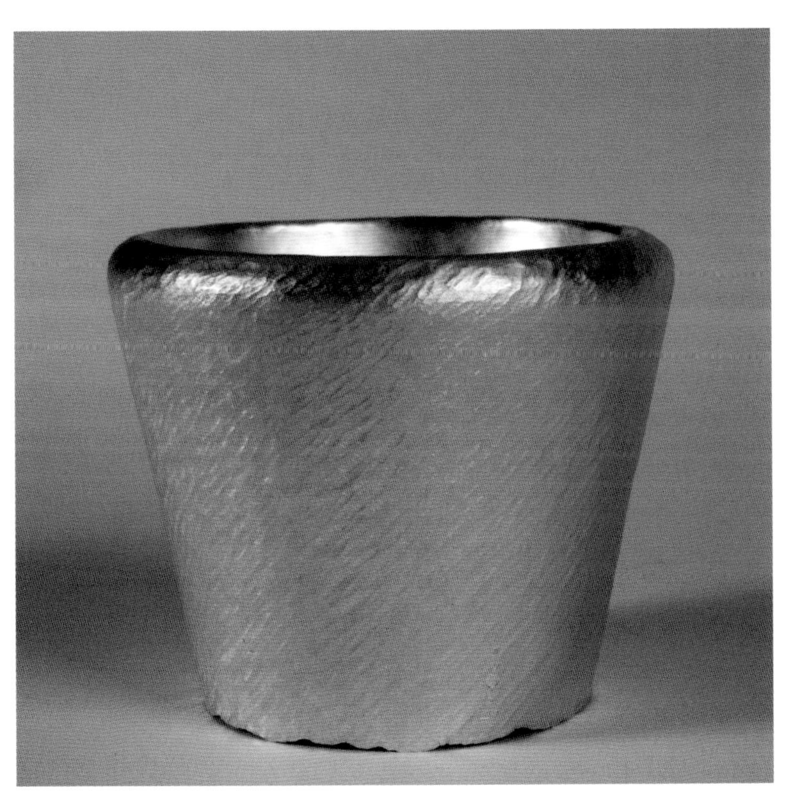

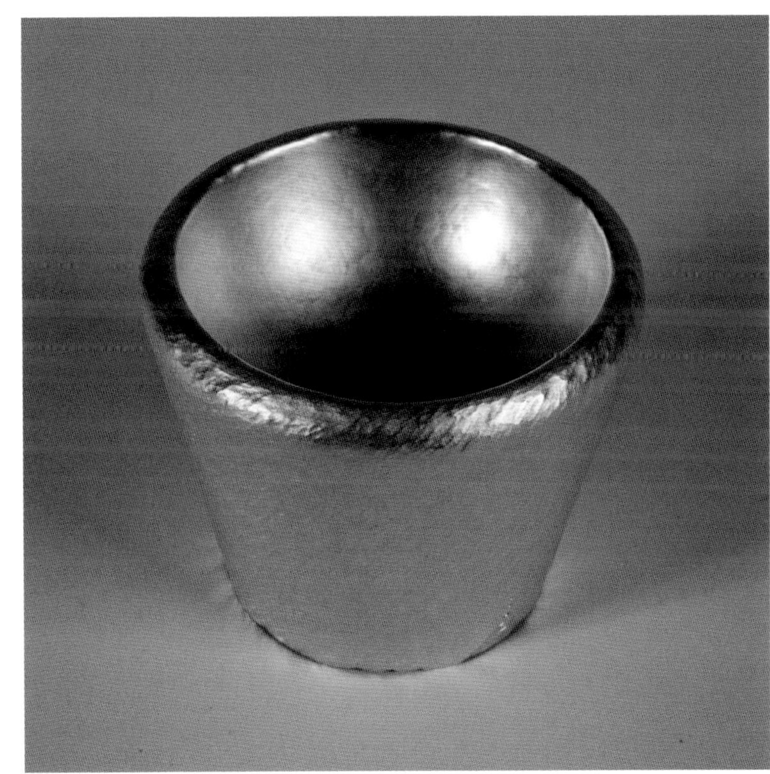

129

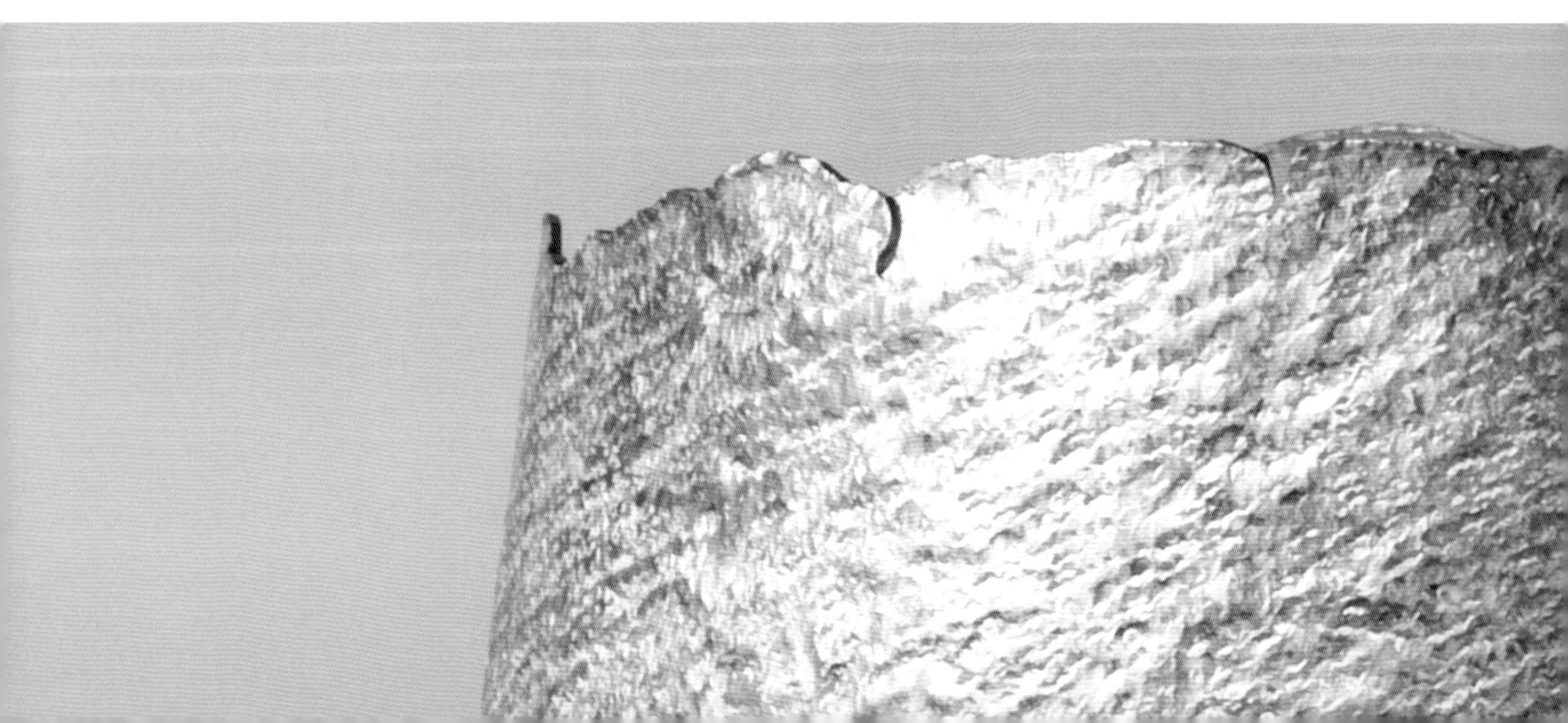

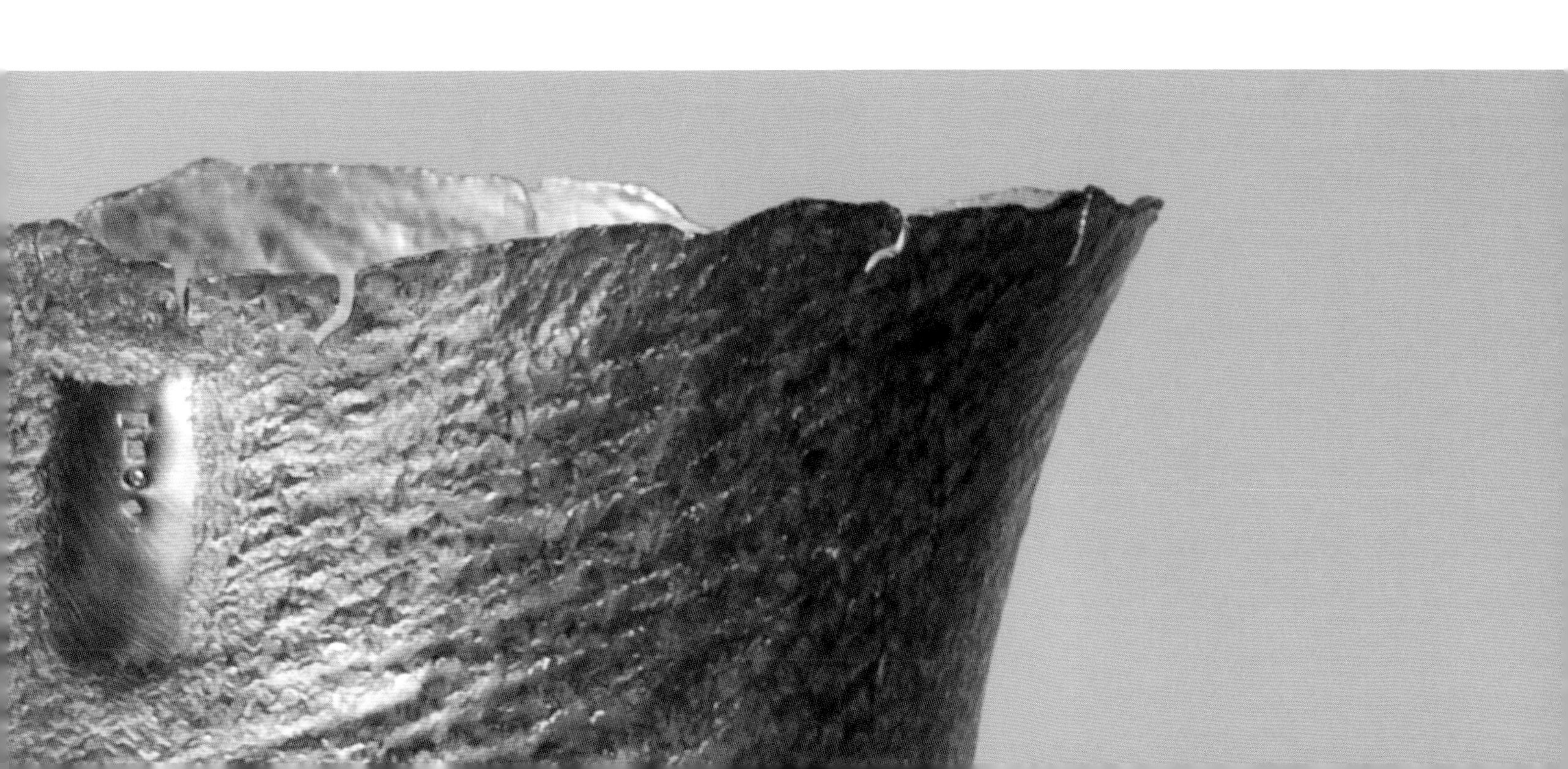

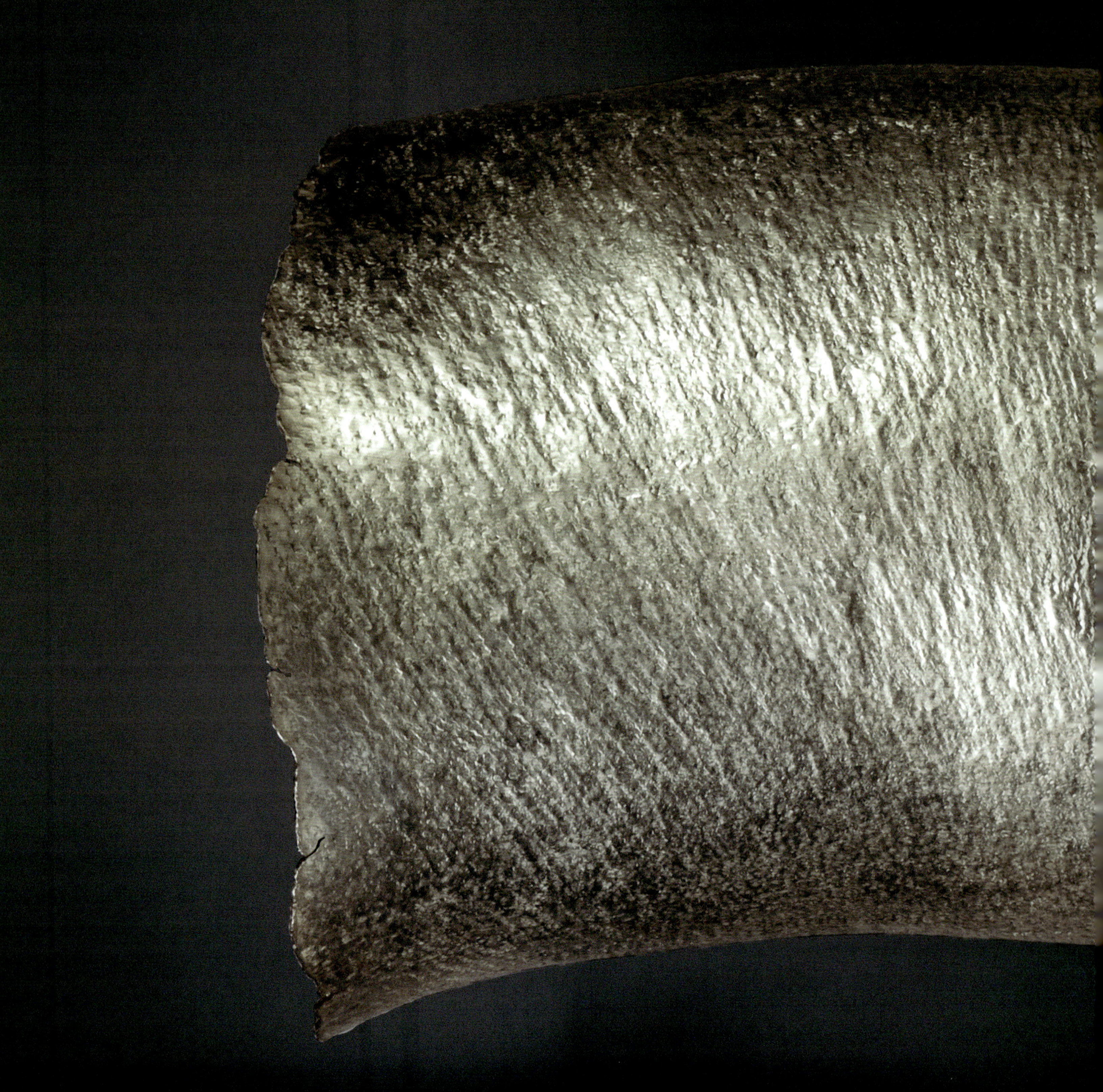

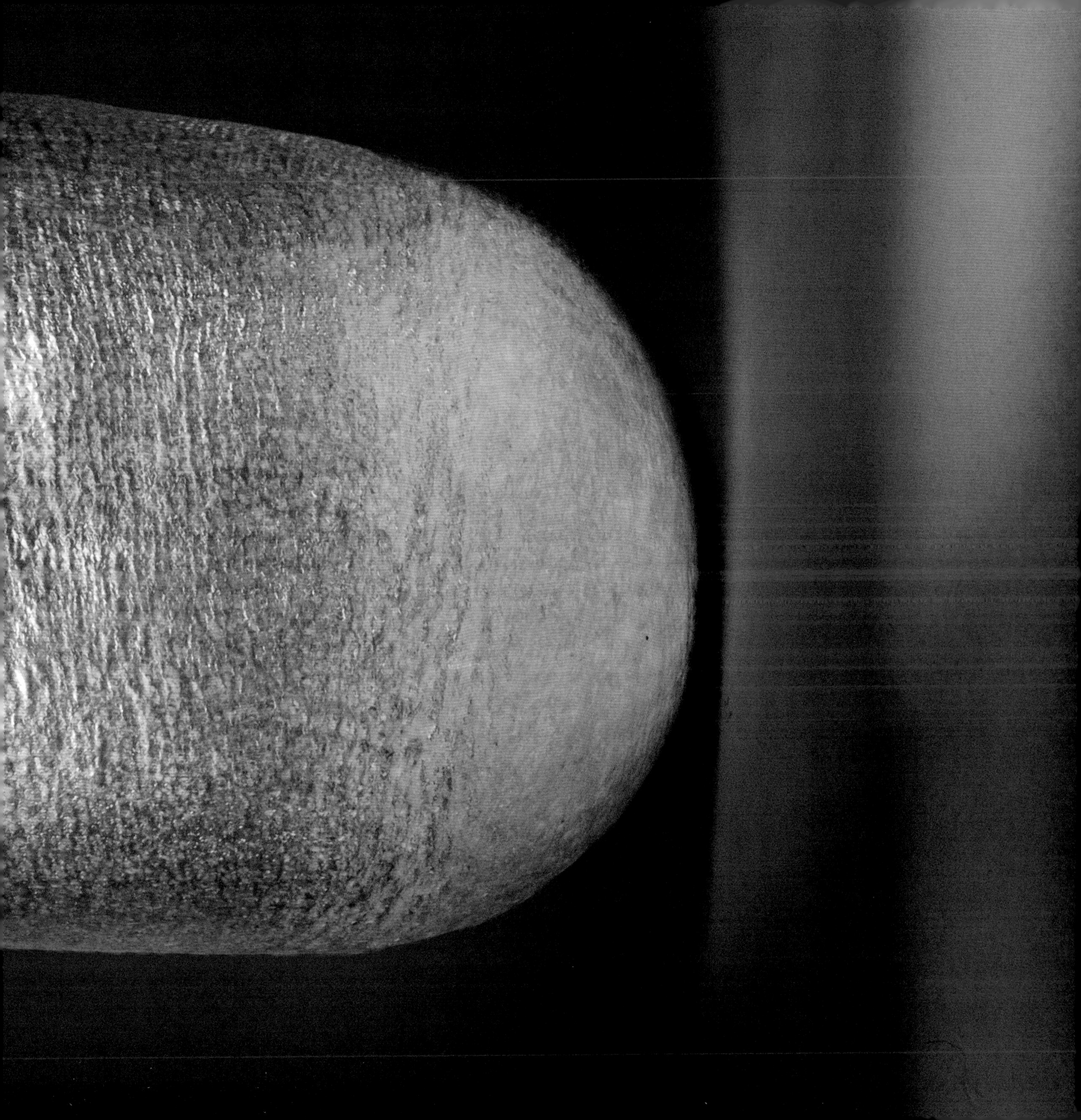

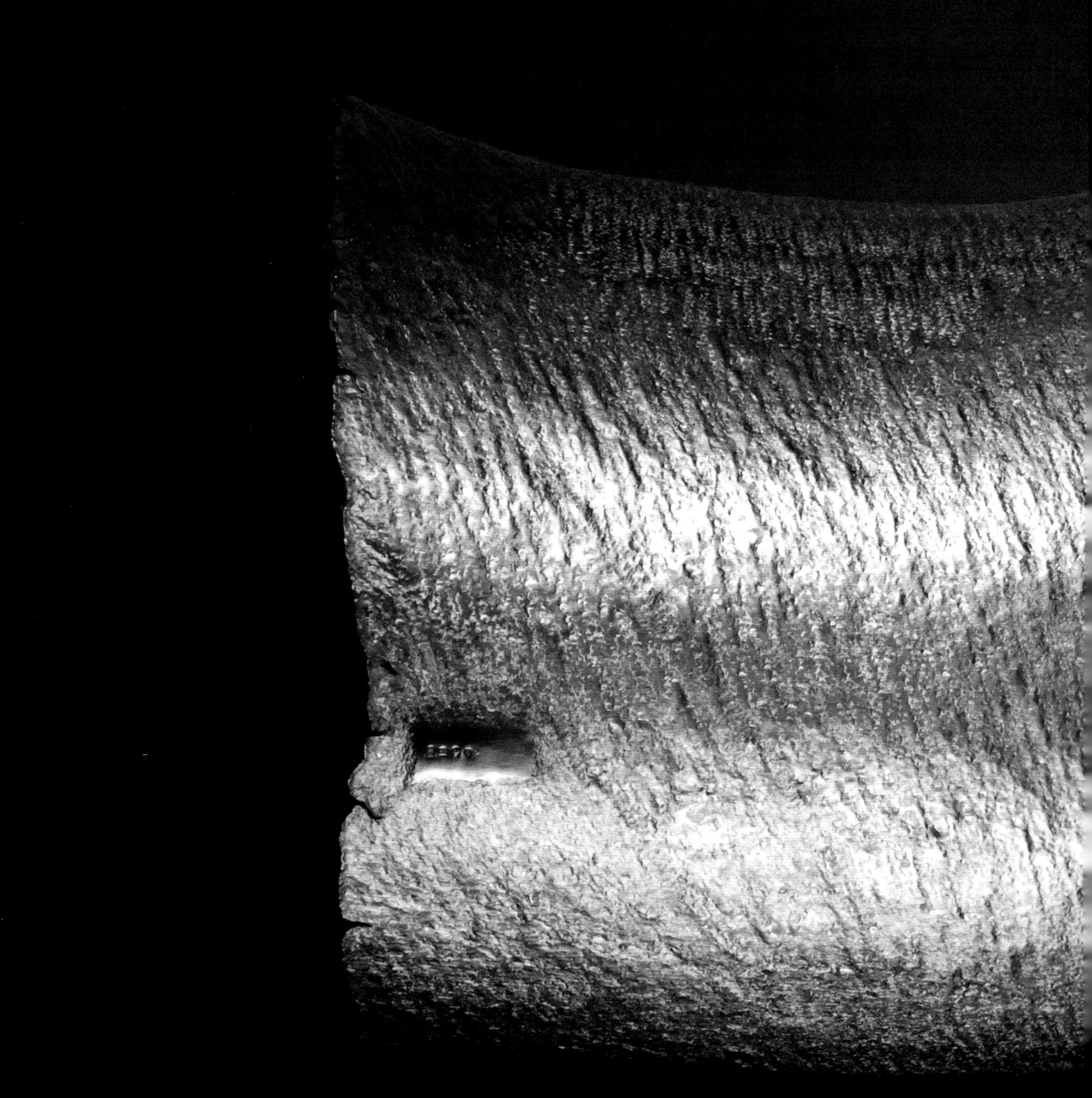

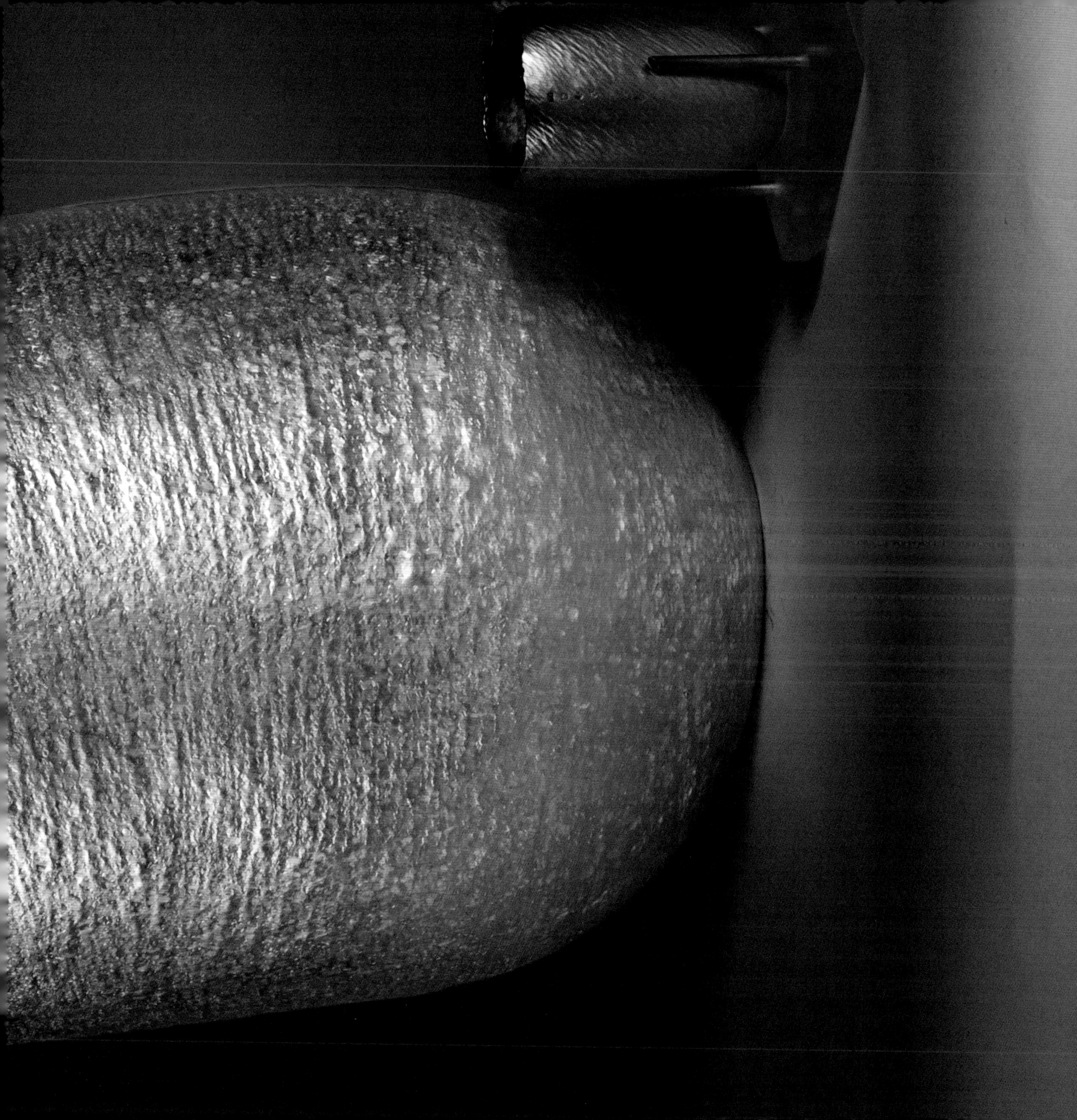

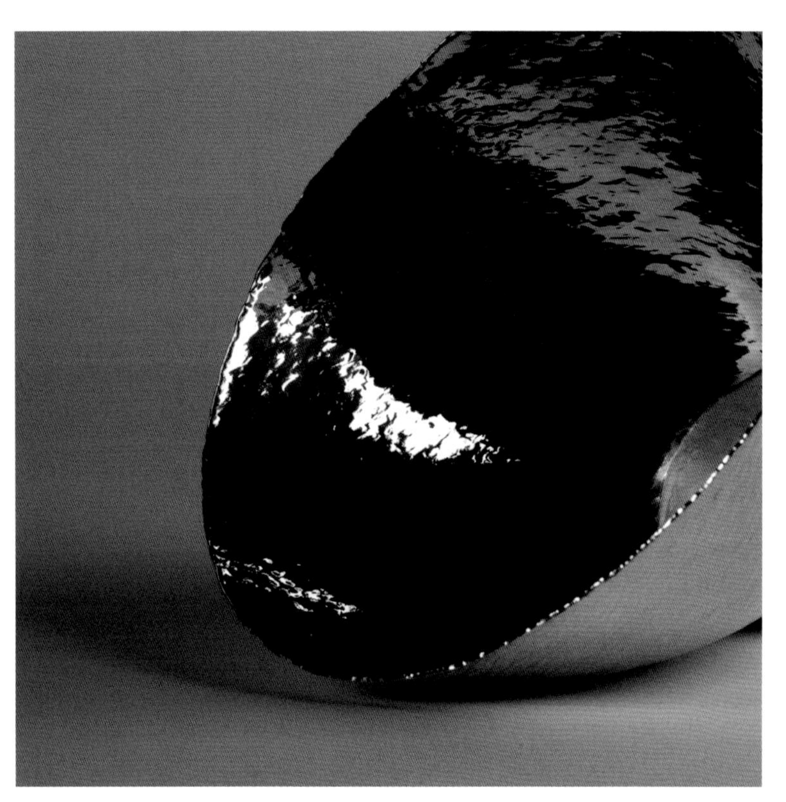

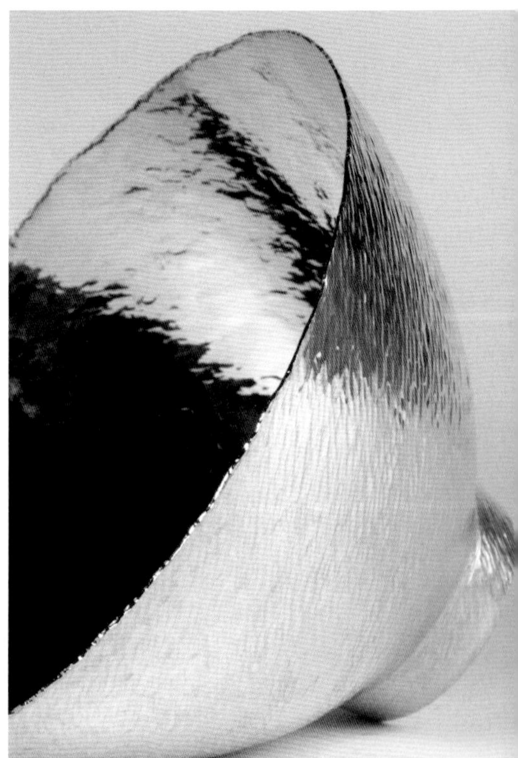

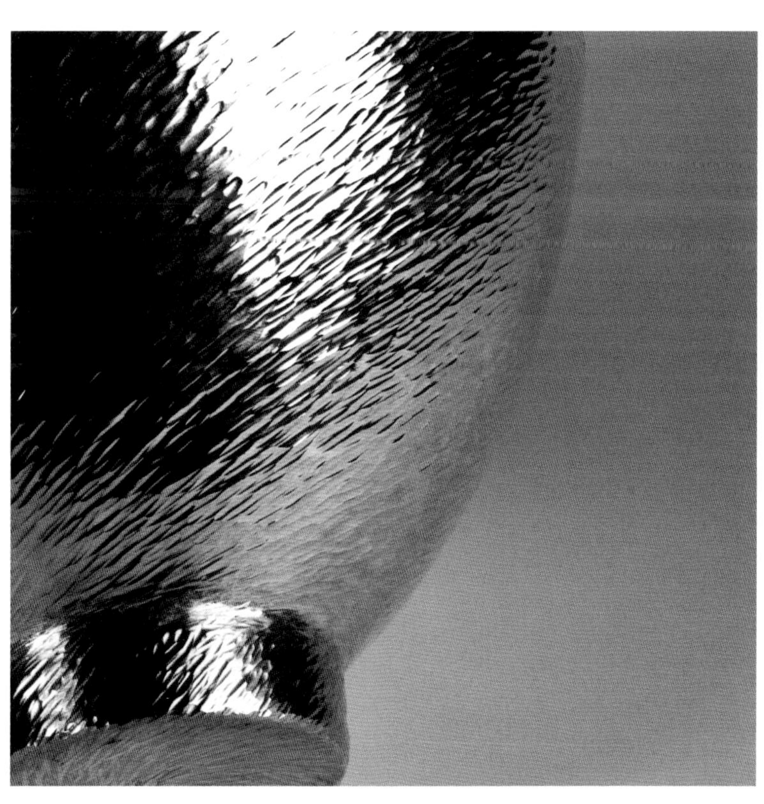

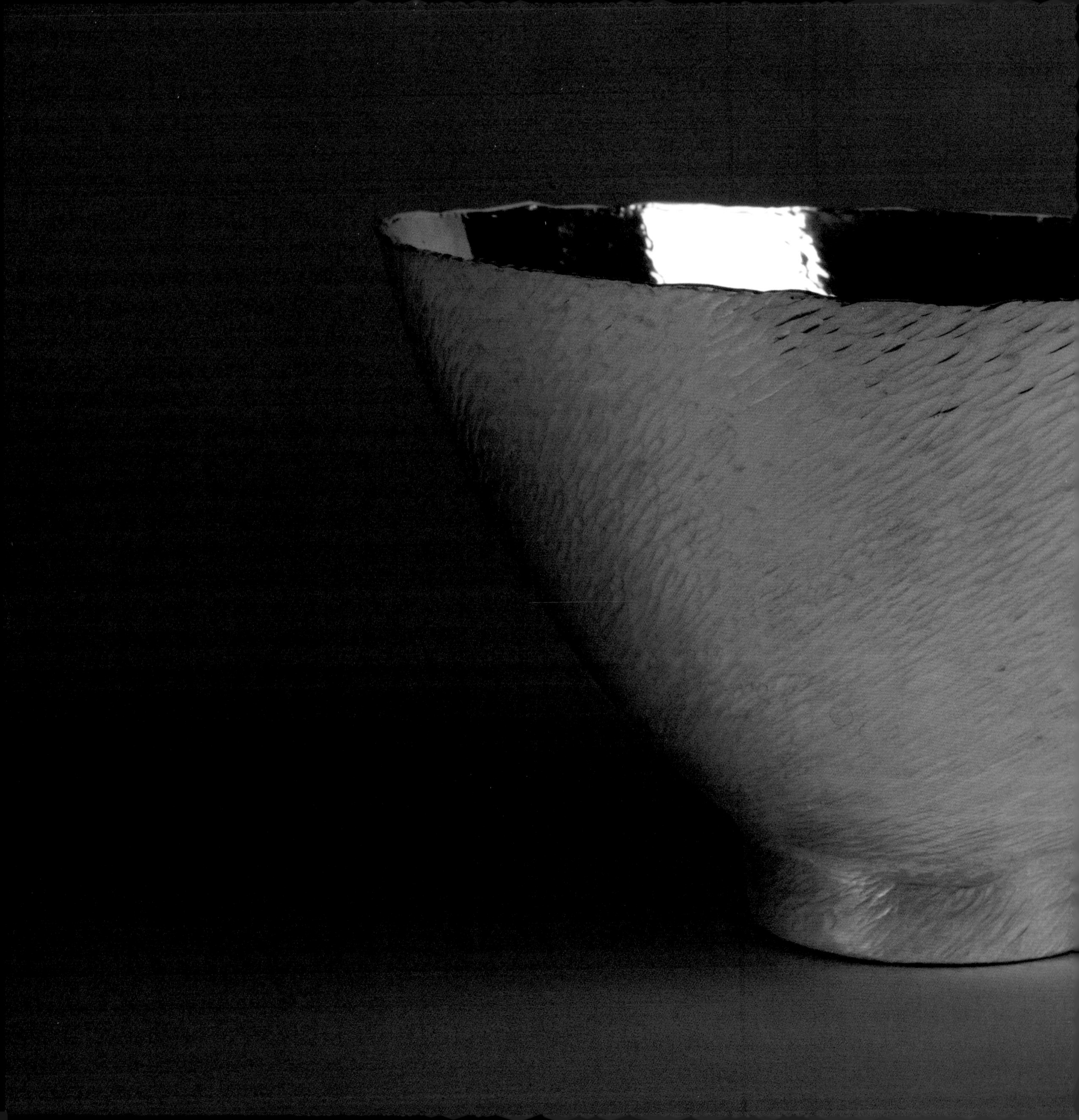

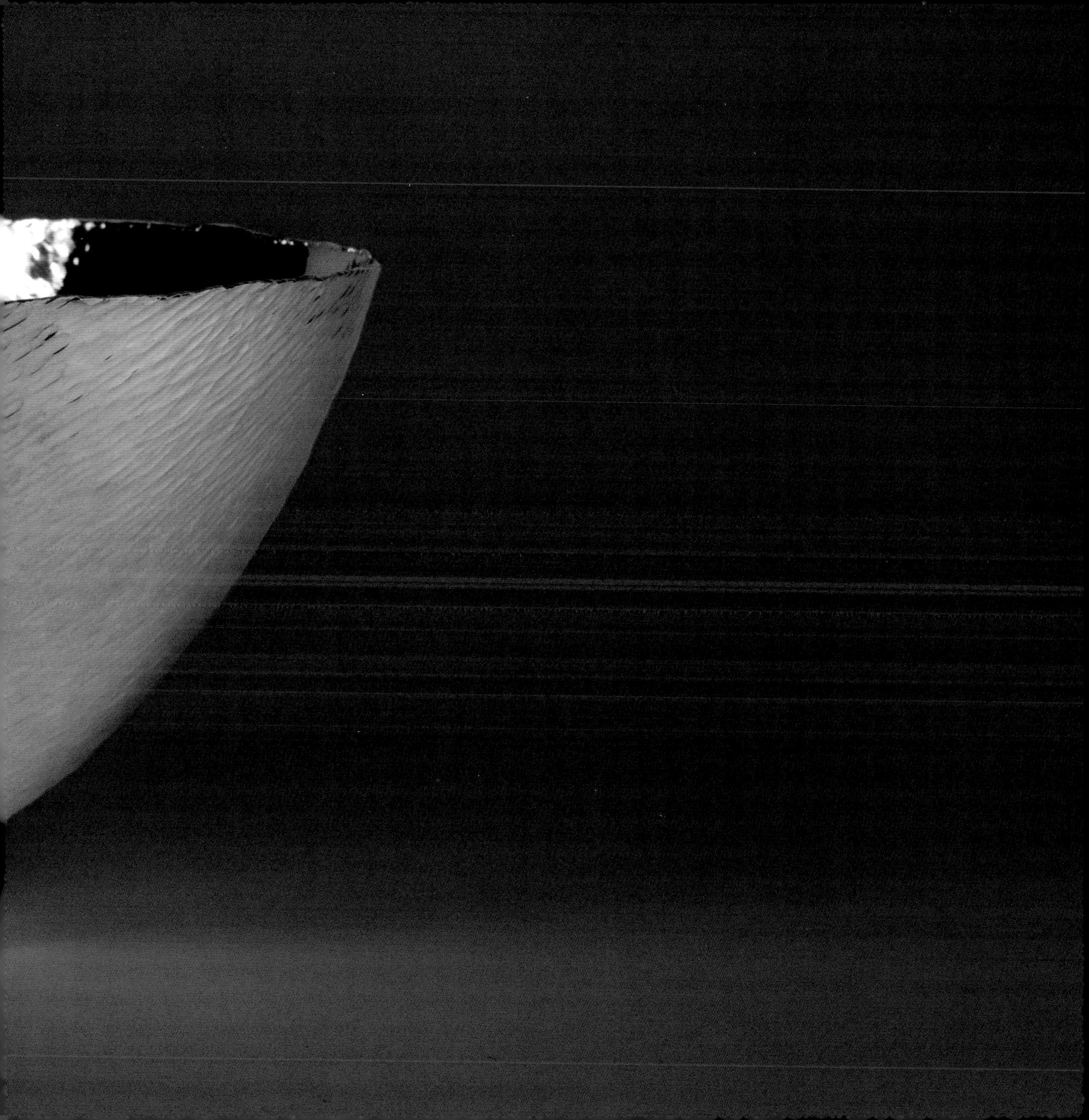

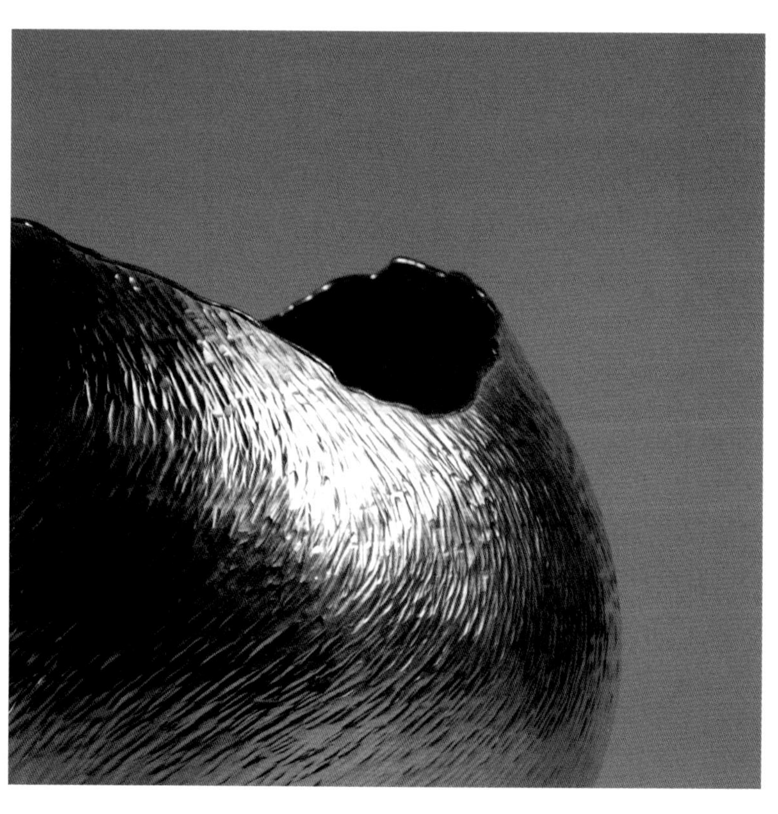

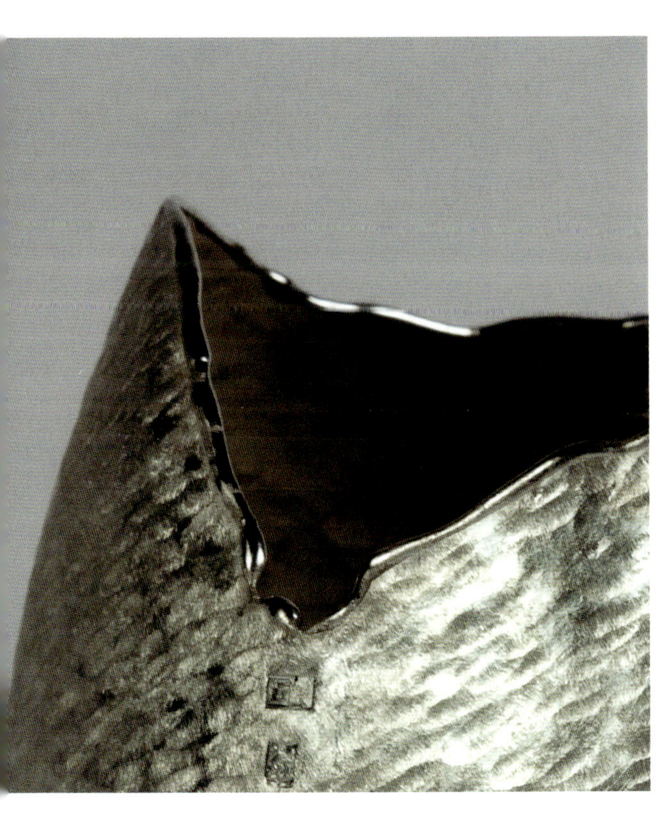
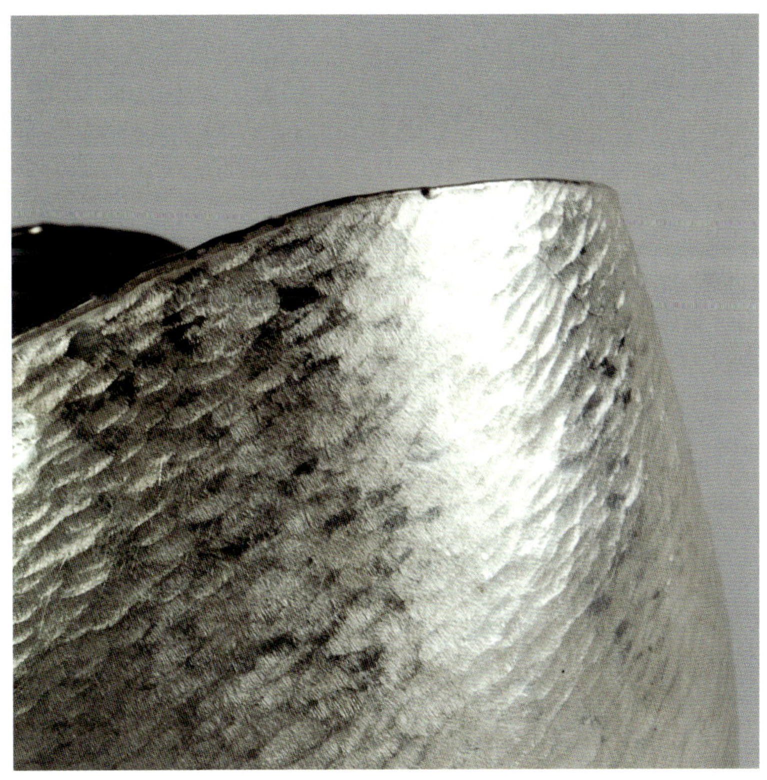

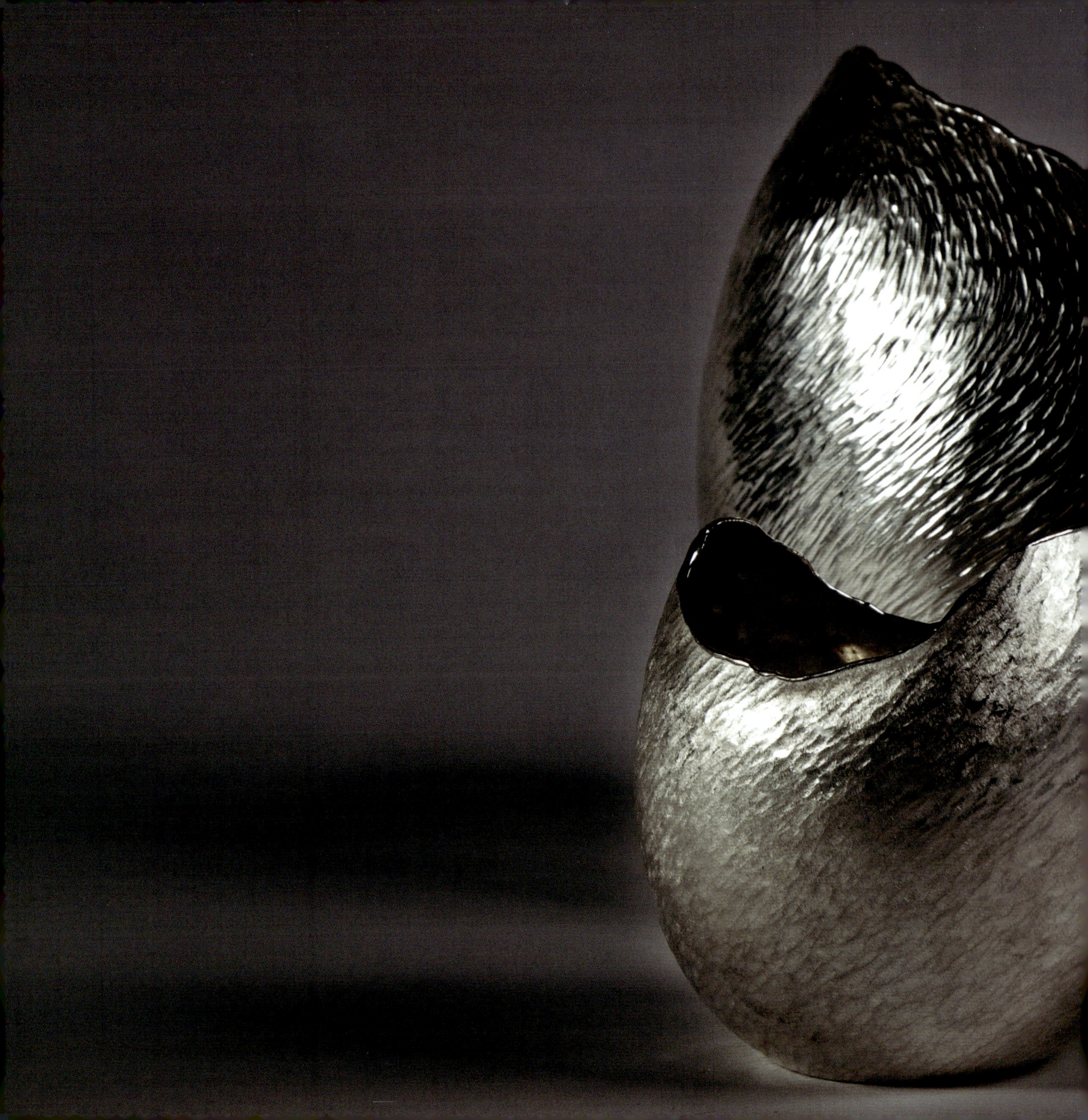

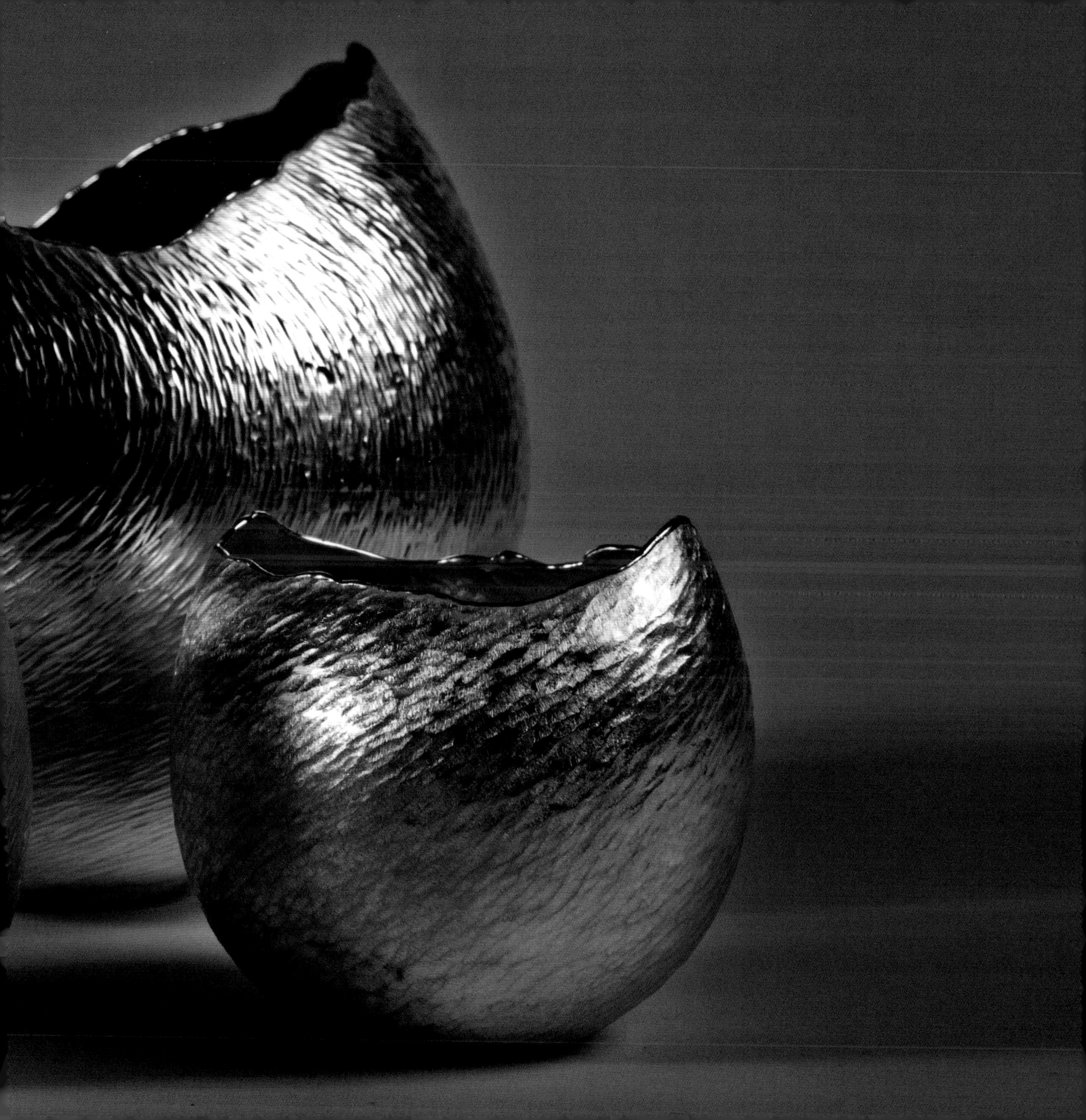

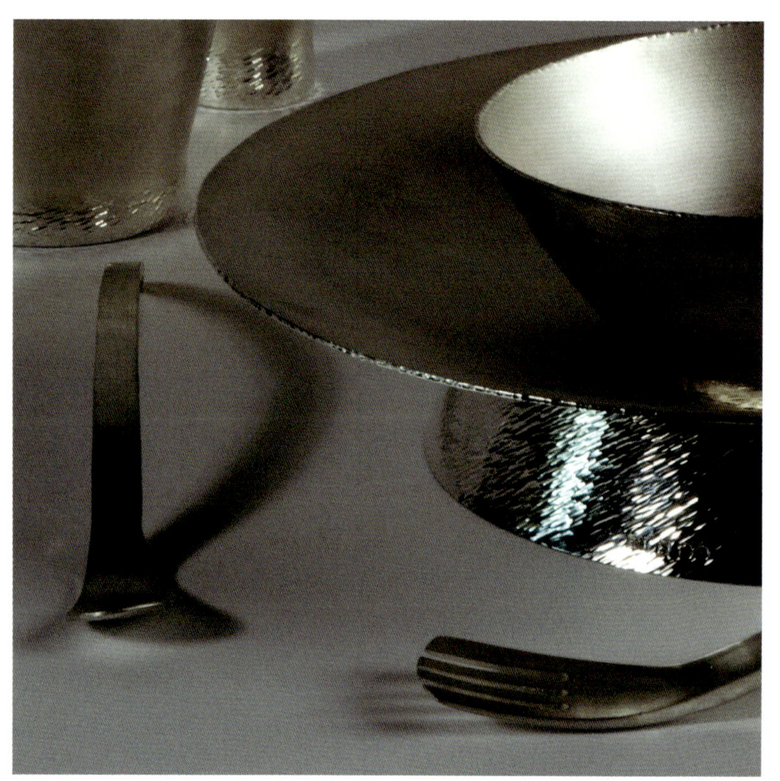

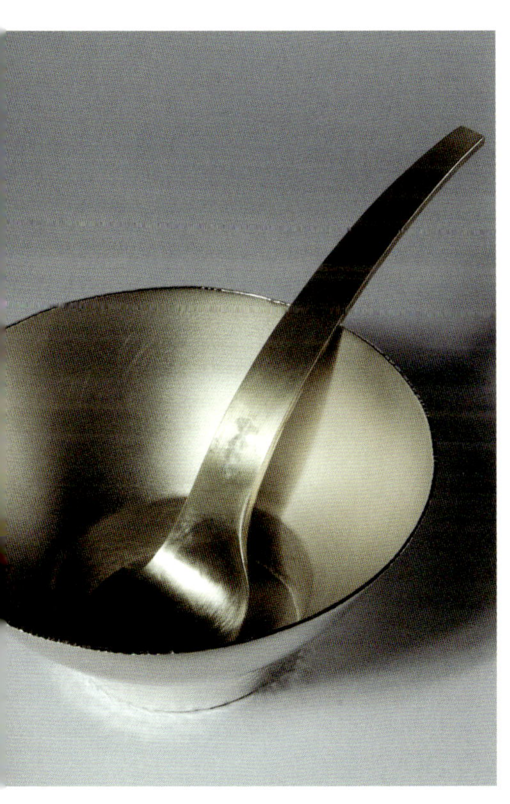

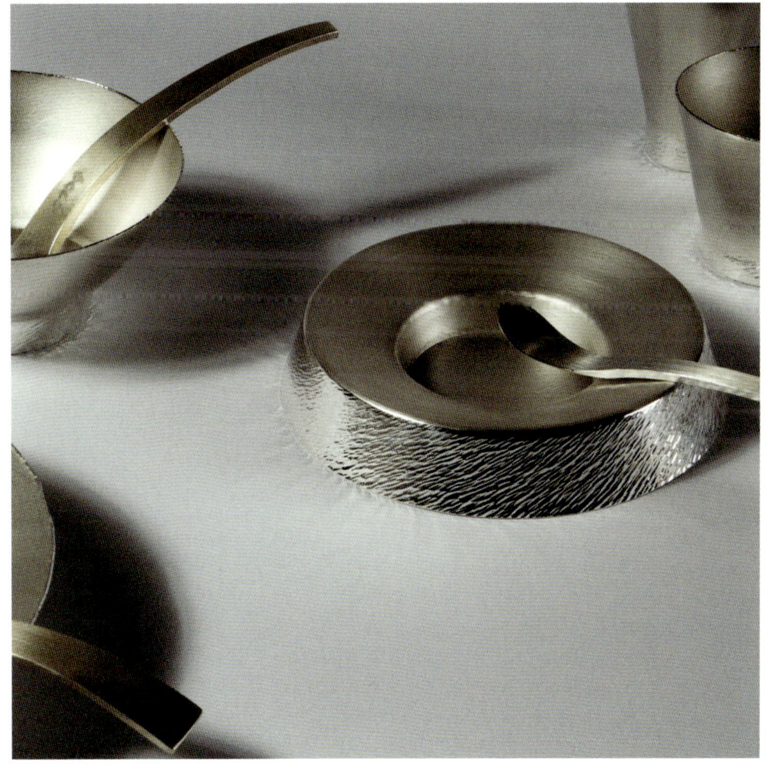

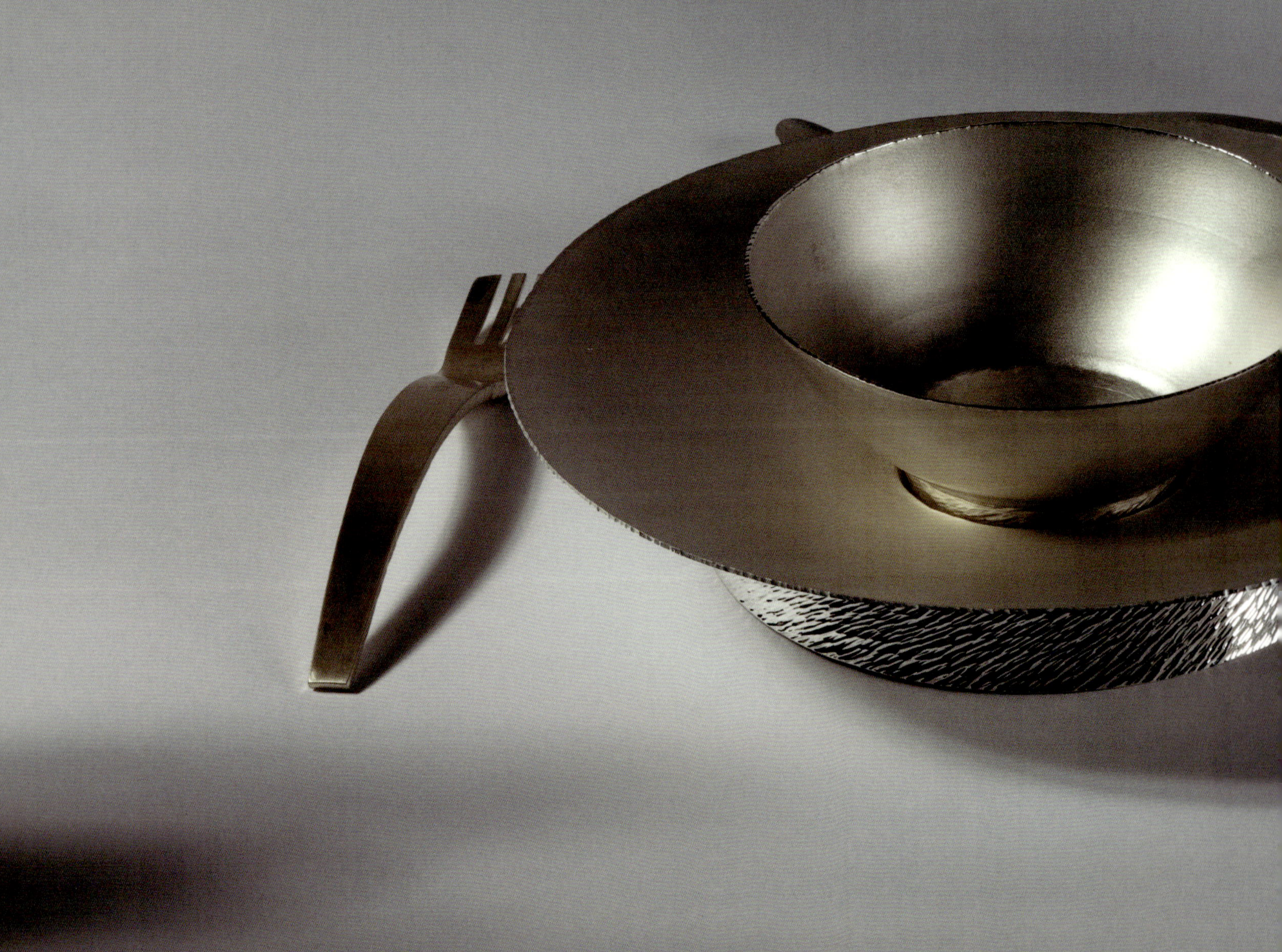

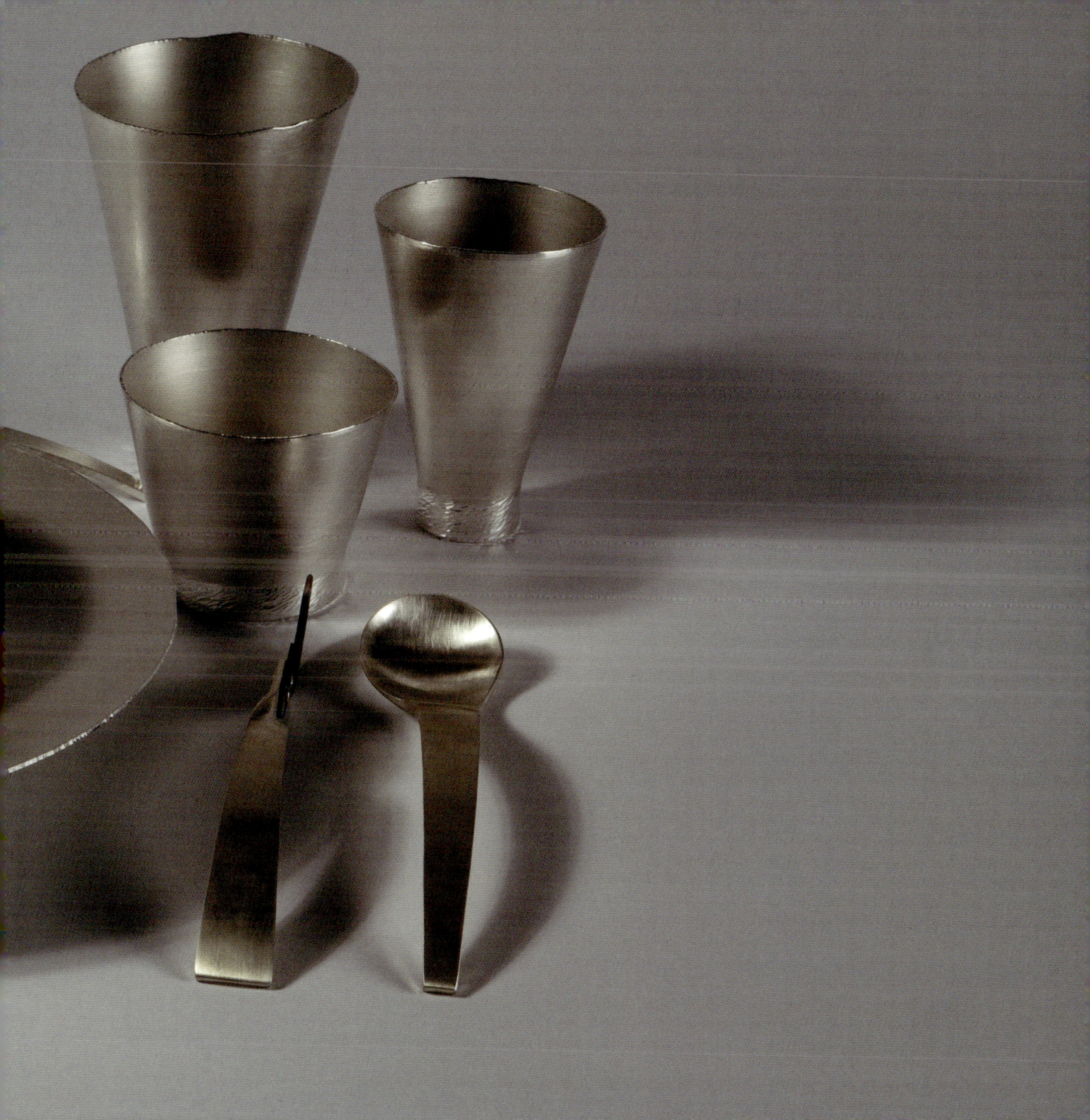

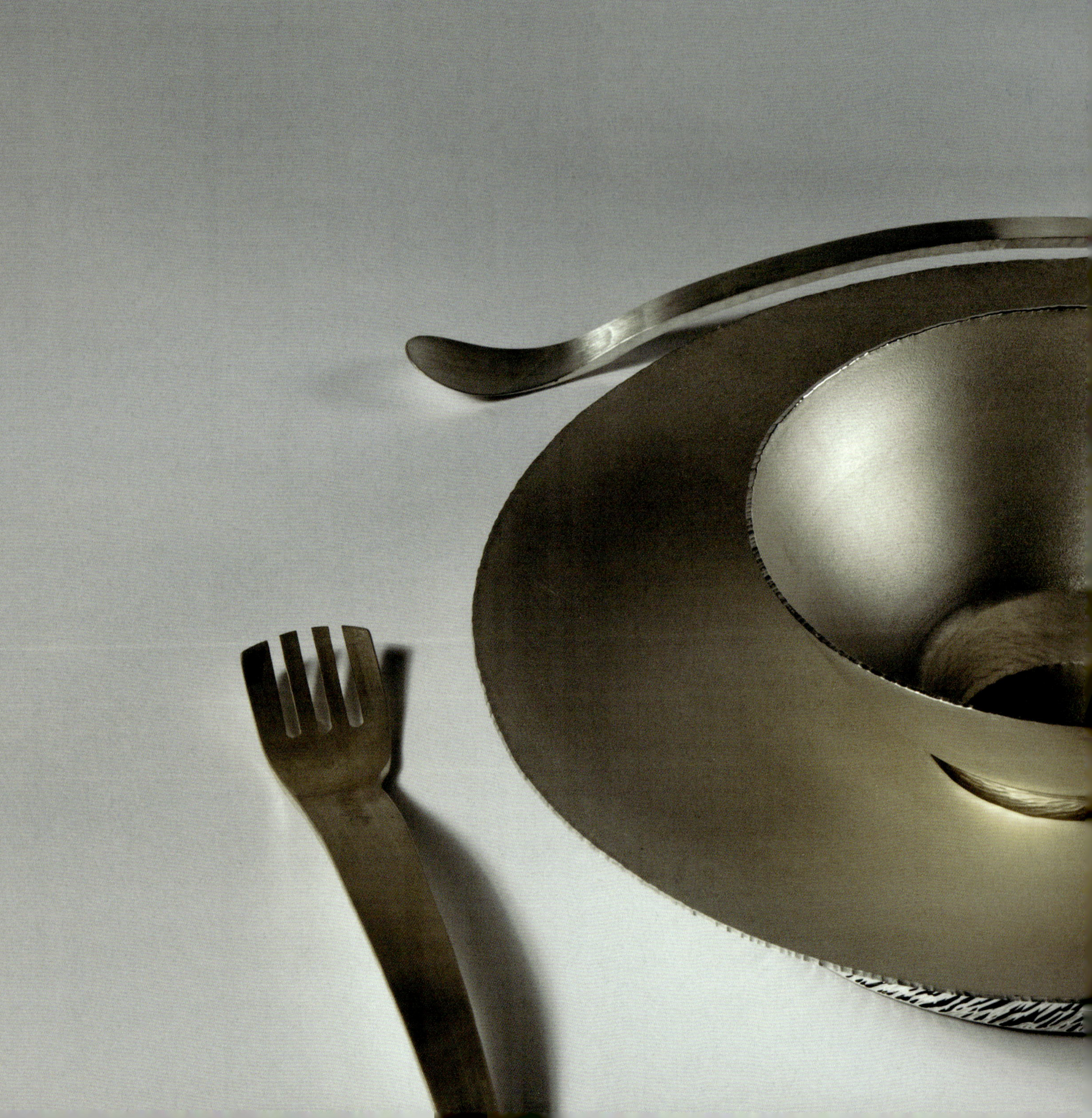

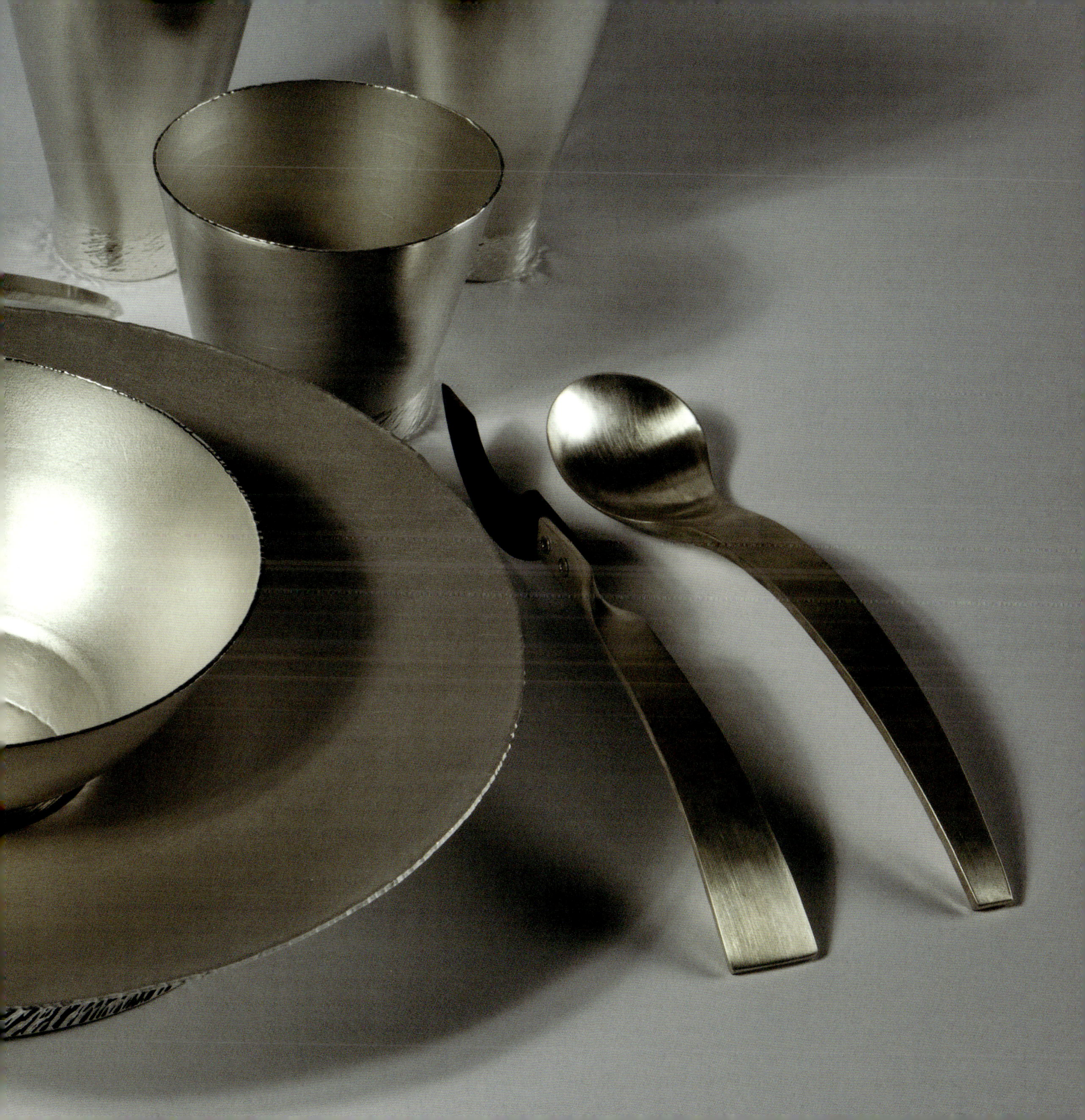

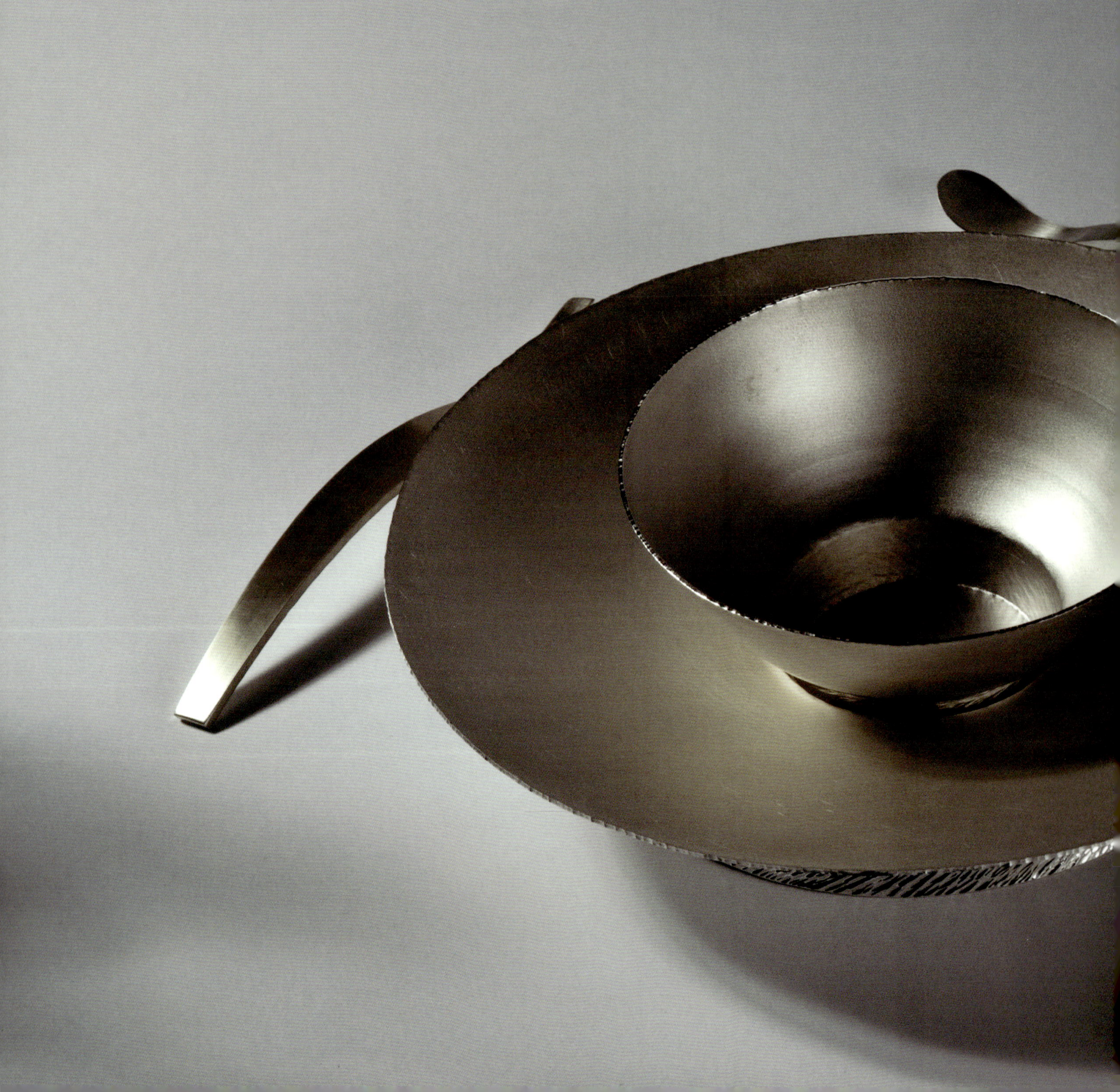

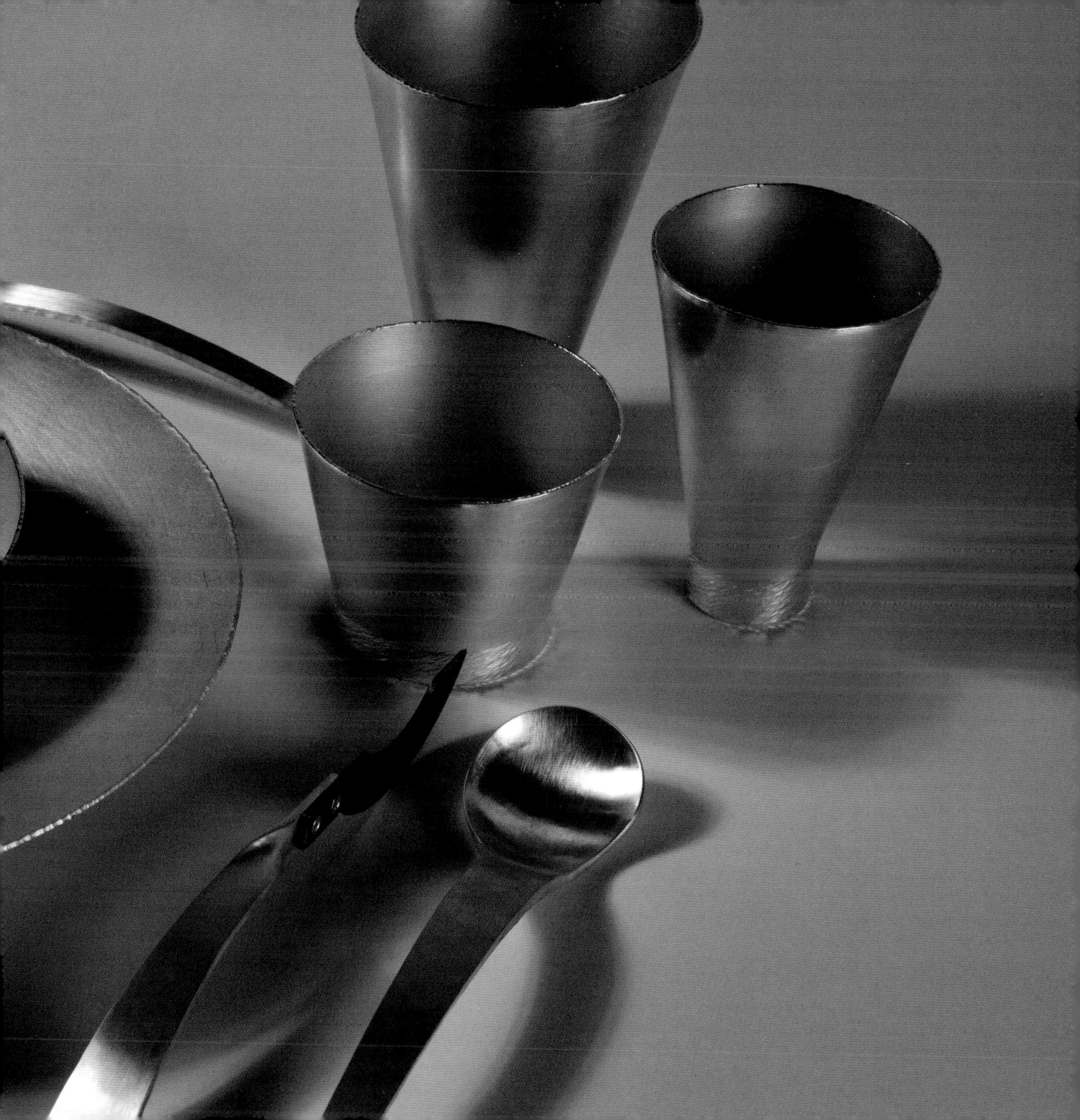

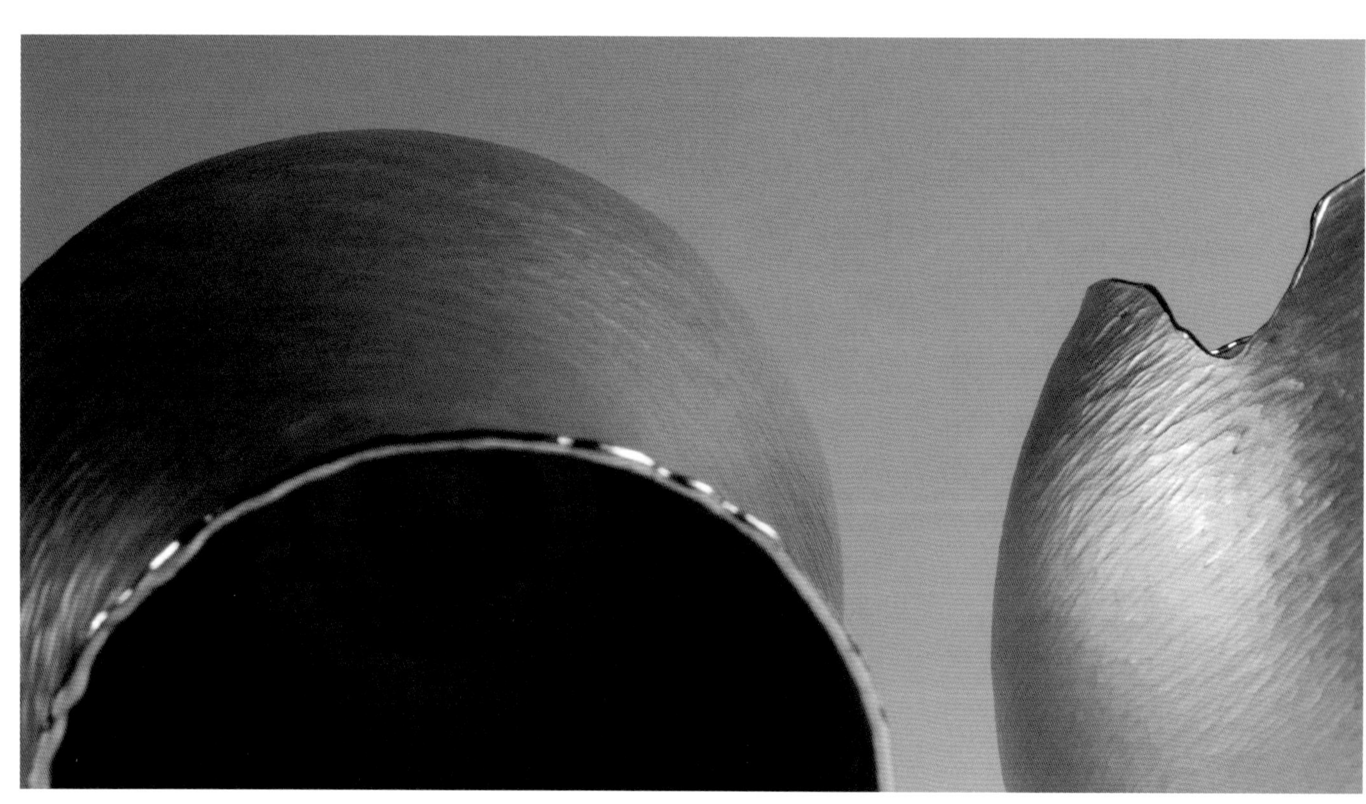

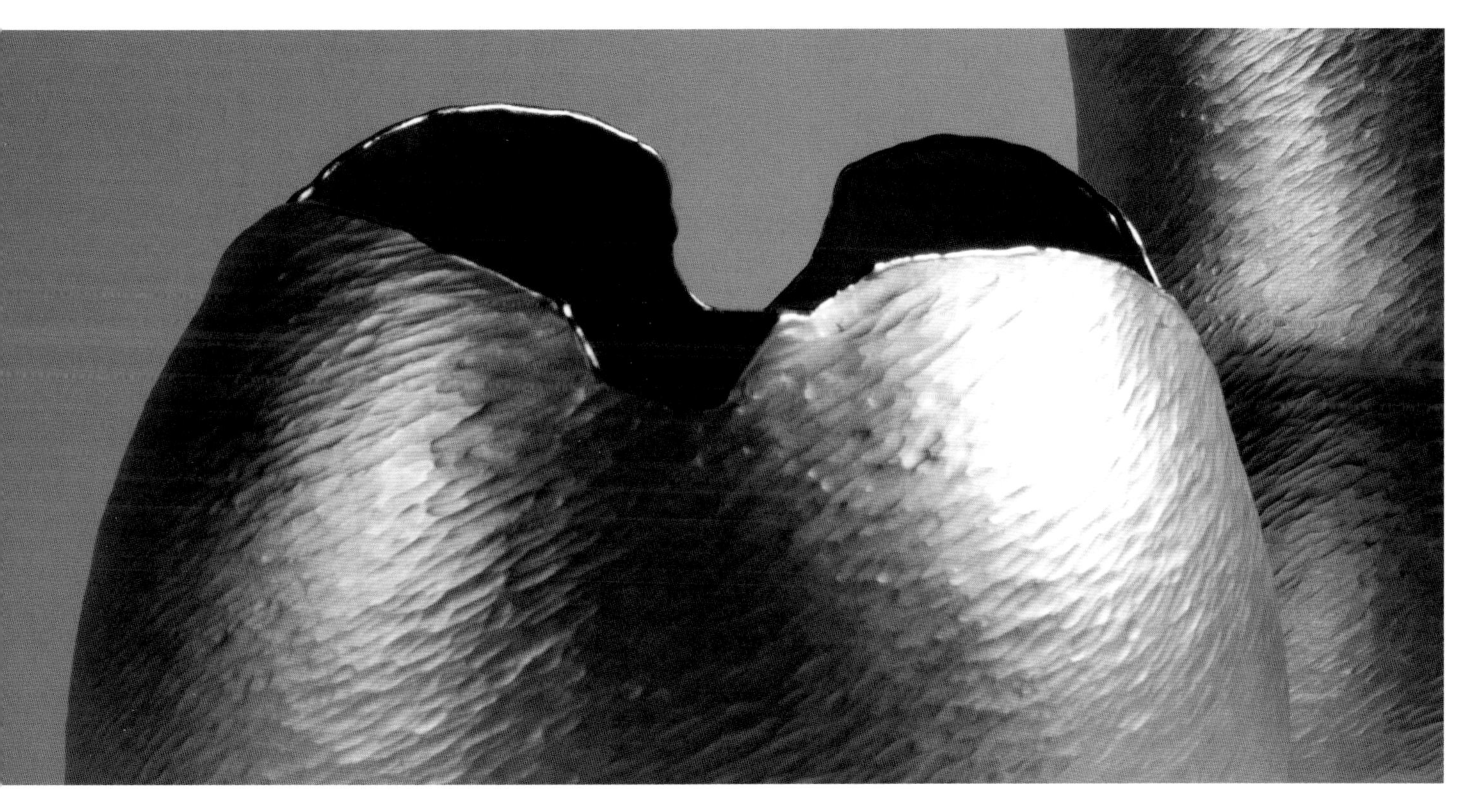

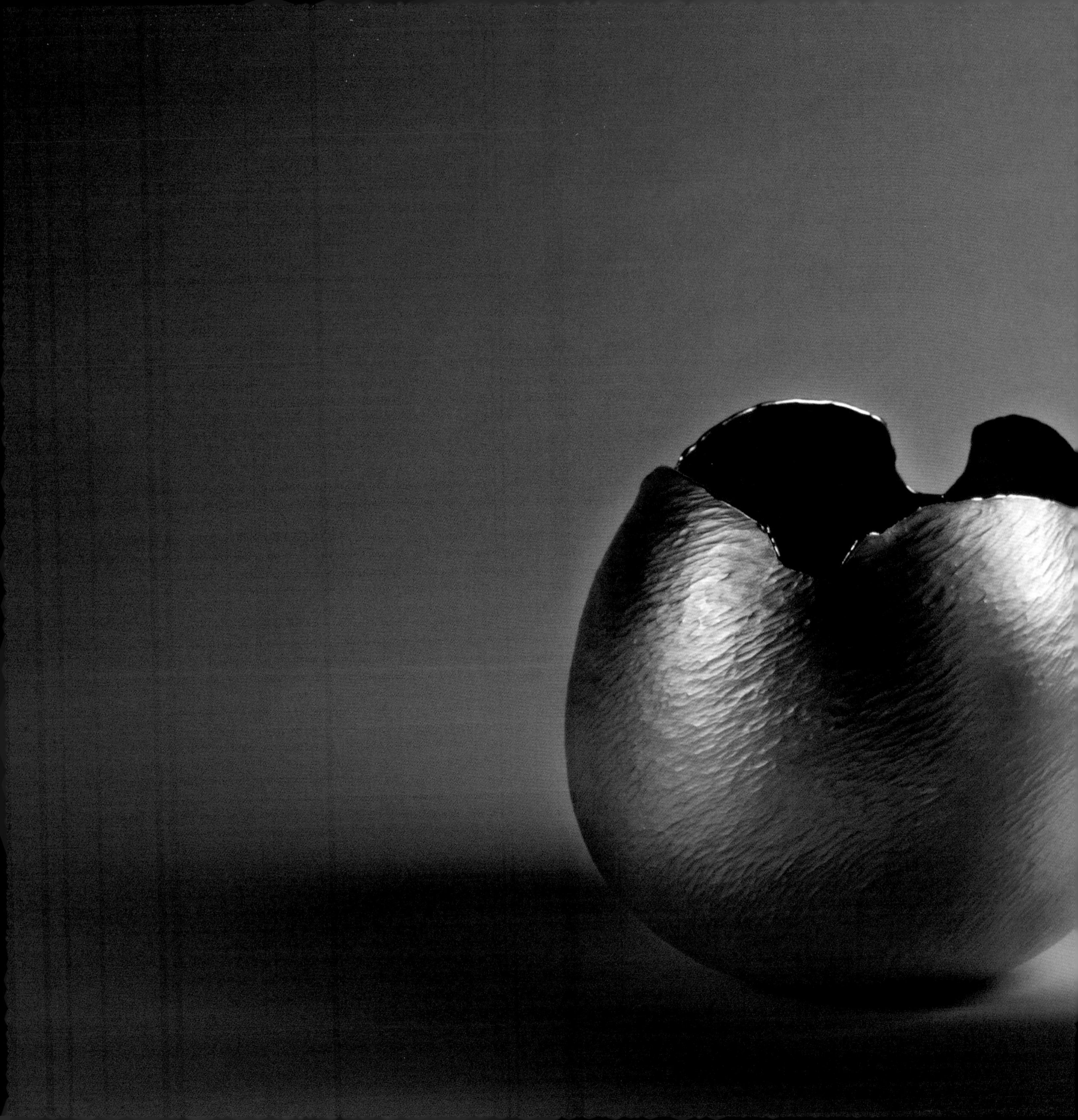

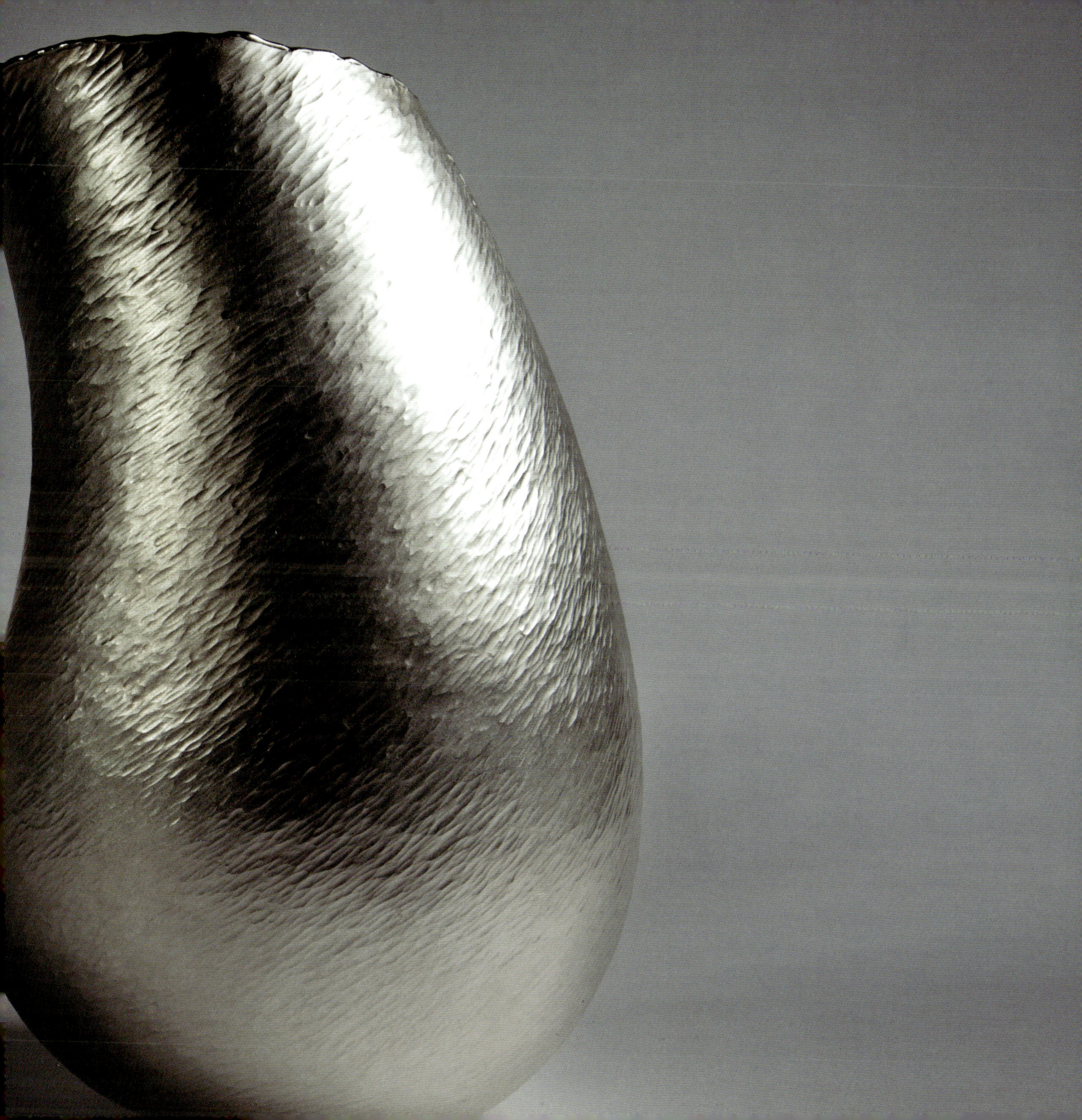

155

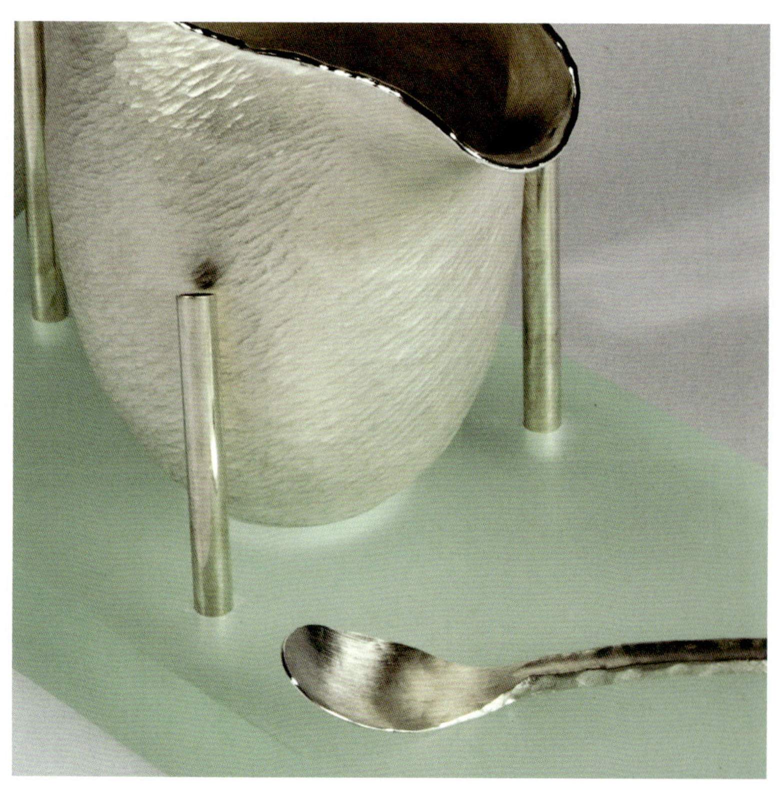

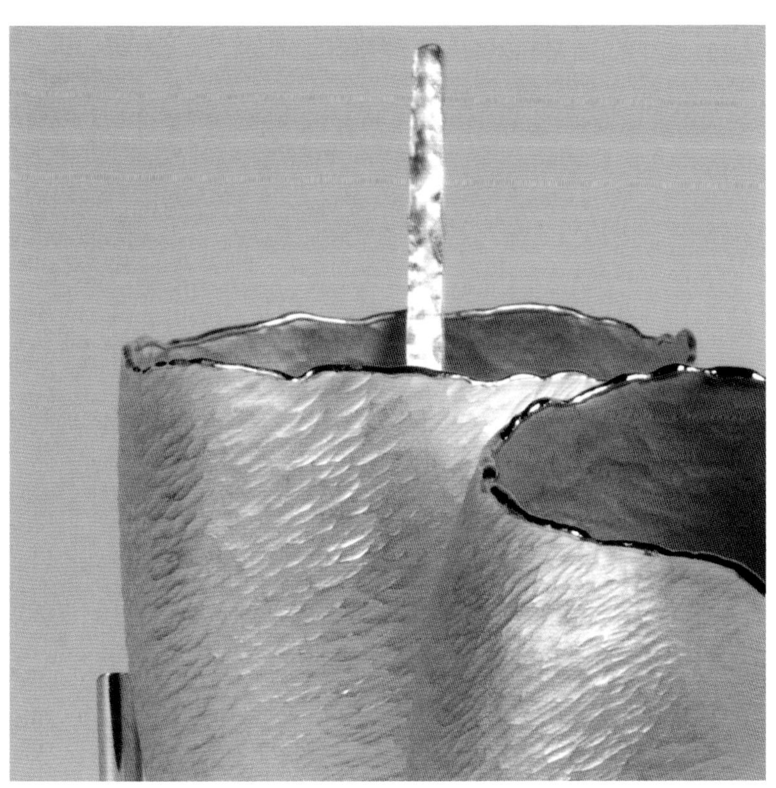

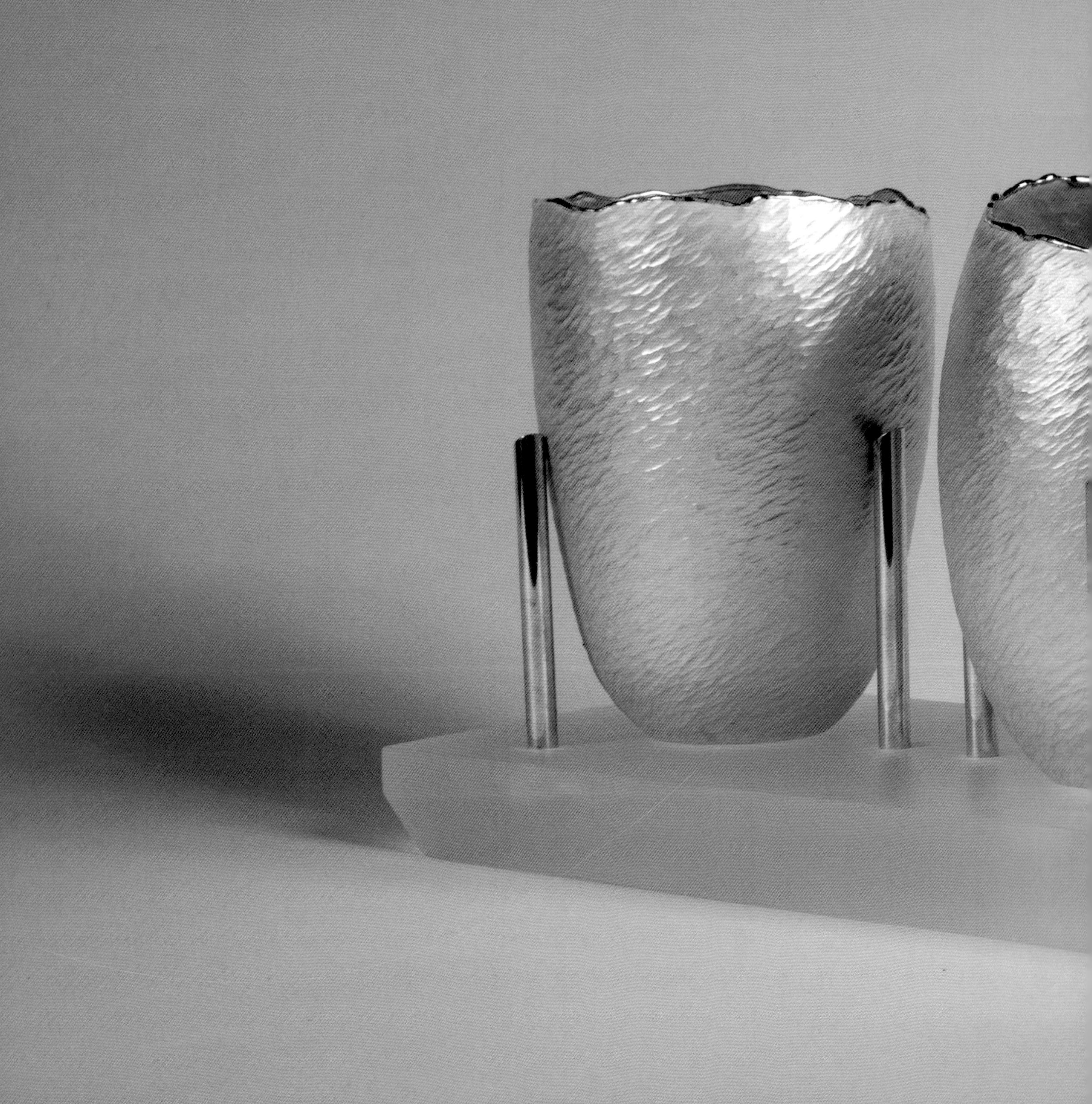

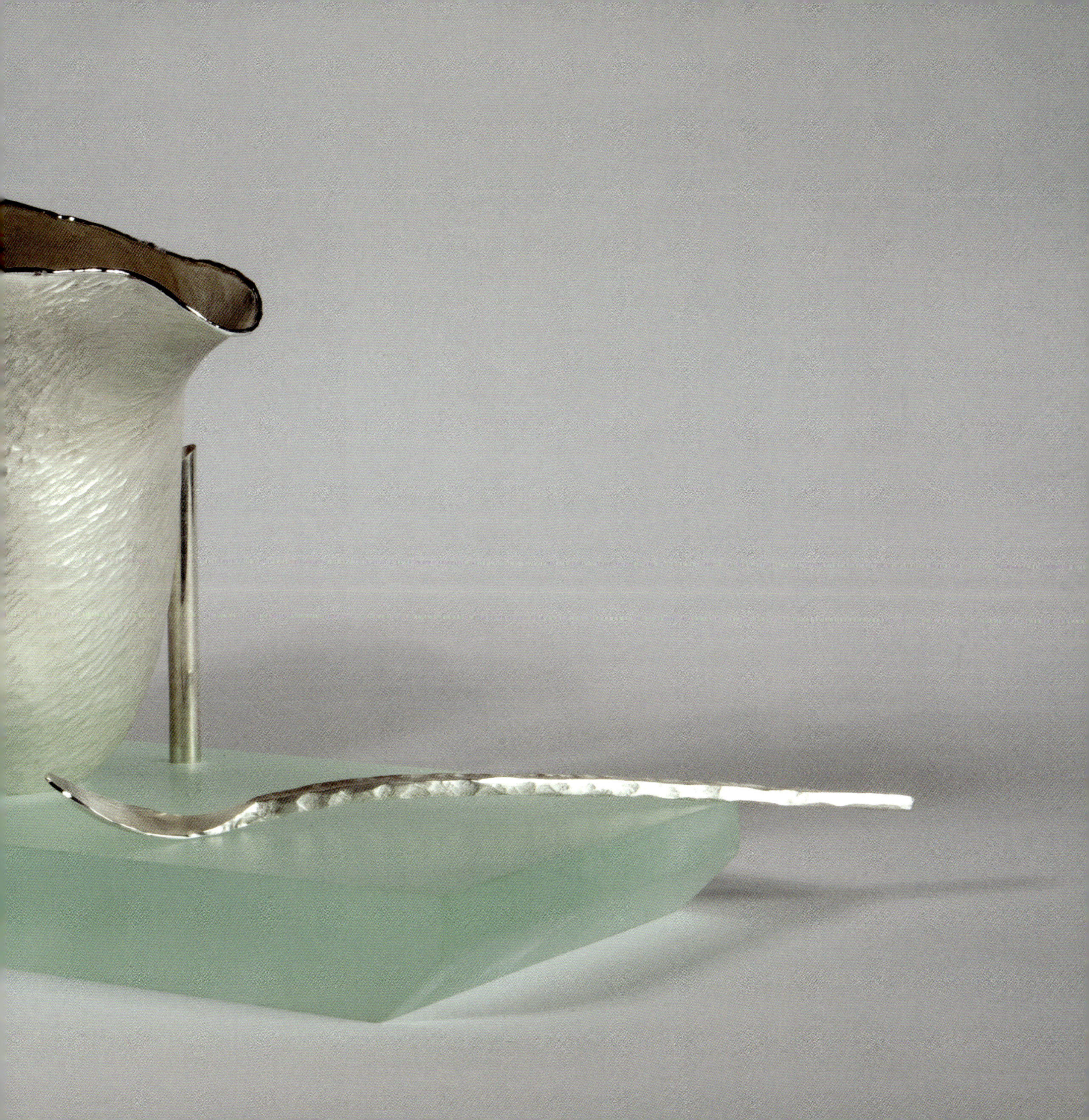

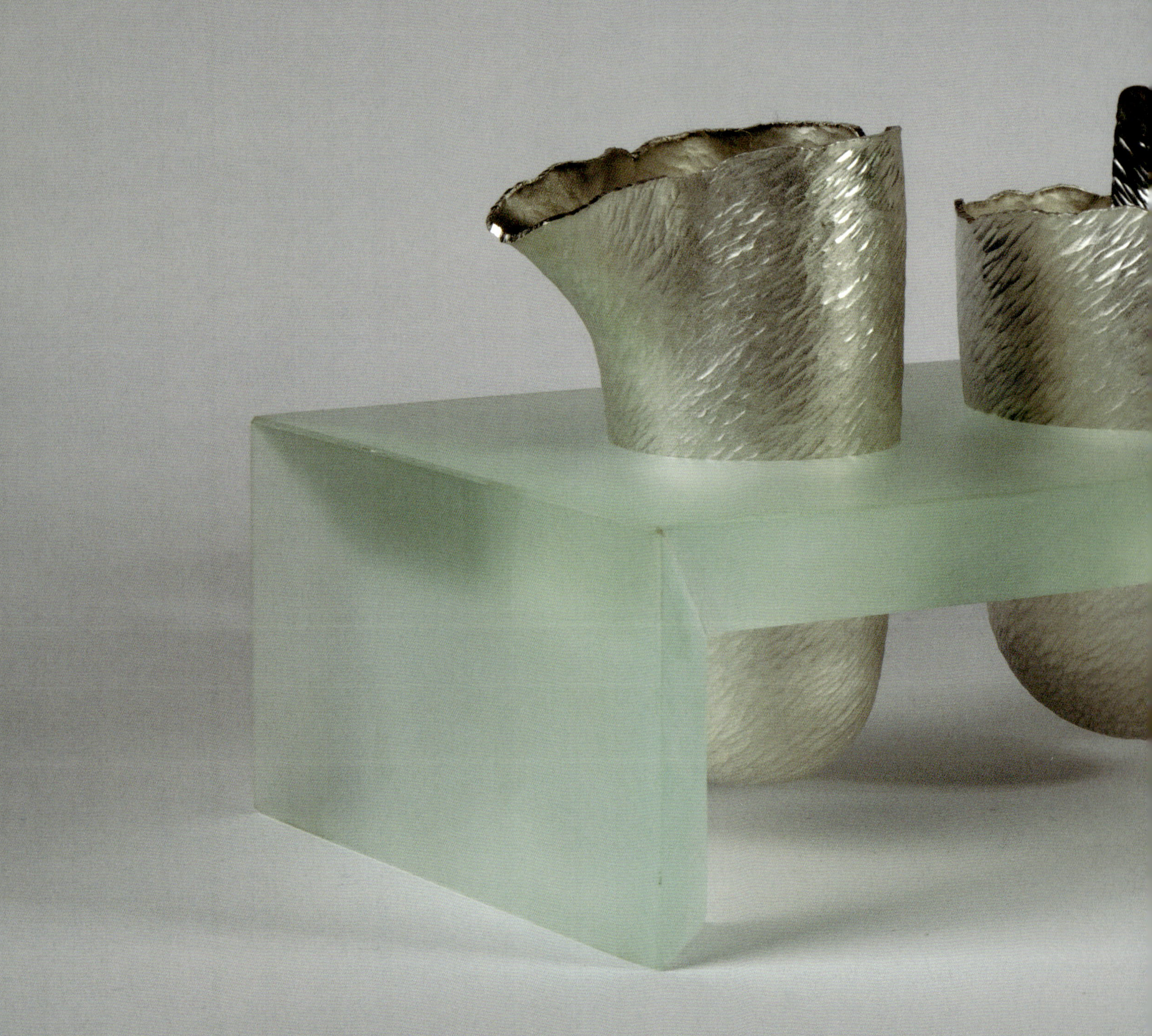

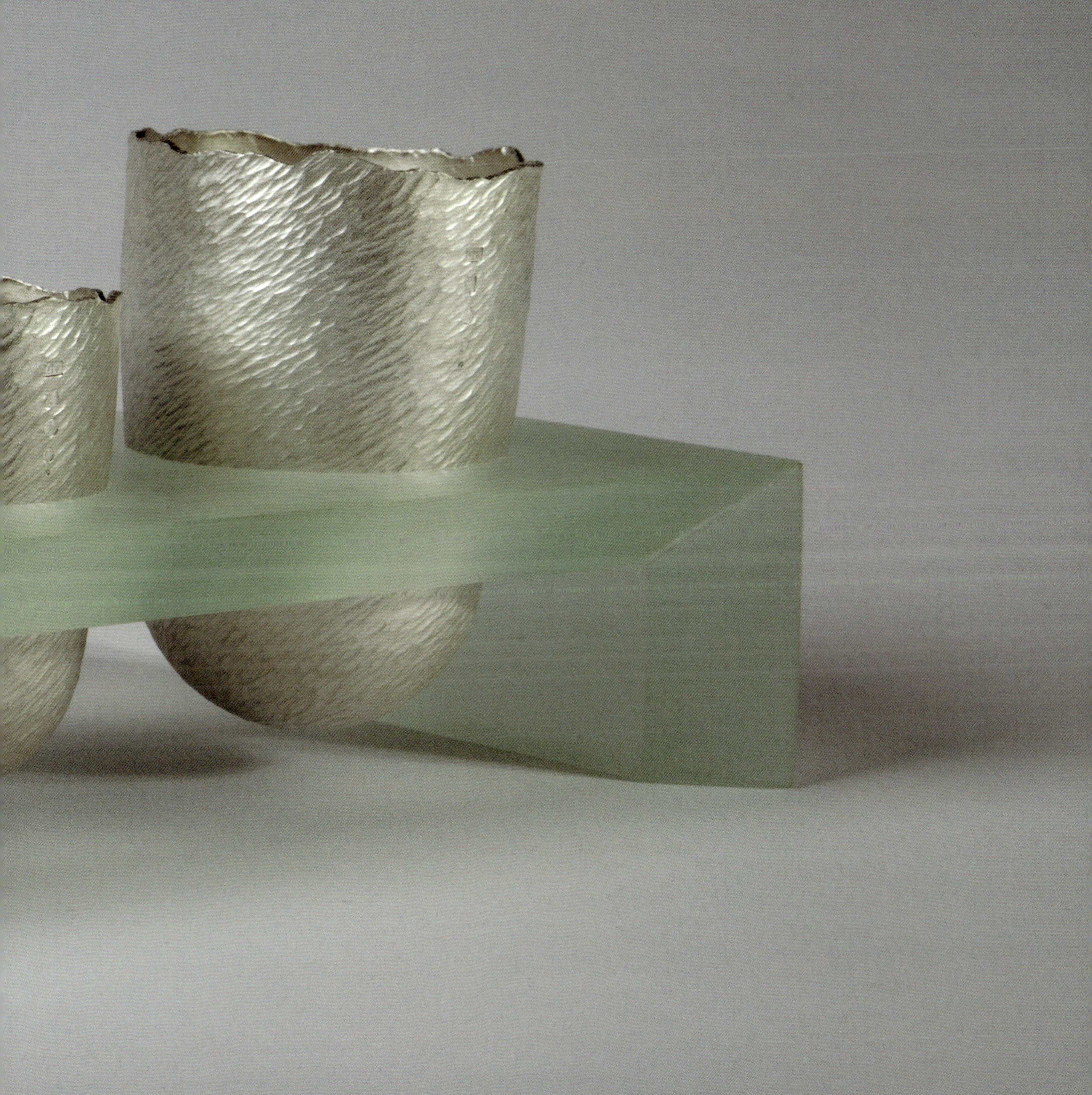

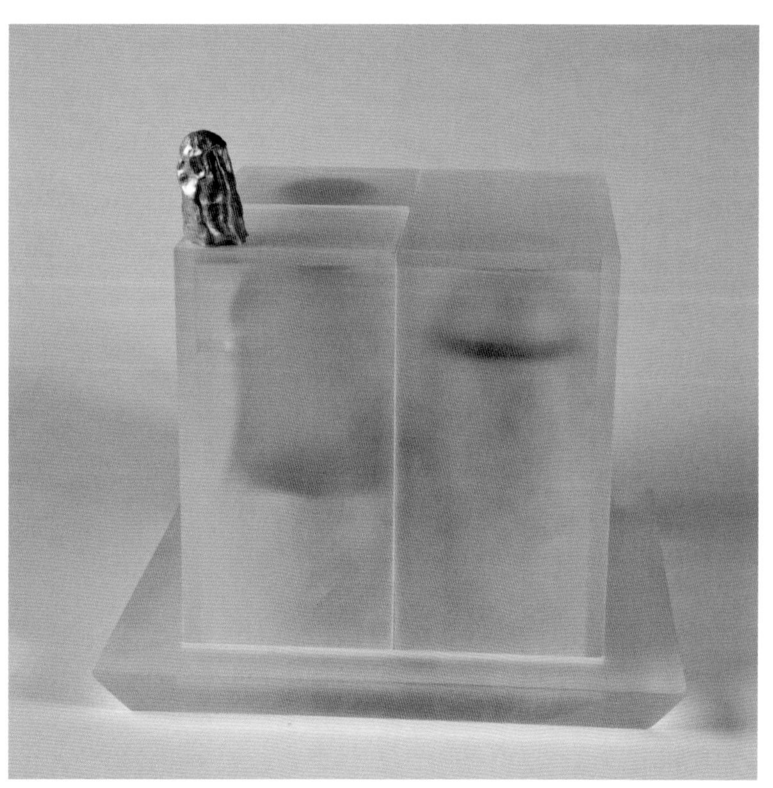

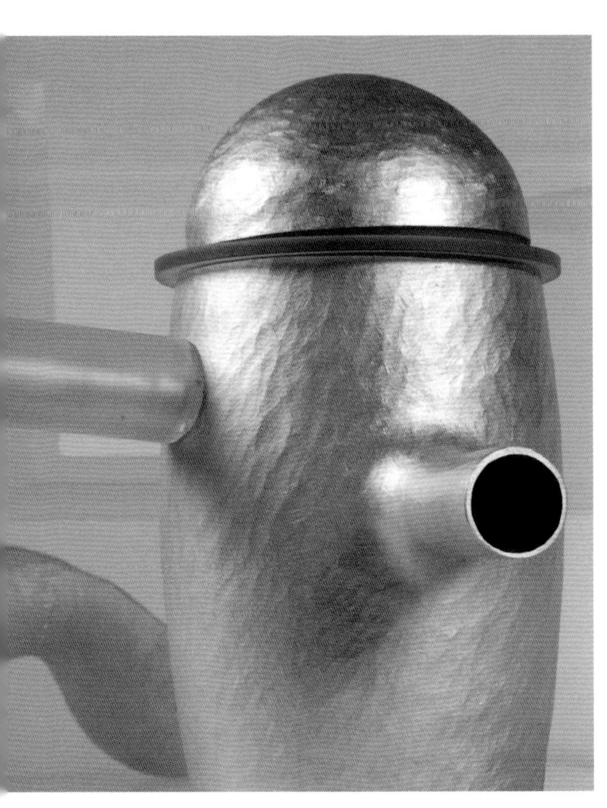

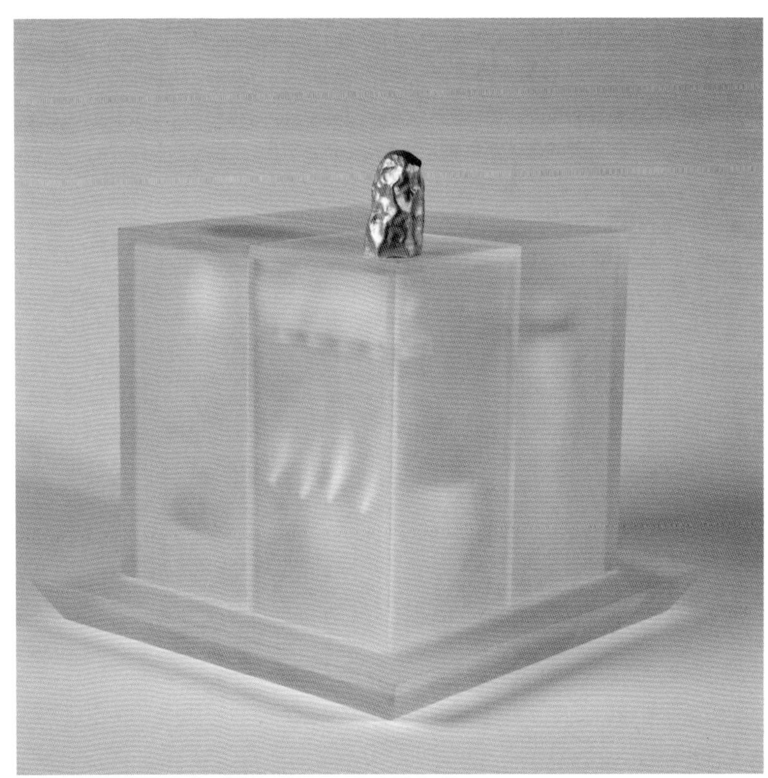

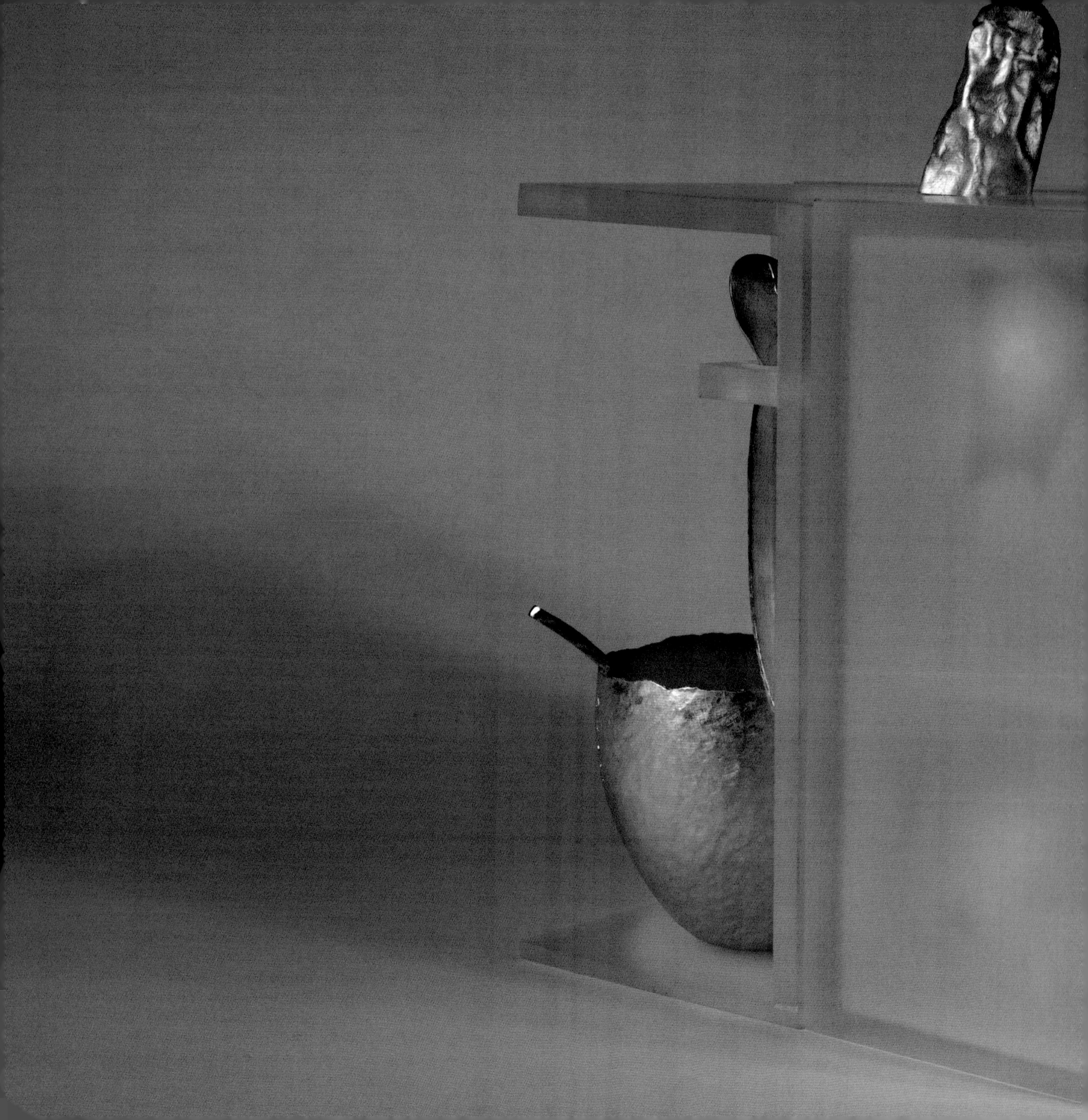

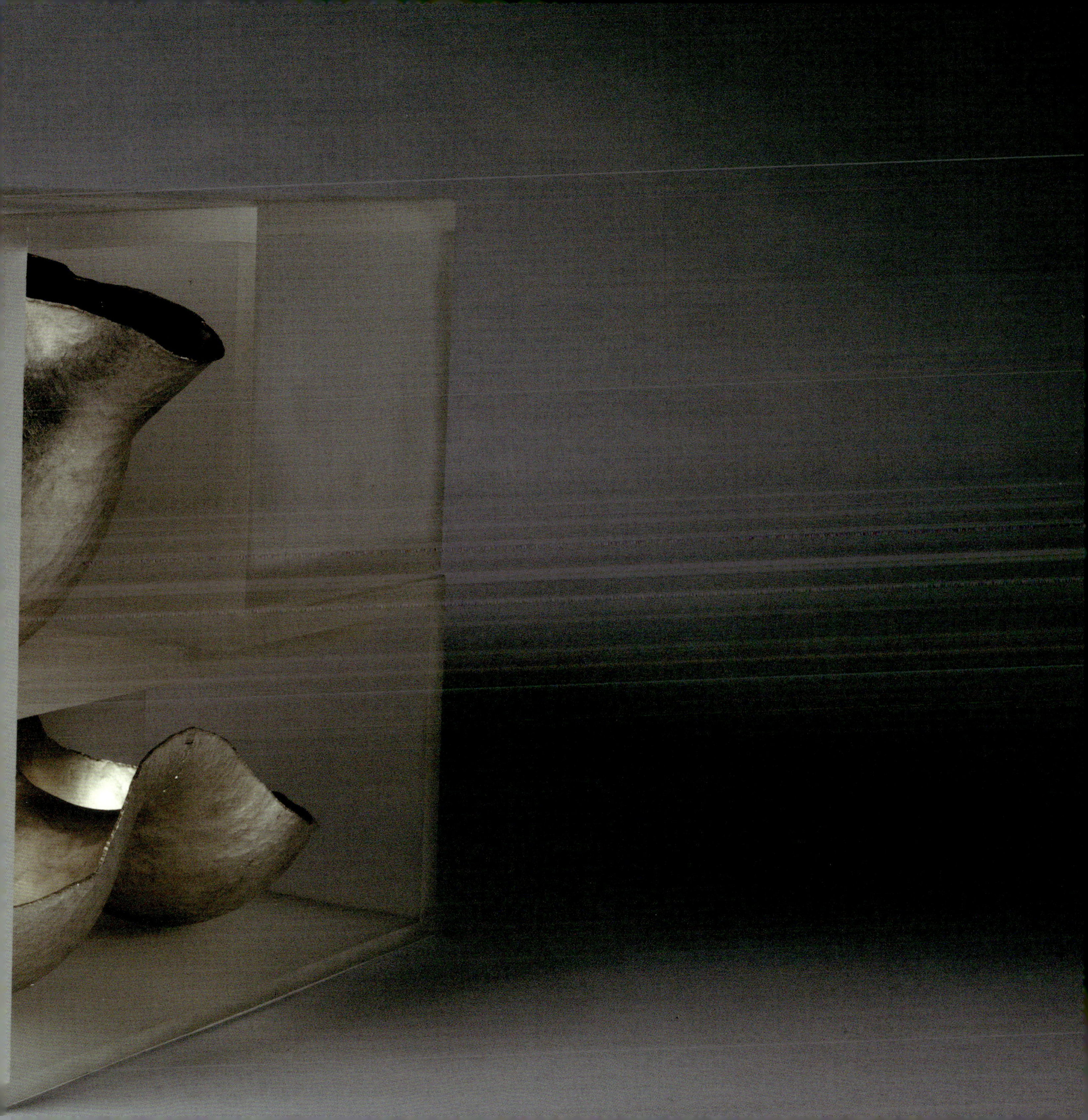

165

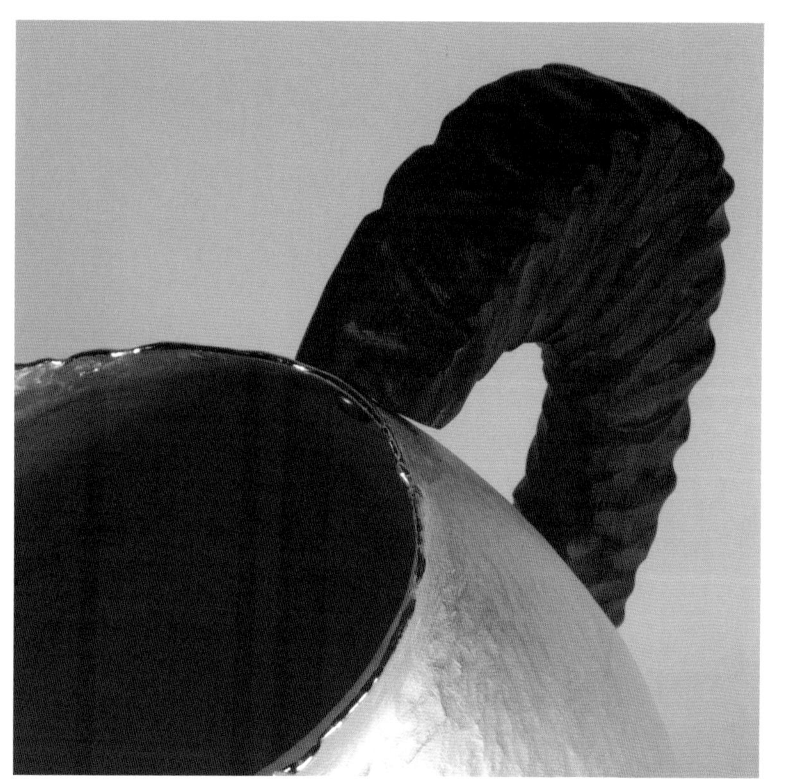

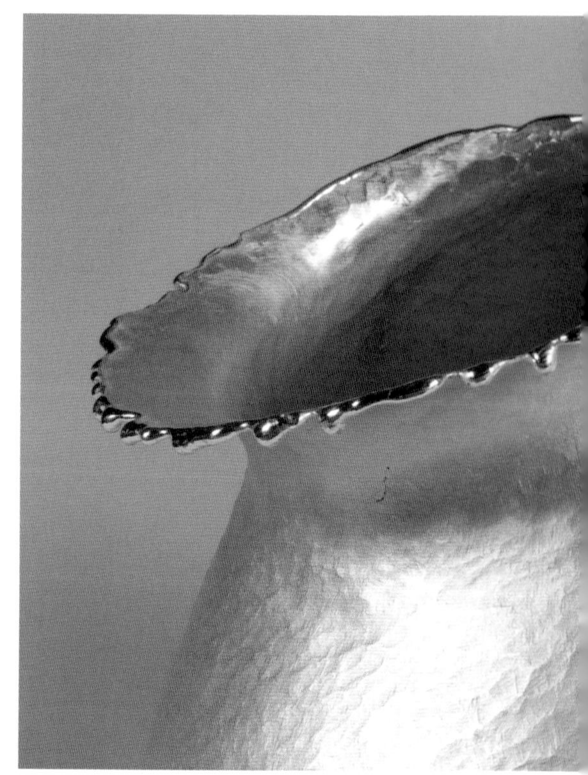

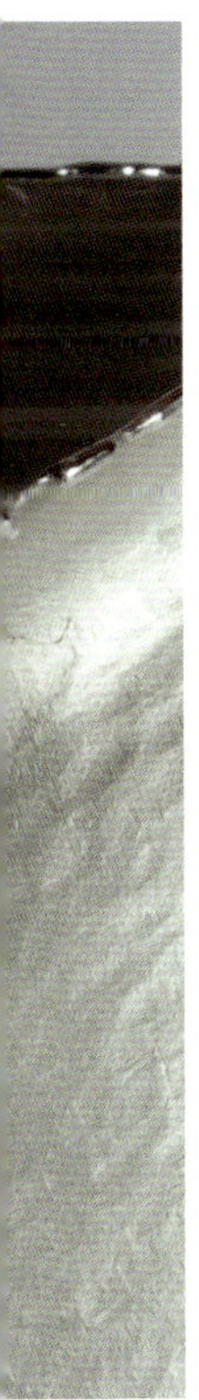

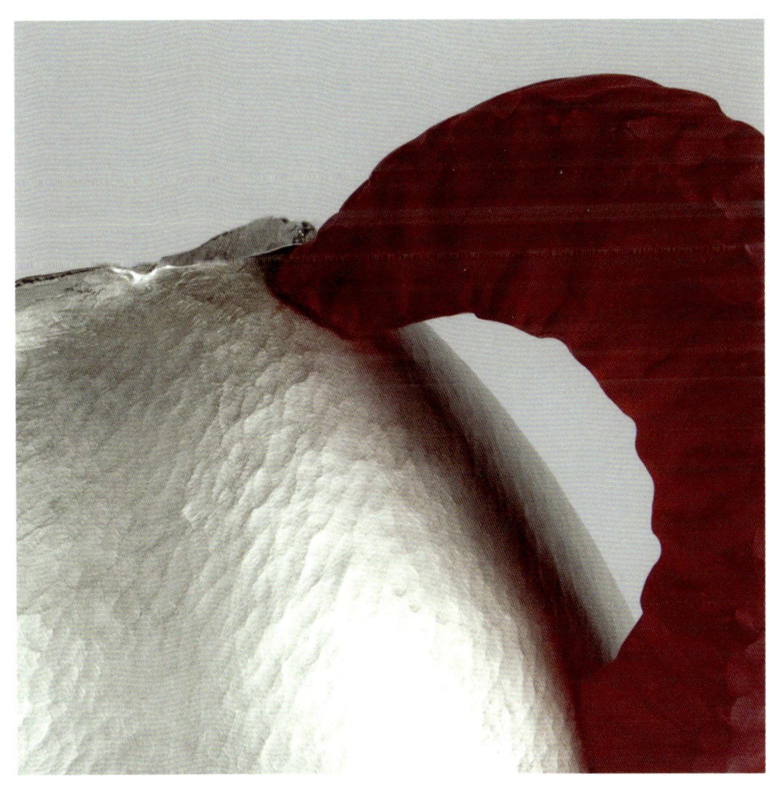

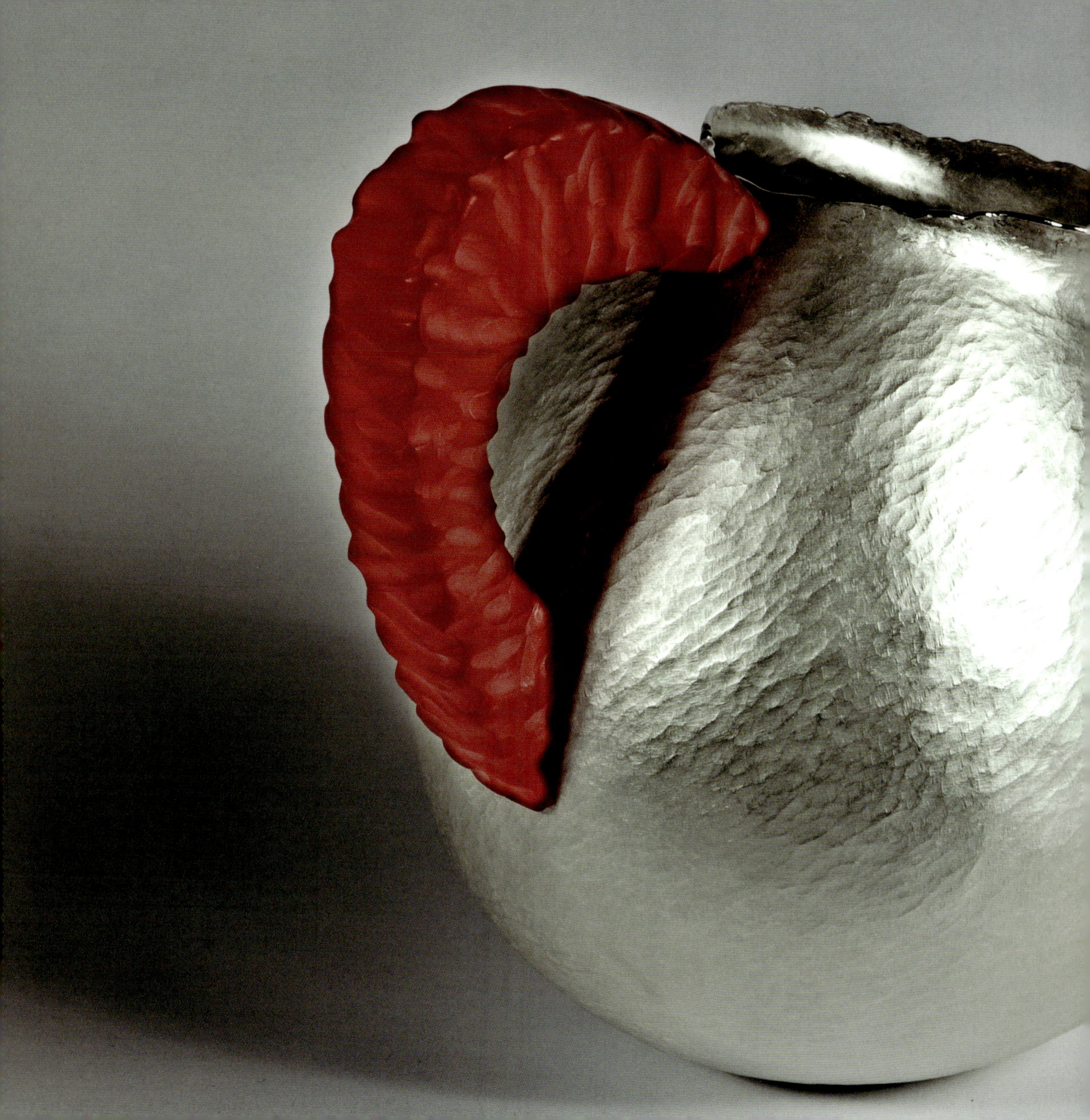

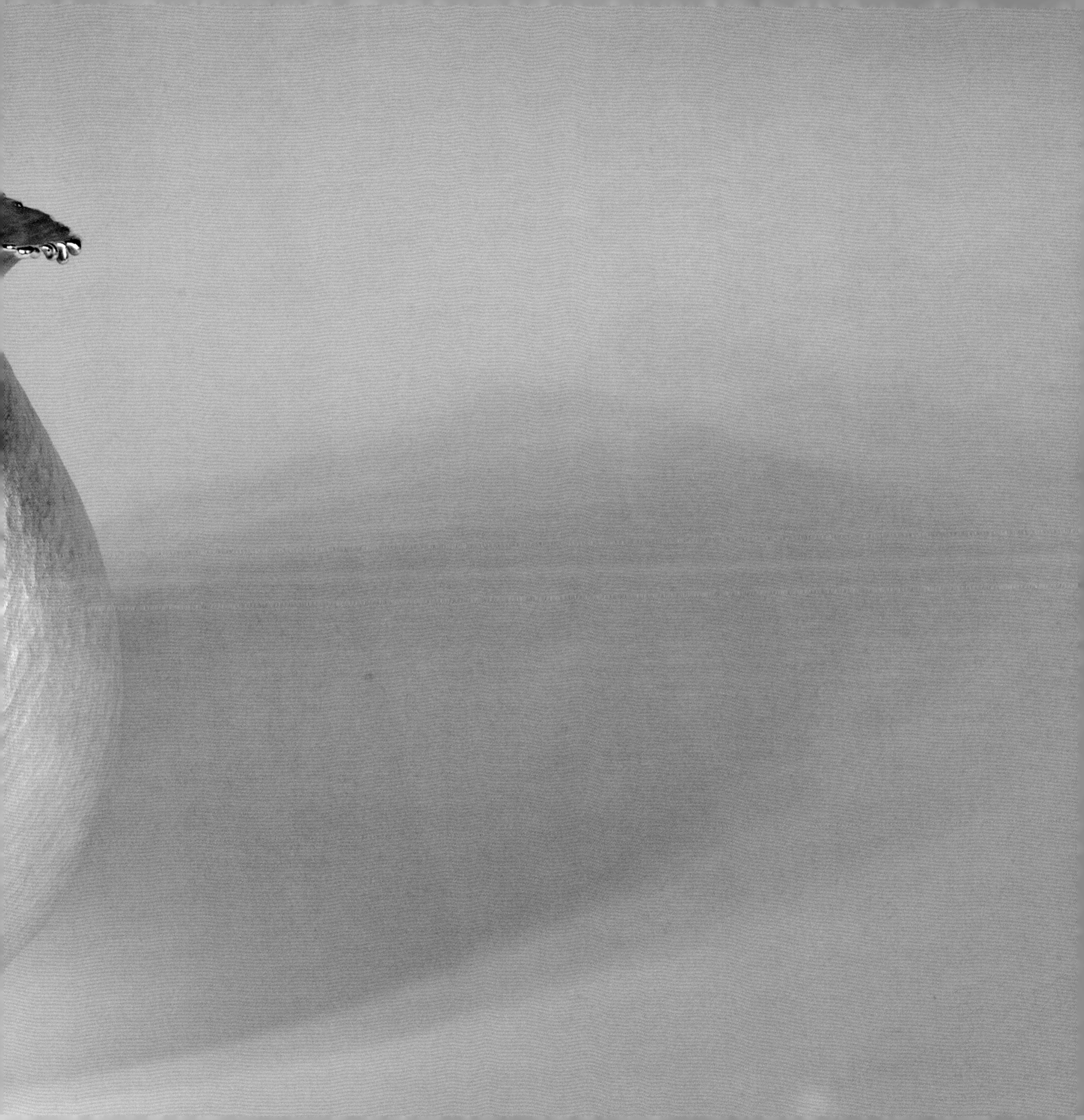

169

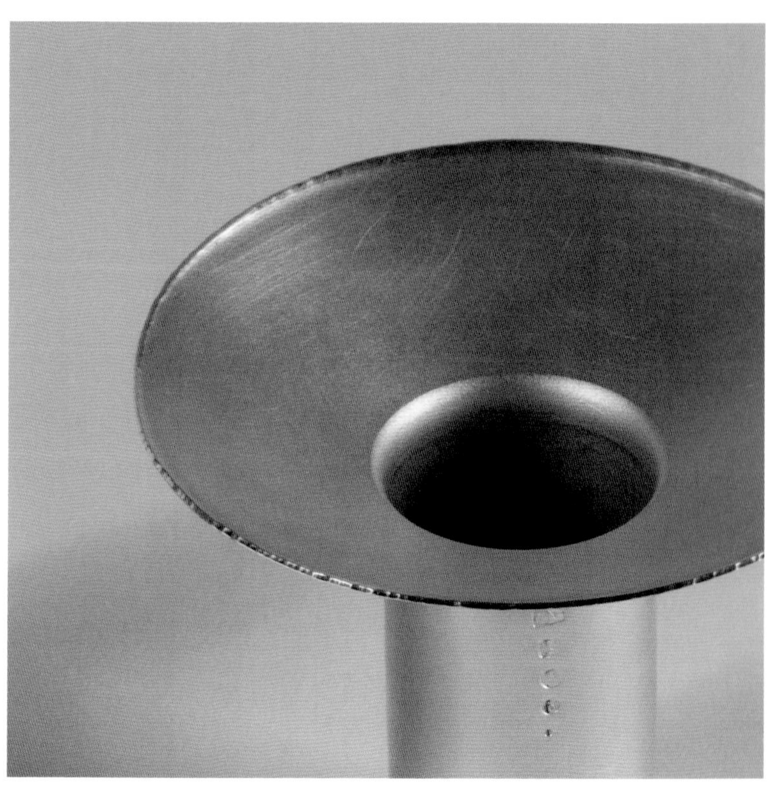

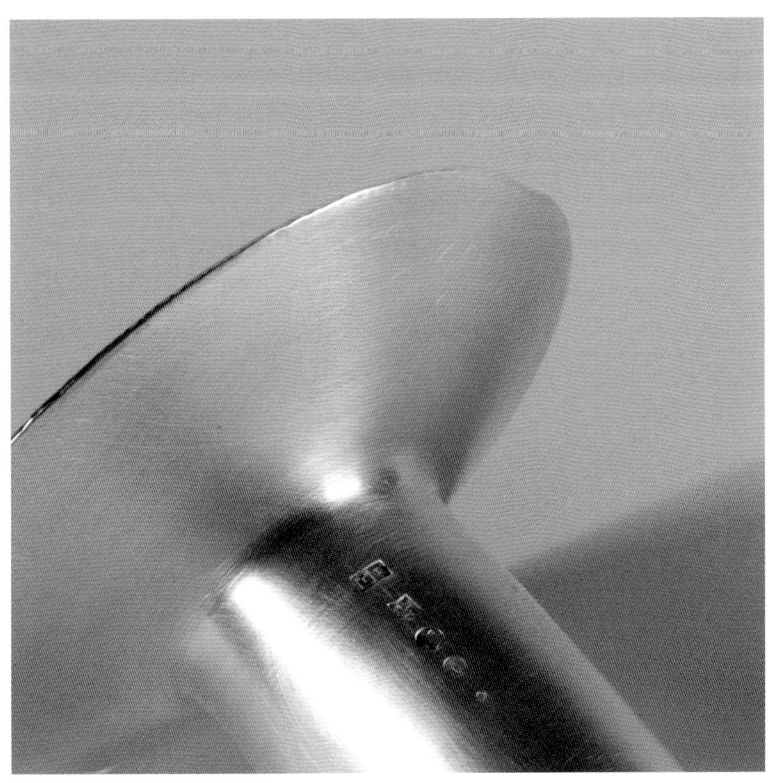

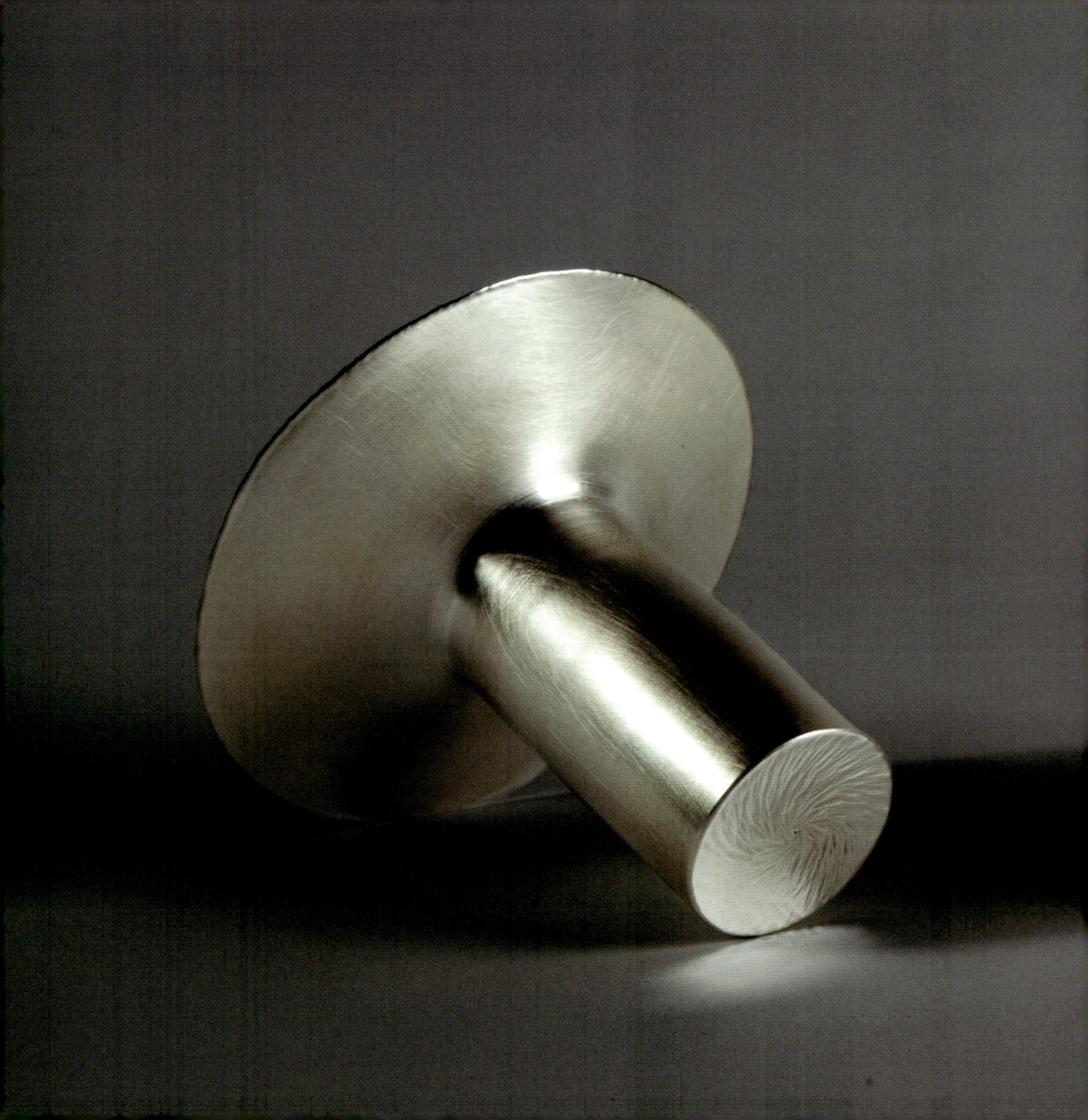

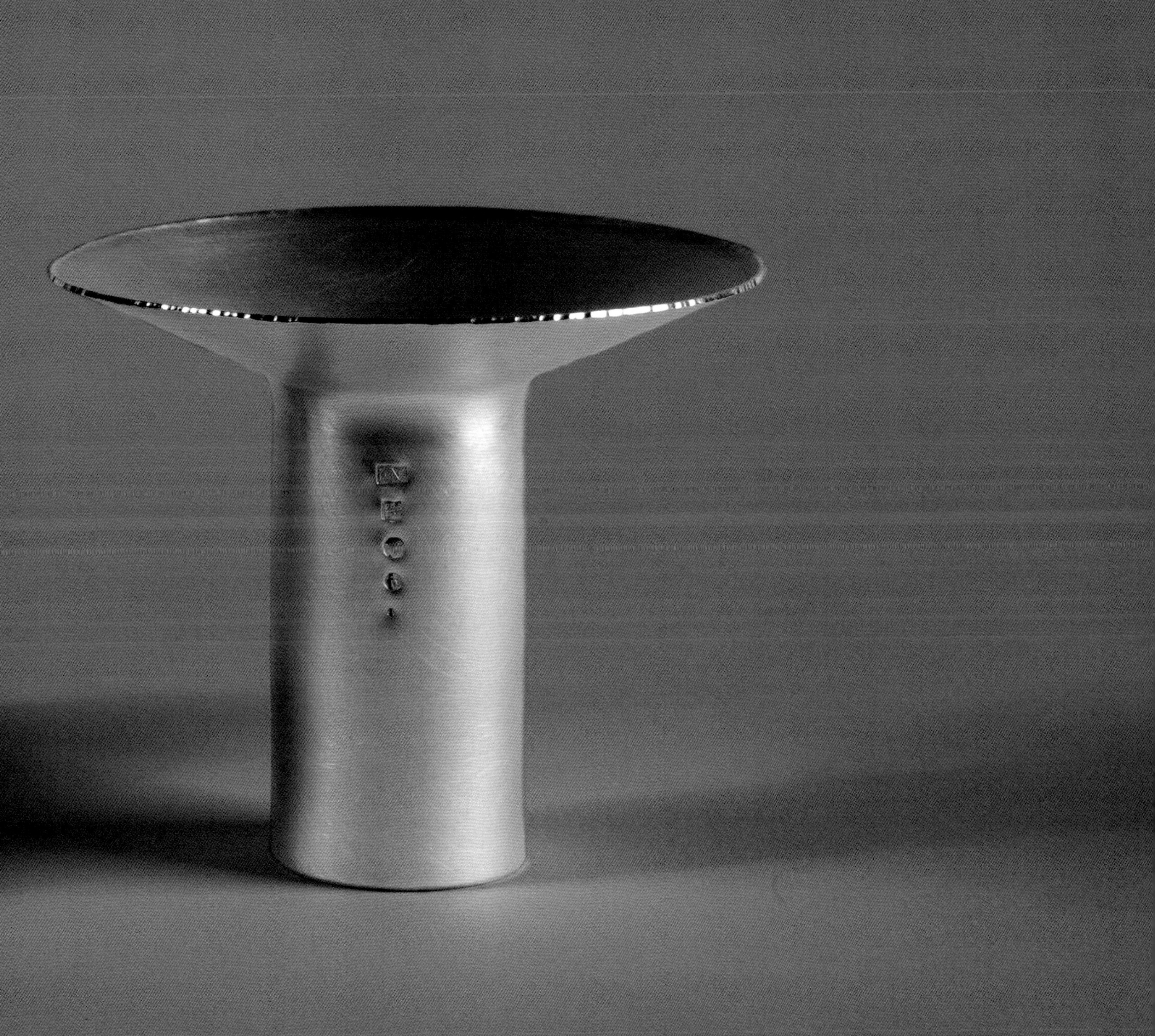

173

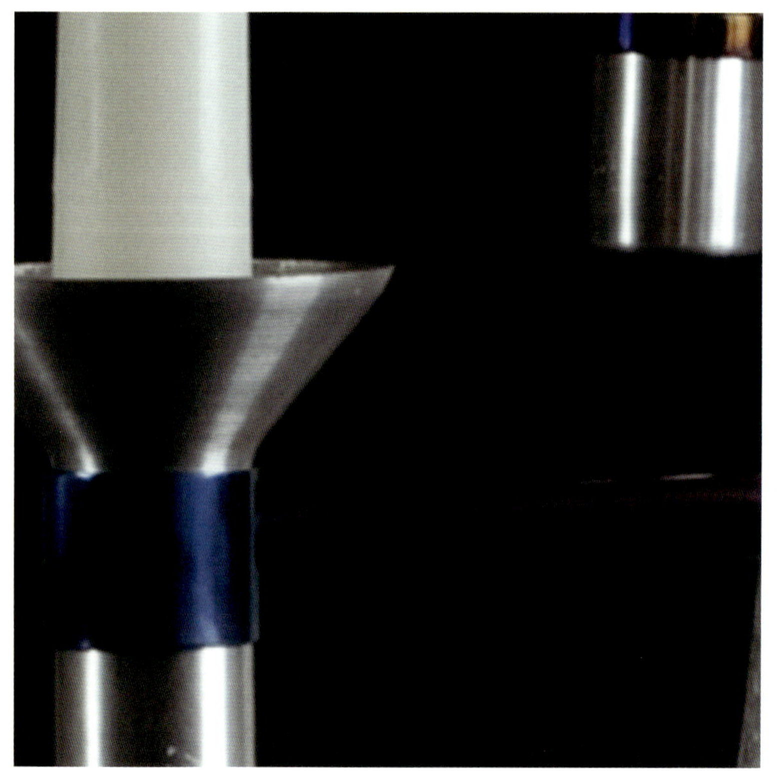

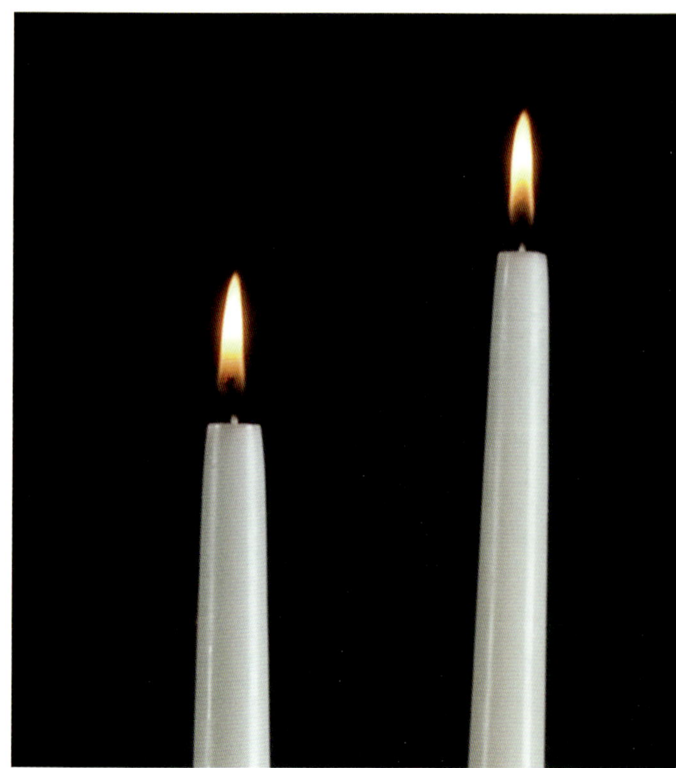

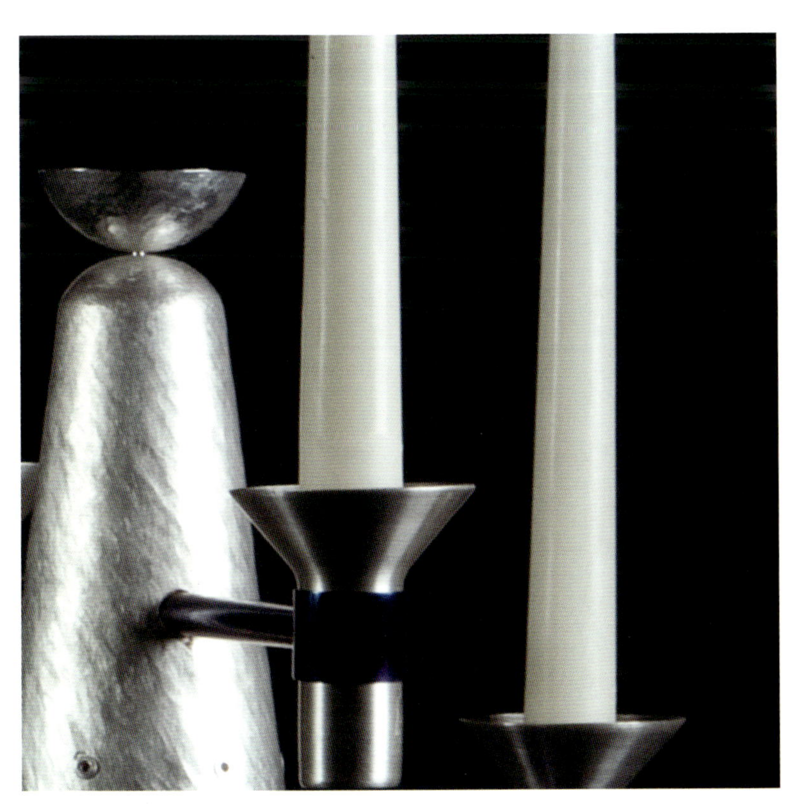

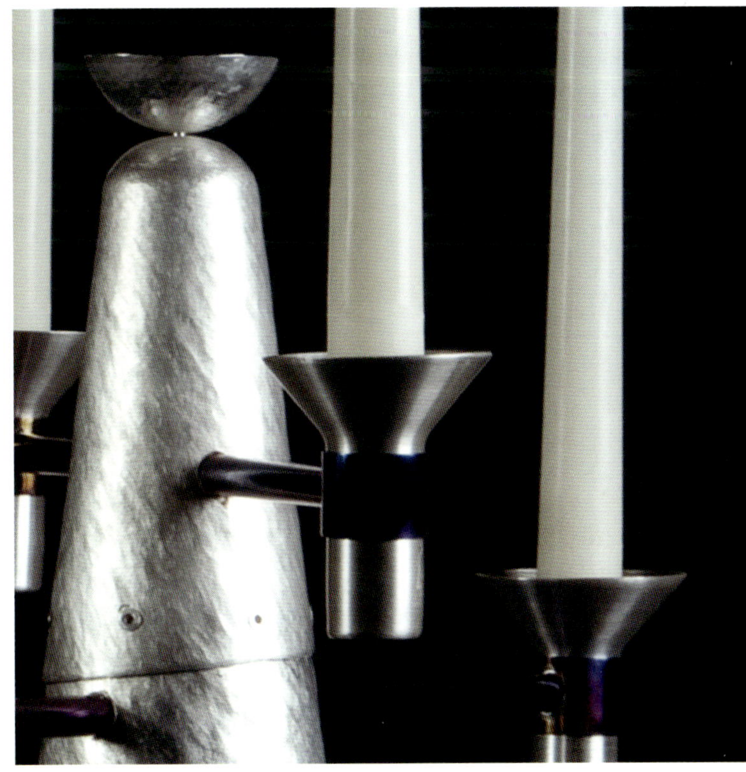

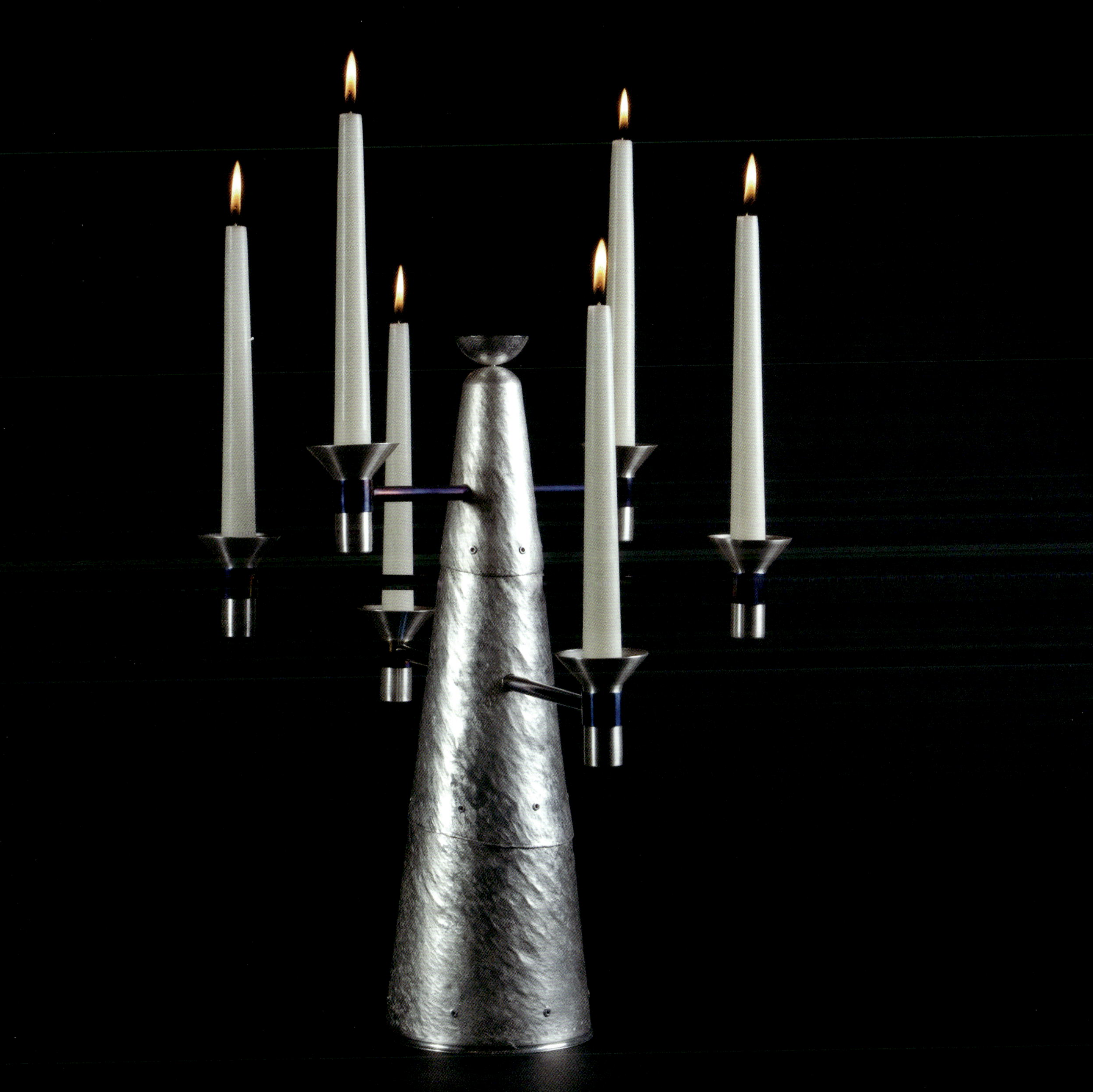

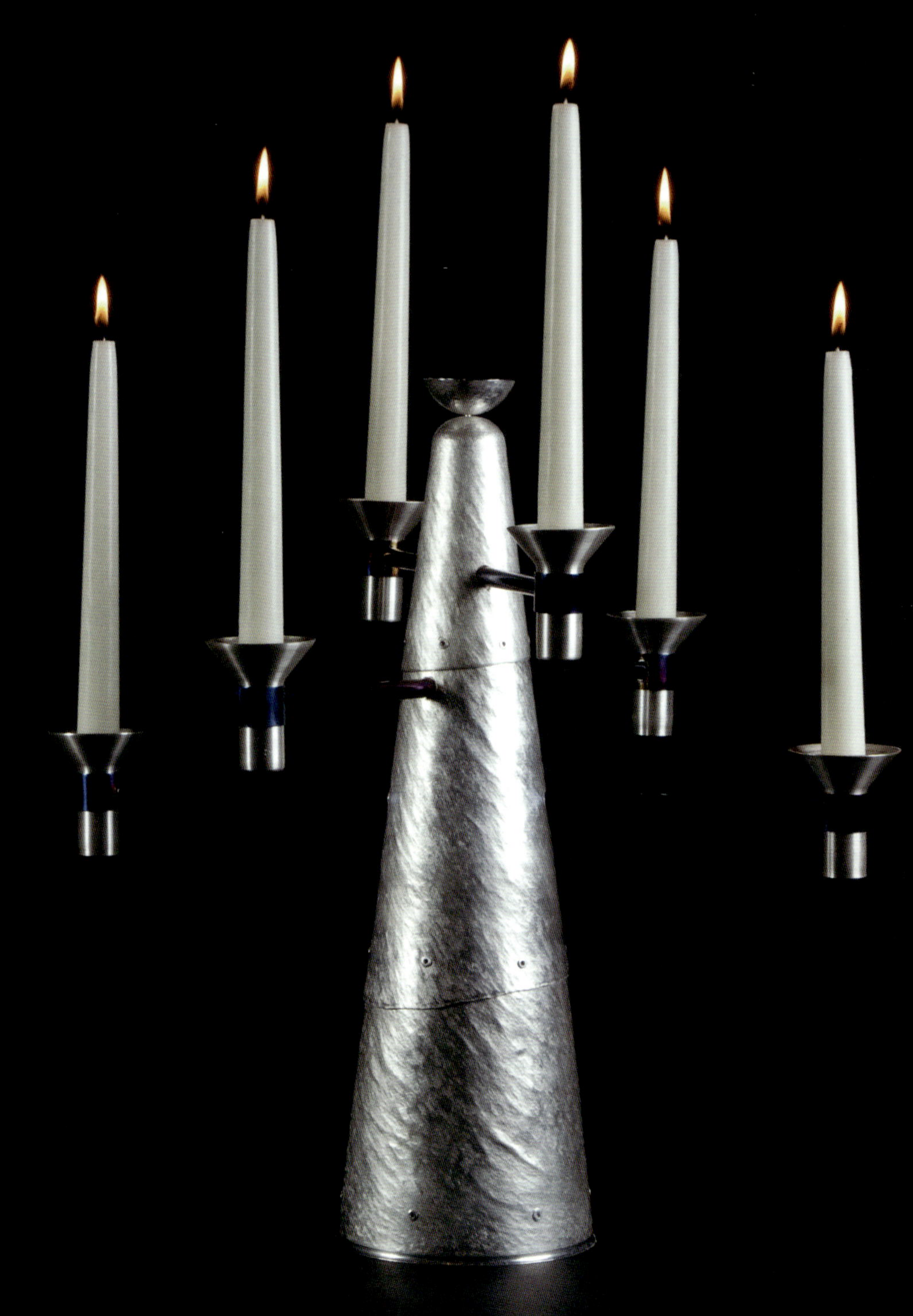

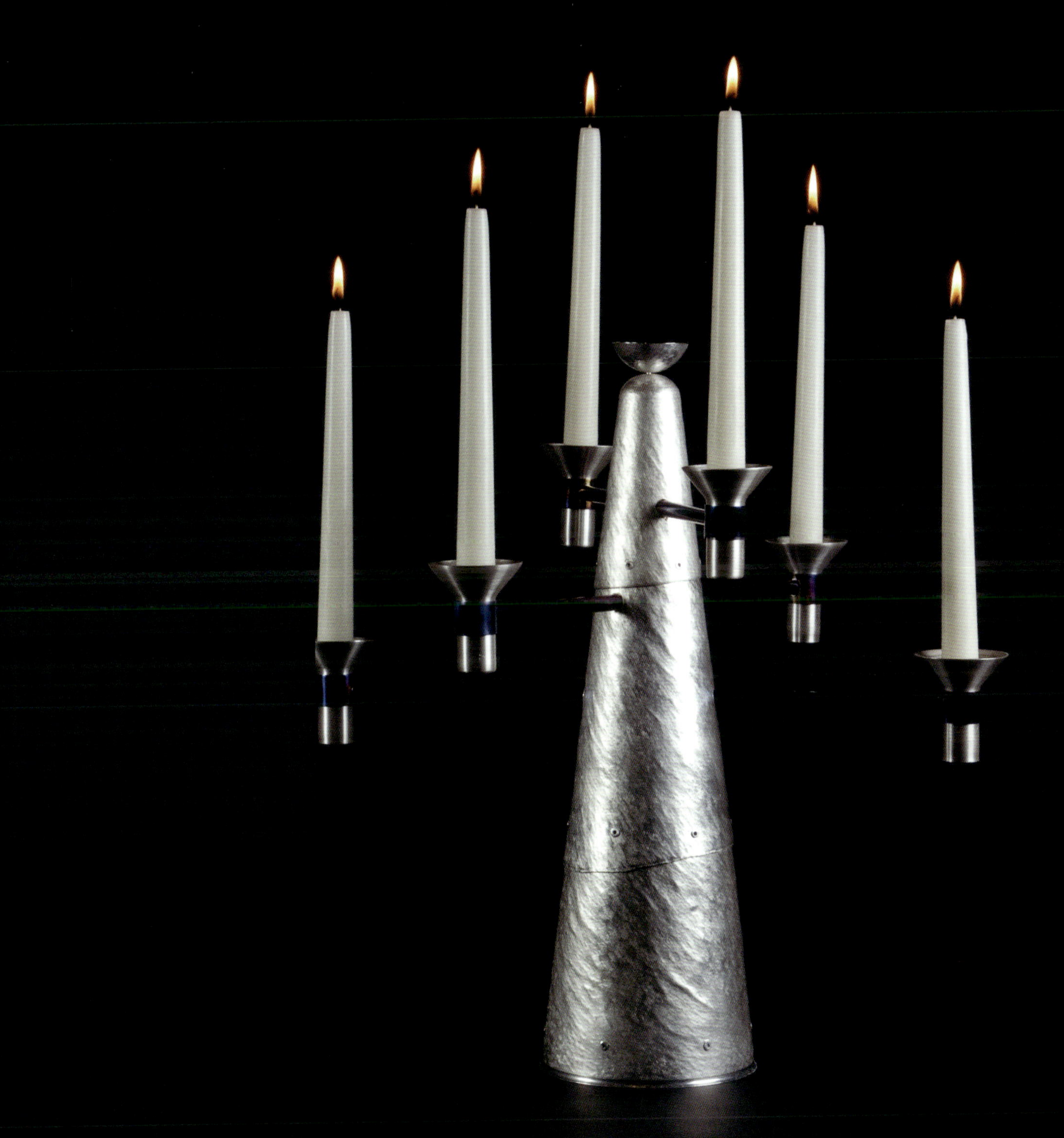

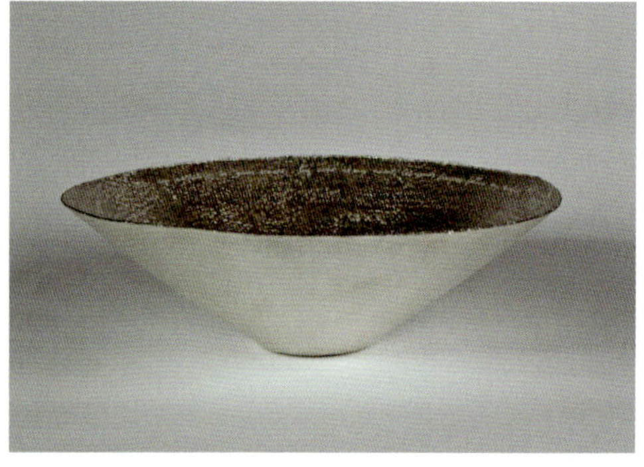

page 03
Big Cone
fine silver 999‰, year 2012
Ø 37 cm, H 14 cm

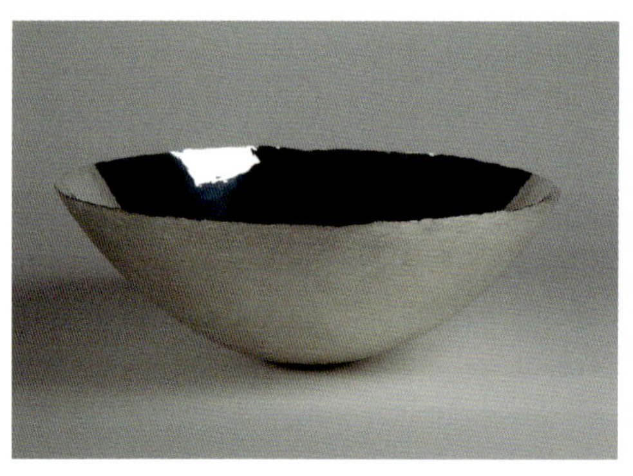

page 43 - 46
Scratch
fine silver 999‰, year 2013
Ø 47 cm, H 18 cm

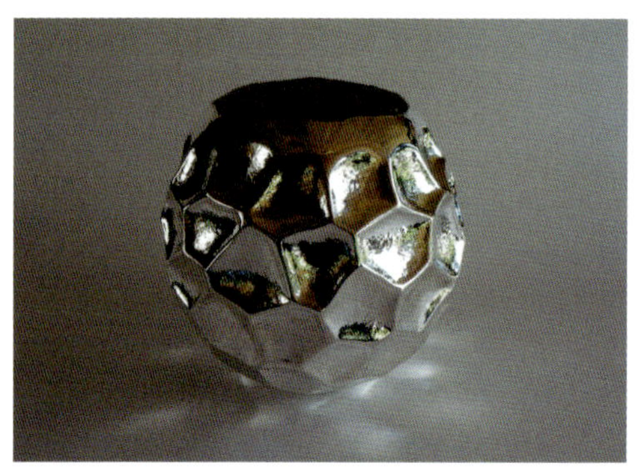

page 47 - 50
Ball Shape Landscape bowl
fine silver 999‰, year 2013
H 30 cm, W 31 cm, Ø 31 cm

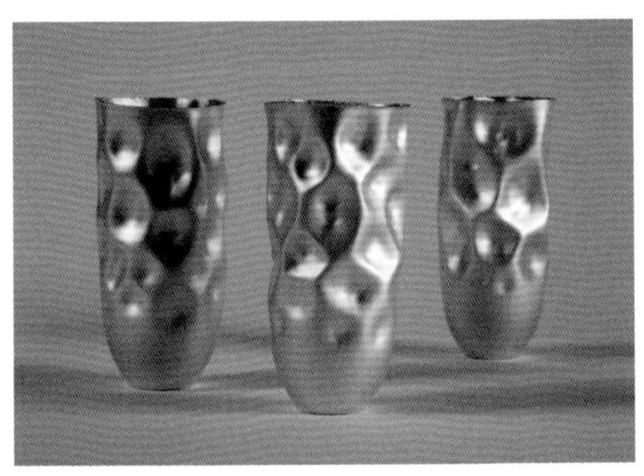

page 51 - 52
Landscape wine beakers
fine silver 999‰, year 2013
Ø 7 cm, H 14 cm

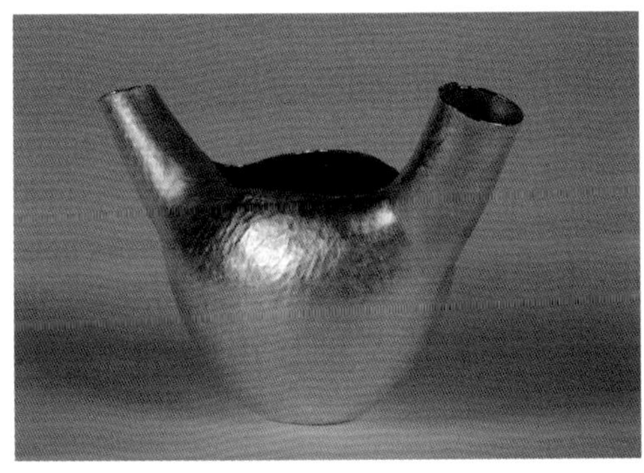

page 53 - 56
Bigger Twisted
fine silver 999‰, year 2013
H 23 cm, W 25 cm, D 10 cm

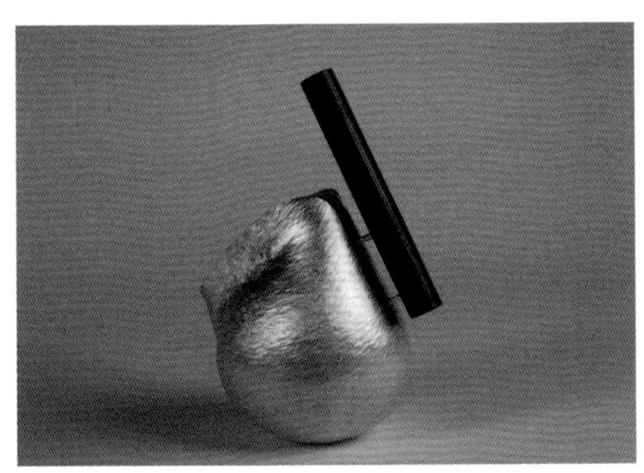

page 57 - 60
Not even thick cream...
fine silver 999‰, snakewood, year 2013
H 25 cm, W 15 cm, D 7 cm

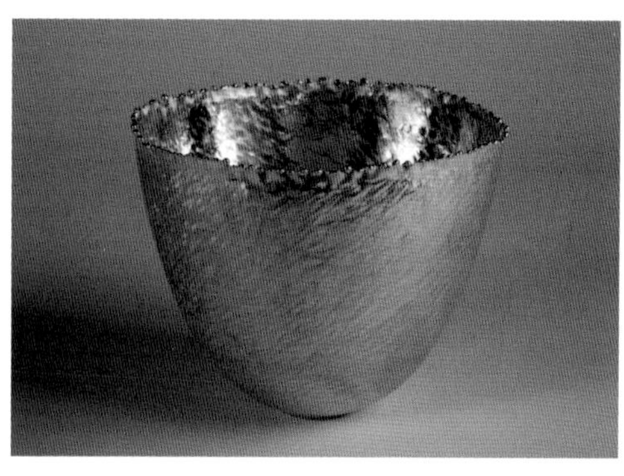

page 61 - 64
Pearl rim bowl
fine silver 999‰, year 2013
Ø 15 cm, H 20 cm

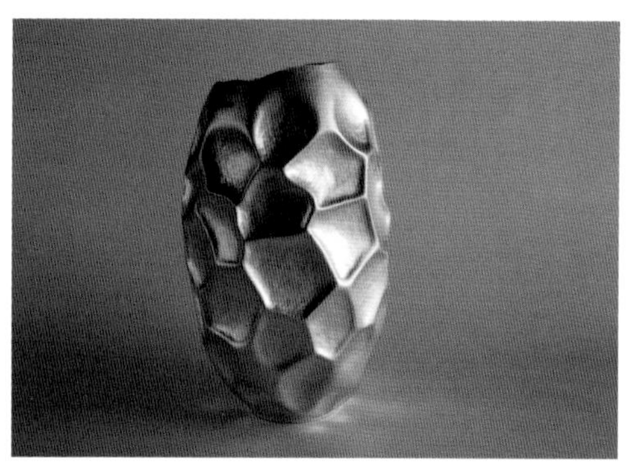

page 65 - 68
High Landscape vessel
fine silver 999‰, year 2013
H 45 cm, W 25 cm, Ø 25 cm

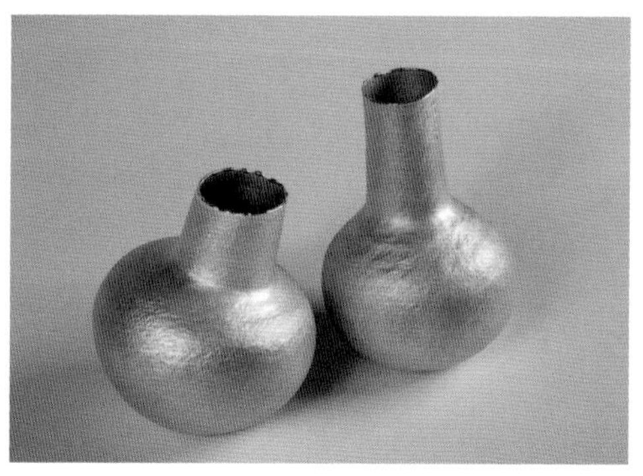

page 81 - 84
Smelling Vessels
fine silver 999‰, year 2013
various dimensions

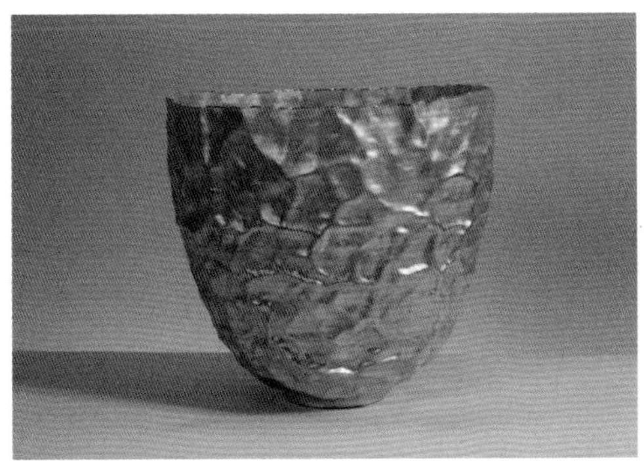

page 85 - 88
Landscape I bowl
fine silver 999‰, year 2012
Ø 23 cm, H 32 cm

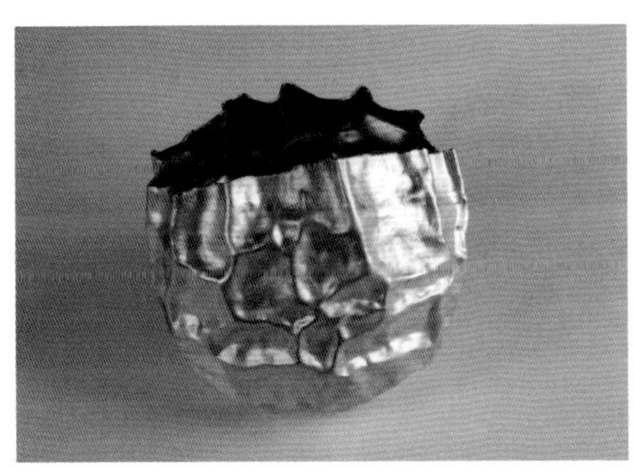

page 89 - 92 and cover
Landscape III bowl
fine silver 999‰, year 2012
H 26 cm, W 30 cm, D21 cm

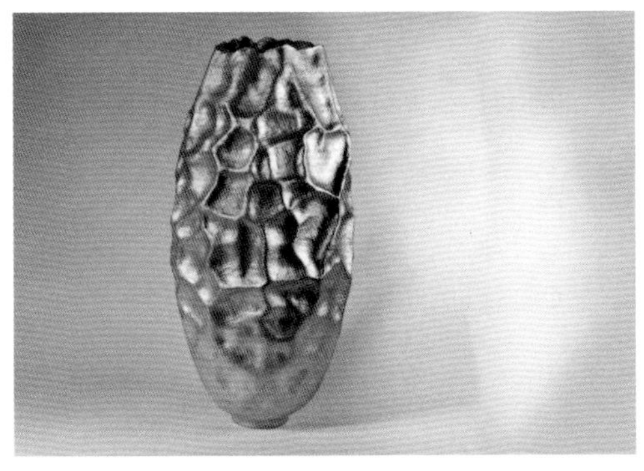

page 93 - 96
Mega Landscape bowl
fine silver 999‰, year 2013
Ø 37 cm, H 85 cm

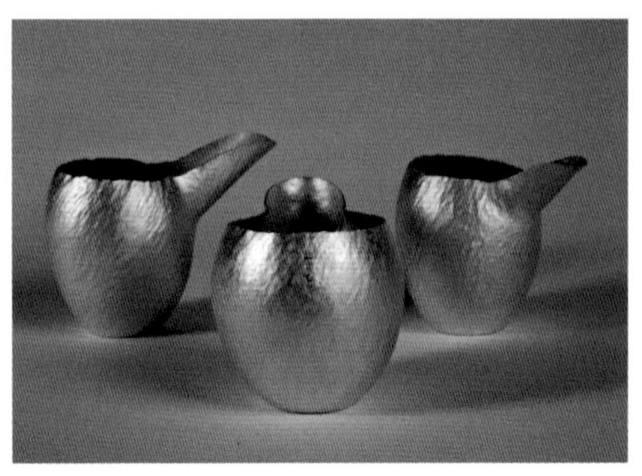

page 97 - 100
Creamers
fine silver 999‰, year 2012
various dimensions

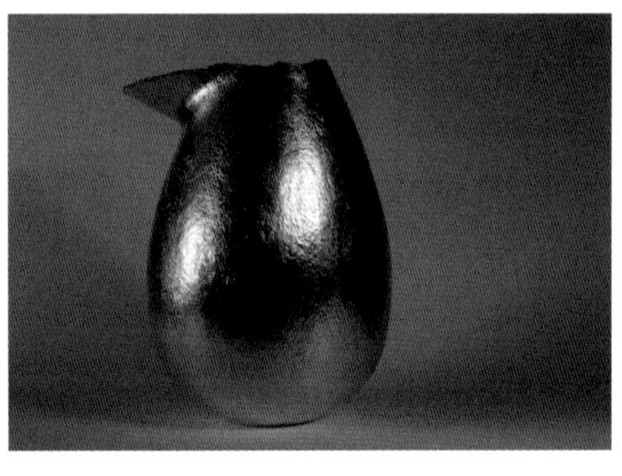

page 101 - 104
Mega bowl 01
fine silver 999‰, year 2011
H 70 cm, W 45 cm, Ø 37 cm

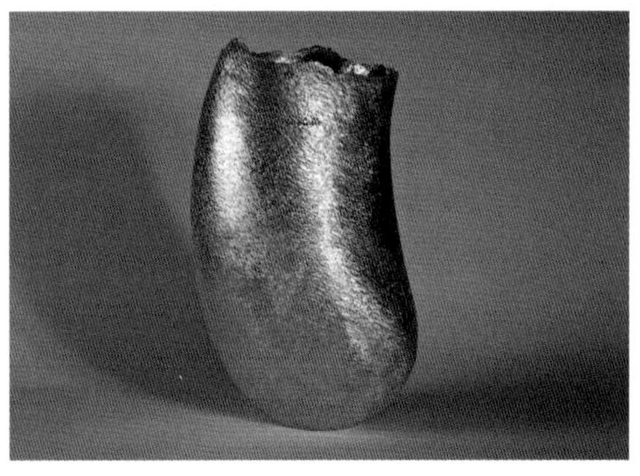

page 105 - 108
Touchable
fine silver 999‰, year 2012
H 55 cm, W 34 cm, Ø 29 cm

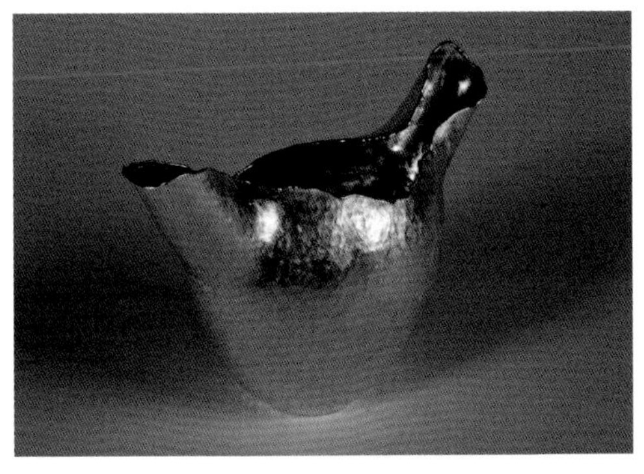

page 109 - 112
Twisted
fine silver 999‰, year 2012
H 20 cm, W 20 cm, D 10 cm

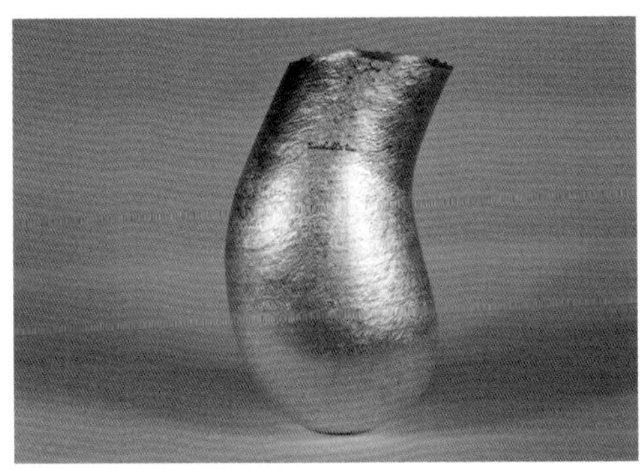

page 113 - 116
Touchable too
fine silver 999‰, year 2012
H 40 cm, W 25 cm, Ø 20 cm

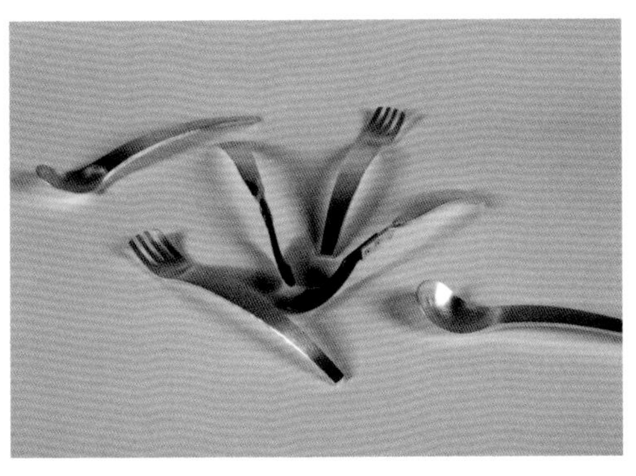

page 117 - 118
Tools with a twist
fine silver 999‰, titanium, year 2012/2013
various dimensions

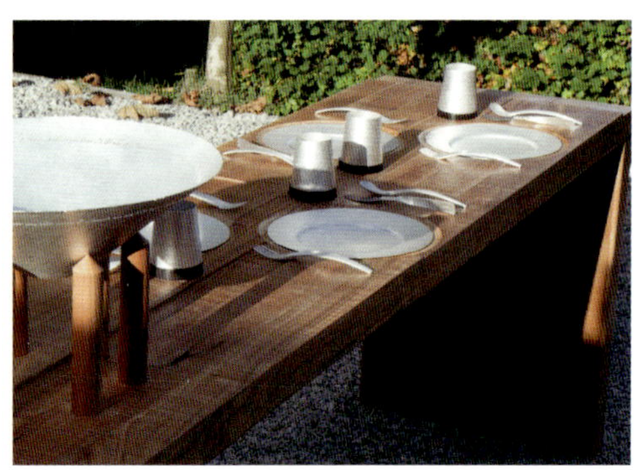

page 119 - 120
Table four four
fine silver 999‰, titanium, cherry wood, year 2012
H 110 cm, W 220 cm, D 60 cm

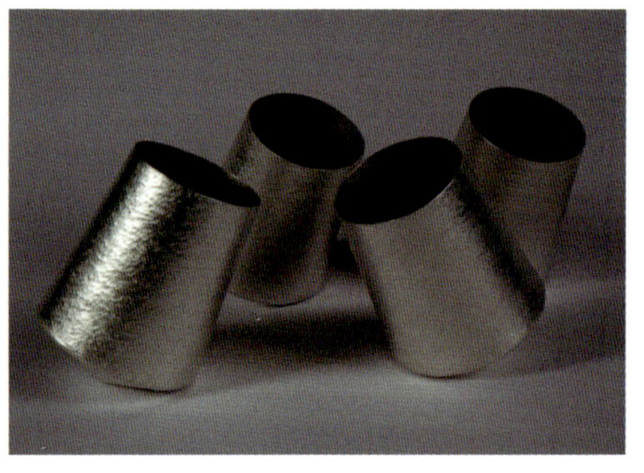

page 121 - 122
Wine tumblers
fine silver 999‰, year 2012
H 12 cm, W 7 cm, Ø 7 cm

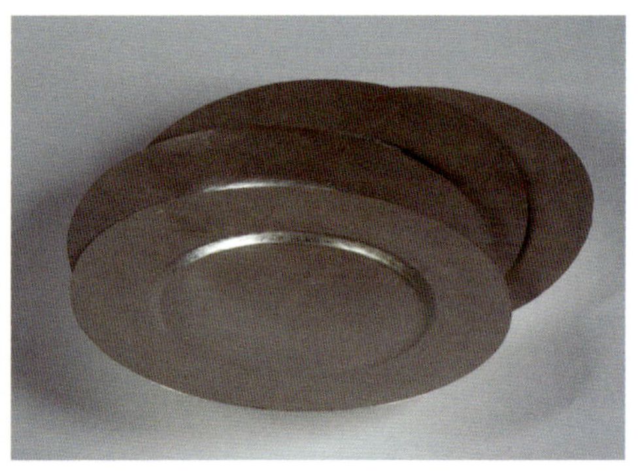

page 123 - 124
Plates
fine silver 999‰, year 2012
Ø 25 cm, D 3 cm

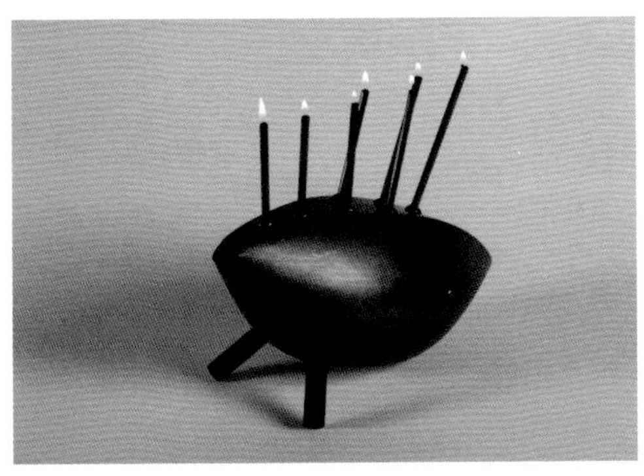

page 125 - 126
I Light you
silver 925‰, year 2010
H 27 cm, W 25 cm, D 12 cm

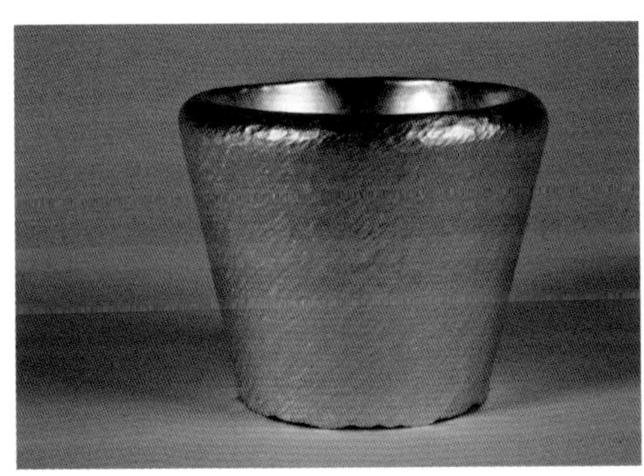

page 127 - 128
Mixing
fine silver 999‰, year 2012
Ø 14 cm, H 17 cm

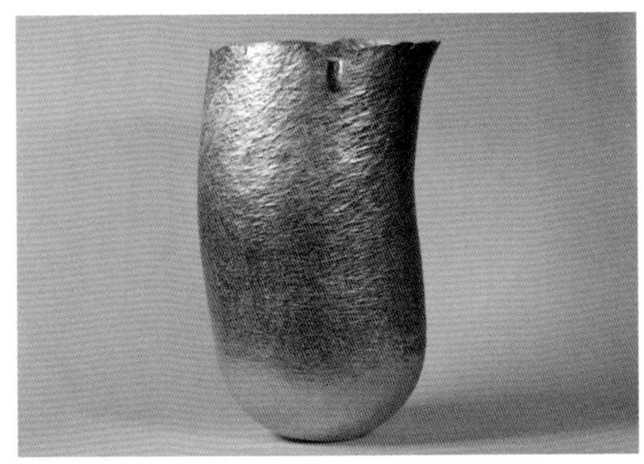

page 129 - 134
WindyCityBowl
fine silver 999‰, year 2011
H 76 cm, W 37 cm, Ø 35 cm

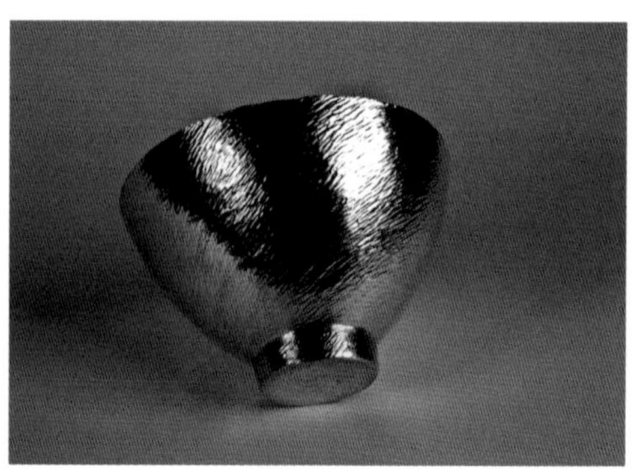

page 135 - 138
Parabolic bowl
fine silver 999‰, year 2013
Ø 12 cm, H 14 cm

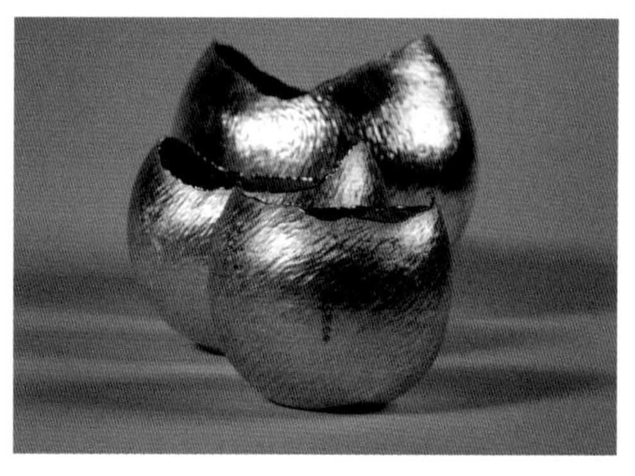

page 139 - 142
Just some ovals
fine silver 999‰, year 2013
various dimensions

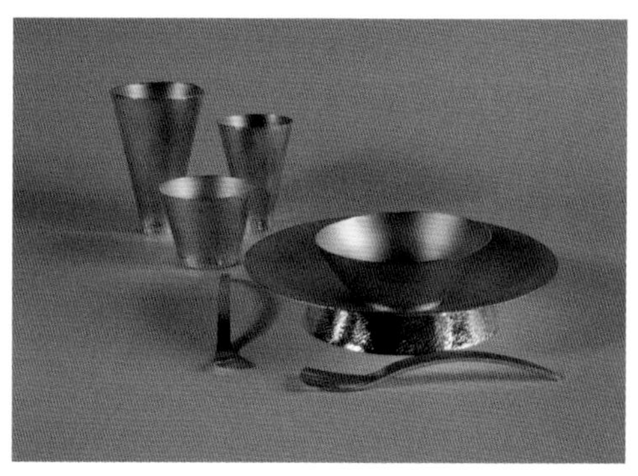

page 143 - 150
Placesetting
fine silver 999‰, titanium, year 2013
various dimensions

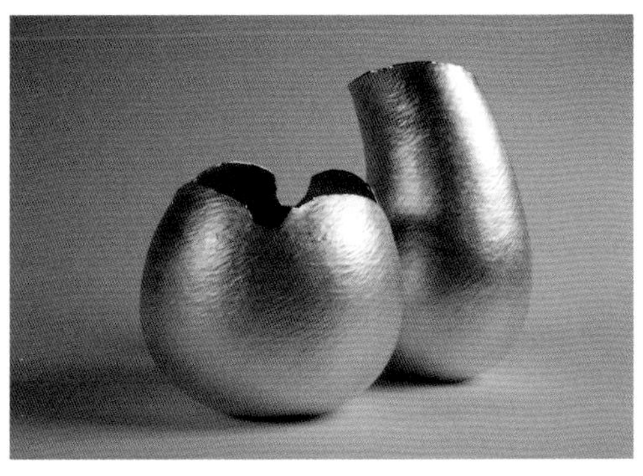

page 151 - 154
Lina's bowls
fine silver 999‰, year 2012
various dimensions

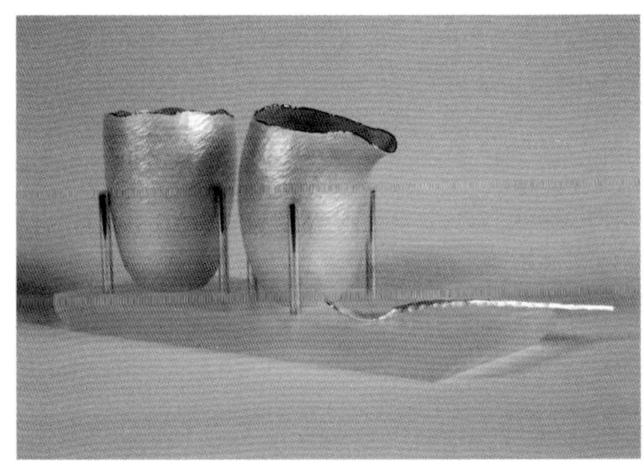

page 155 - 158
Milk & sugar
fine silver 999‰, acrylic, year 2011
various dimensions

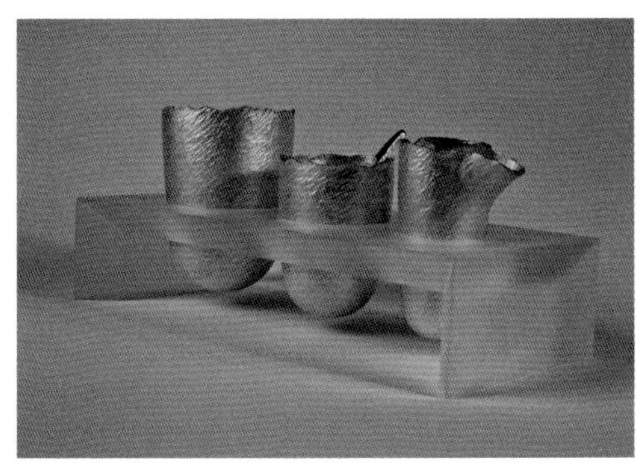

page 159 - 160
Sweets & Milk
fine silver 999‰, acrylic, year 2012
various dimensions

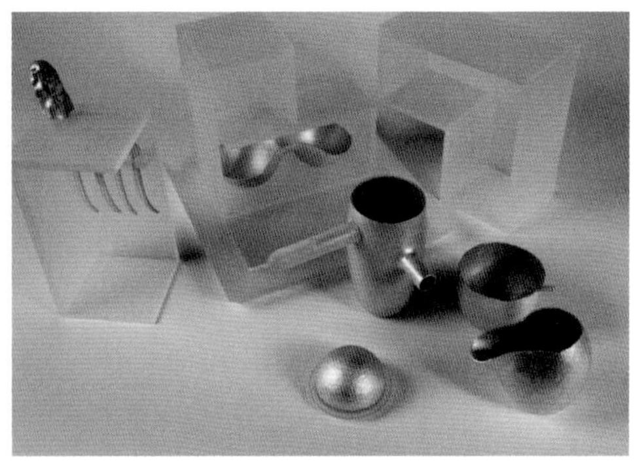

page 161 - 164
Tea Cube ...
fine silver 999‰, acrylic, year 2013
in closed situation H 20 cm, W 20 cm, D 20 cm

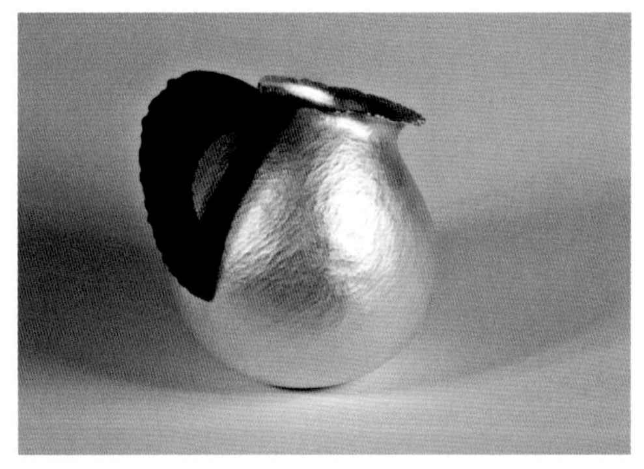

page 165 - 168
Water jug
fine silver 999‰, acrylic, year 2011
H 25 cm, W 27 cm, D 20 cm

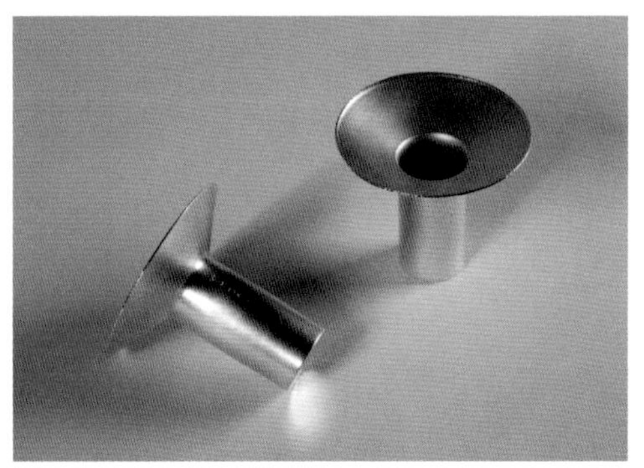

page 169 - 172
Champi .....
fine silver 999‰, year 2013
Ø 7 cm, H 7 cm

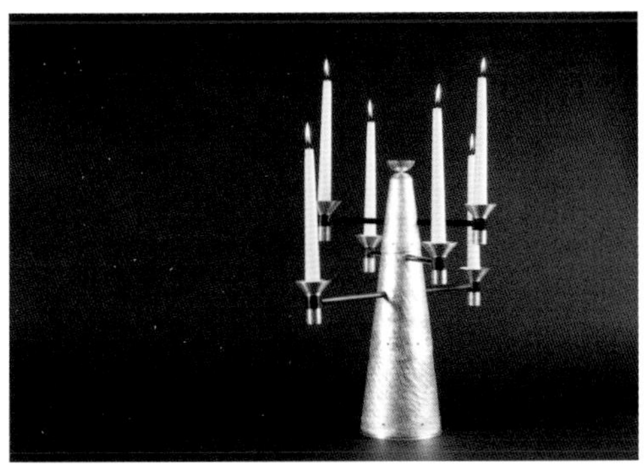

page 173 - 178
The balance of light & smell ...
fine silver 999‰, titanium, year 2013
H 47 cm, W 43 cm, D 30 cm

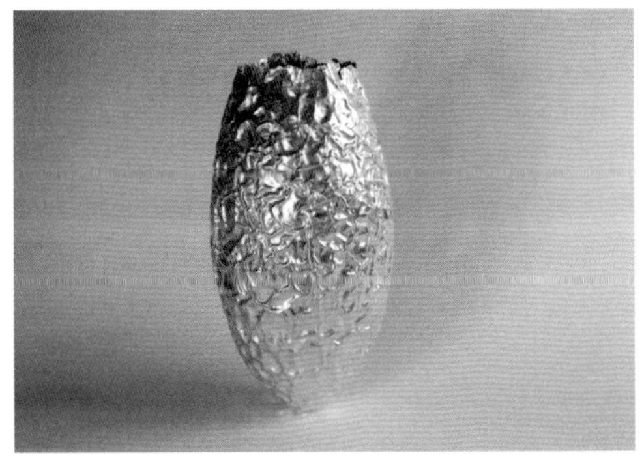

page 33, 38, 39 - 42
Sterckshofopdracht 2013
fine silver 999‰, year 2013
H 45 cm, Ø 21 cm

191

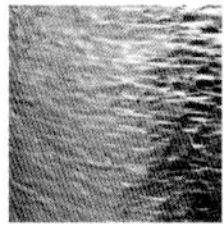

Dit boek werd mede mogelijk gemaakt met de vriendelijke hulp van:
This book was realized with the kind help of:
Cet ouvrage a été réalisé avec l'aimable soutien de:
Dieses Buch wurde realisiert mit der freundlichen Unterstützung von:

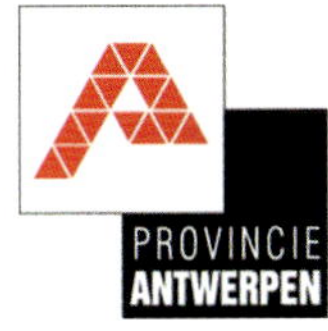

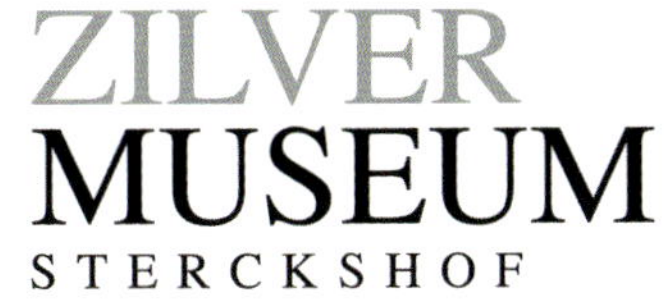

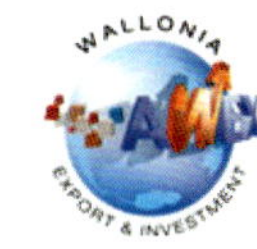

homepage:
www.belgiansilverworks.com
www.thalen-thalen.com

contact:
mail: thalen.thalen@skynet.be
mail: thalen.thalen@gmail.com